DEMOCRACY and PLURALISM in AFRICA

CONTRIBUTORS

Elliott Abrams
United States

Colin Legum
United Kingdom

Austin Amissah
Ghana

David N. Magang
Botswana

John A. A. Ayoade
Nigeria

Bona Malwal
Sudan

Pauline H. Baker
United States

Davidson Nicol
Sierra Leone

Pathé Diagne
Senegal

Victor A. Olorunsola
Nigeria/United States

Ali Khalif Galaydh
Somalia

Dov Ronen
United States

John W. Harbeson
United States

Richard L. Sklar
United States

Lansiné Kaba
Guinea/United States

W. A. E. Skurnik
United States

Ilunga Kabongo
Zaire

Winston B. Tubman
Liberia

This volume was prepared under the auspices of the
Africa Research Program of the Center for
International Affairs, Harvard University.

DEMOCRACY and PLURALISM in AFRICA

edited
by DOV RONEN

LYNNE RIENNER PUBLISHERS, INC.

HODDER and STOUGHTON

Published in the United States of America in 1986 by
Lynne Rienner Publishers, Inc.
948 North Street, Boulder, Colorado

Published in Great Britain by
Hodder and Stoughton Educational,
a division of Hodder and Stoughton Ltd
Mill Road, Dunton Green, Sevenoaks, Kent

Library of Congress Cataloging-in-Publication Data

Democracy and pluralism in Africa.

   "Papers presented at a symposium organized by
Harvard University's Center for International Affairs'
Africa Research Program . . . in November of 1984, at
the Wye Plantation in Queenstown, Maryland"—Introd.
   Includes bibliographies and index.
   1. Africa—Politics and government—Congresses.
2. Africa—Constitutional law—Congresses.   3. Pluralism
(Social sciences)—Congresses.   4. Democracy—Congresses.
I. Ronen, Dov.   II. Harvard University.   Africa Research
Program.
JQ1872.D46   1986   320.96   86-10114
ISBN 0-931477-65-4

US ISBN 0-931477-65-4
UK ISBN 0-340-40390-X

Printed and bound in the United States of America

To my mother,
with love

Contents

Part 2   Practice and Problems

Part 3   Prospects

Tables

Acknowledgments

Among the many individuals who must be thanked, I wish first to mention Ambassador Gerald Helman, U.S. Department of State, who was instrumental in obtaining funds for the symposium where all the papers, save the one by the editor, were presented and discussed. For the success of the symposium, additional thanks are due to the United States Information Agency for assisting with its organization; to the participants; and to the staff of the Wye Plantation, Queenstown, Maryland, where the symposium was held. I wish also to thank Malorye Allison, Rachel Bayly, Lem Coles, Mary Ellen Connell, Jefferey Davidow, William Krug, Jonathan Moore, and Donald Norland for their work and commitment to the success of the project. Thanks also go to John Heilbrunn for the translation of a French text.

The project was organized and the volume prepared at the Center for International Affairs' Africa Research Program. I wish to thank Professor Samuel P. Huntington, director of the Center, and Dr. Chester Haskell, its executive officer, for their advice and support.

My special thanks are due to Paul Psychas for editorial assistance and to Deborah Kvam for her editorial work, typing, indexing, and guiding of this undertaking through its various stages.

Dov Ronen

1

Dov Ronen

The Challenges of Democracy in Africa: Some Introductory Observations

Democracy and pluralism are not concerns of scholars alone. They matter to political actors, who are charged with the governance of peoples. They are of concern to lawyers, because democracies are often built upon a legal document—a constitution—that outlines rights and obligations. Democracy is of concern to scholars because the meanings, implications, and implementation of "rule by the people" continue to provide an intellectual challenge.

Both "democracy" and "pluralism" appear in the title of the book. My initial intention had been to use the term "democracy" to denote a principle; by "pluralism," on the other hand, I referred to the observable fact of cultural or ethno-cultural heterogeneity in African states. In my view, it is this ethno-cultural heterogeneity that makes implementation of democracy in Africa problematic. However, most contributors to this volume, quite significantly, use democracy and pluralism interchangeably. Pathé Diagne is the exception; if I read him correctly, he uses "plurality" for heterogeneity and "pluralism" for the method of governing a pluralistic society. The various interpretations of the two words introduce one thought-provoking aspect of the various contributions. This multiplicity and ambiguity cannot be accidental, for "democracy" poses a dual challenge. The implementation of a functioning democracy in Africa is one challenge: the first quarter-century of independence for many African states has clearly demonstrated its enormity. The second challenge, I would argue, is to derive the meaning of democracy. It seems evident to me that for at least the last quarter-century, democracy has meant an ideological commitment to a system quite different from other systems. Thus a stand for democracy is a stand against systems such as tyranny or dictatorship. In this context, which is probably the predominant one, democracy means an open society, a society in which all sections of the citizenry participate in political life, as opposed to other

1

societies in which they do not.

Attaching such a loose meaning to democracy is, in my view, unfortunate because it leaves too open the means of its implementation. For example, some argue in favor of a single-party system that allows the expression of plurality of views within the party; others oppose such a "democratic" system, for it excludes the organization of additional parties that hold different views.

Because of such an ambiguous definition, a related problem also arises. If the meaning of democracy is not clear-cut, proponents of democracy often tend to support specific institutions which are associated in their minds with democratic institutions elsewhere. The Westminster model of parliamentary government, for example, has stood as a criterion for success or failure in Africa, because it has long been a functioning institution in the British democratic system. Democracy, of course, does not require a Westminster model, and the absence of such need not mean the absence of democracy. Indigenous African cultures may themselves have produced institutions that also fit the criteria of democracy. This is to say that we must have a clearer notion of the meaning of democracy. In my contribution to this volume I shall say more on this subject.

Democracy poses an additional problem of a different nature. It is that democracy—its implementation as a functioning system—is a challenge in and of itself. It does not depend on the level of economic development. This view is not shared by everyone, as several of the contributors indicate. Hence, I wish to clarify what I mean.

It is evident that famine-stricken people cannot easily establish and maintain a democracy; for them, functioning in one is equally difficult. First, the famine-stricken do not tend to aspire to anything more than survival. Second, famine-stricken people are by definition dependent on others for food and health care. Thus, a system of food distribution and health care need not be democratic in the eyes of the recipients; it must only be efficient.

When and if a given population rises above the strictly defined famine level, above the conditions, for instance, that prevailed recently in Ethiopia and the Sahel, then the relevance of democracy (or any other political system) needs to be examined in an entirely different context. My proposition is this: Human beings aspire to freedom *and* to economic well-being; there is not any clear-cut historical evidence that once famine is no longer a consideration either of the two aspirations precede the other. African peoples aimed for the termination of colonial rule, i.e., freedom; there is no evidence to suggest that prospects for accelerated economic development under colonial rule would have been an acceptable substitute for freedom. Nor is there any evidence, in my view, that economic development is a road to or a prerequisite for democracy. What I am arguing is that democracy and economic development are and should be taken as separate challenges, and therefore should be aimed at separately. Democracy should not be put aside with the excuse that it will be the eventual by-product of economic development.

Last, I wish to propose that democracy in itself is not, after all, a goal. It is a means for the attainment of something far more abstract which one might call human freedom, contentment, happiness, or a life free from fear. This distinction holds great importance for democracy. Democratic institutions and processes often require sacrifices and compromise, which are worthwhile making only for the attainment of this higher ideal. Remembering this essential difference is important, because such a view of democracy may free those of us who are interested in Africa from our often too rigid attachment to well-tried models elsewhere.

This volume is a collection of papers presented at a symposium organized by the Africa Research Program at Harvard University's Center for International Affairs with the assistance of the U.S. Department of State and the United States Information Agency (U.S.I.A.), in November of 1984, at the Wye Plantation in Queenstown, Maryland. For these two-and-a-half days of discussion, analysis, and exchange of views, the Africa Research Program invited the participants, set the topics, and provided general guidelines.

The result is a variety of perspectives on the problems facing democracy and pluralism in Africa. The contributors—Africans, Europeans and from the United States—come from different government, professional and academic backgrounds. Lansiné Kaba, Ilunga Kabongo, David N. Magang, and Bona Malwal argue that colonialism suppressed the democratic systems inherent in traditional African societies. John Harbeson likewise points to the deleterious effects of colonization, and argues that political stability can only be attained when the process of decolonization is complete. That is, until African political systems are modified to suit African traditions, Africans will continue to view constitutionalism as an obstacle to rather than a means of political empowerment.

A variation of this viewpoint is held by Colin Legum. He maintains that since no African state was a democracy at the time of its independence, present democratic institutions are not rooted in indigenous societies. John A. A. Ayoade, Ali Khalif Galaydh, and Victor Olorunsola believe that most Africans do not understand the democratic system and hence have unrealistic expectations of the democratic state. When these expectations go unfulfilled, political stability is threatened. According to Ayoade, smaller-scale governments are needed to attract the disillusioned back into the political process and to create national unity.

In contrast, Richard Sklar holds that constitutionalism is firmly rooted in at least one African nation, Zimbabwe, despite its Marxist government. Because its independent judiciary system has continually upheld the constitution even in cases where the government is the defendant, Sklar believes Zimbabwe may, in practice, embody both communist and liberal principles.

The role of ethnicity must be considered in any discussion of African democracy. Elliot Abrams and Pauline Baker point out that political instability has been exacerbated by ethnic unrest, a feature that Pathé Diagne says traditional societies did not have. Diagne and Davidson Nicol both advocate education as one means of overcoming racial, religious, and ethnic differences. W. A. E. Skurnik advocates properly supervised government use of the media to help foster national unity.

An important factor in African politics is the role of the military. Nicol and Austin Amissah see temporary military intervention as necessary for maintaining order during times of ethnic hostilities, as well as for the forced removal of a government that has lost the support of its people and yet refuses to dissolve itself. Furthermore, Amissah believes such intervention may actually support constitutionalism, since even a military regime must legitimize its rule. Winston Tubman, on the other hand, argues that the military could better safeguard constitutional democracy by decreasing in size and turning its activities from preparation for combat toward economic development functions.

It is hoped that this collection, however controversial some viewpoints may be (or because they are), will everywhere provoke thought and debate among scholars, government officials, businessmen, and students.

Part 1

Theory
and
Concepts

2

John W. Harbeson

Constitutions and Constitutionalism in Africa: A Tentative Theoretical Exploration

An inquiry into African constitutional development is one means of asking to what extent African nations have articulated and institutionalized fundamental principles for regulating and defining the character of their political processes. The further question is how the constitution of political life in Africa resembles or differs from constitutional systems elsewhere. Constitutional inquiry as it is understood in Western countries is not, however, the only or necessarily the most appropriate way of viewing this fundamental question. Constitutional analysis of African political development may lead to reliance upon several debatable assumptions about the role of constitutions in particular, and more generally, law in political life.

Among the critical assumptions constitutional analysis of African political life may introduce are: (1) that the basic contours of the term "political" must be defined formally; (2) nations may or must have the opportunity to define governing principles comprehensively and formally at a given point in time; (3) constitutions are an appropriate and effective means of creating, not just confirming, political order in settings of ethnic, linguistic, religious, and developmental diversity; (4) Western-style constitutionalism is transferable to developing-country settings, and that its utility is not conditional upon the presence of particular patterns of economic development and social change; and, (5) that constitutional development is a generic process of political formation not restricted to a process of evolving states founded on broadly construed democratic principles.

The experience of European and American democracies in which constitutionalism has flourished appears to underwrite the validity of the first two assumptions; it lends at least partial support for the third assumption, and leaves the last two open to question. In general terms, the United States, Canada, Great Britain, France, West Germany, and Japan have adopted constitutions formally and comprehensively at their own points in time. To vary-

7

ing degrees, each of these constitutions has been "imposed," yet subject to ultimate acceptance or rejection. Overall, each appears to have been adopted and accepted by those for whom they were proposed. Each of the constitutions has been in some form democratic, leaving unanswered the extent to which constitutionalism is inseparable from the development of democratically governed states. The constitutions of these major industrial democracies have been established in socioeconomic, political, cultural, and historical settings that vary significantly, lending credence to the proposition that these assumptions about constitutional development are generic and not culturally specific. The experience of the major industrial democracies in no way discredits the hypothesis that the empirical validity of the assumptions about constitutional development are specific to particular stages of economic, human resource, and technological development. Many writers have argued as much, following in the footsteps of John Stuart Mill.[1]

My argument is that, to the extent constitutional analysis of African political development embodies the foregoing assumptions, a misleading and perhaps invalid picture of constitutional failure in Africa emerges. One must distinguish between constitutions and constitutionalism in Africa. Constitutional structures inherited from colonial times have been discarded or seriously eroded.[2] The *processes* of evolving constitutional structures in Africa have not reflected the assumptions of Western constitutionalism as outlined above. The proper conclusion, however, is not necessarily that the processes of constitutional building are not at work in Africa, but that they have taken different and unfamiliar forms.

More than one interpretation of recurrent African regime changes and political instability are possible. The following broad hypotheses may explain these phenomena:

1. Regime changes and political instability signify the political decay anticipated by Samuel Huntington nearly twenty years ago. Nationalist movements under colonial rule did not lay the foundations for postindependence African states, or else postindependence regimes have presided over the reversal of embryonic preindependence, nation-building processes.[3] African states have not survived the crisis of legitimacy, identification, penetration, participation, distribution, and integration identified by Lucian Pye.[4]

2. Regime changes and instability reflect a long, tortuous, and still incomplete process of decolonization which is the prerequisite for postindependence state building. Decolonization and independence are processes far deeper and more unbound than a substitution of African for colonial regimes and the subsequent modification, replacement, or discarding of colonially prescribed postindepend-

ence constitutions.[5] Pye's crises of political development require decades, not years, to overcome.

The more optimistic, long-term hypothesis depends on the proposition
that the circumstances of Africa's transition from colonial rule to independence are so fundamentally different from those in which industrial countries' constitutions were established that it is unrealistic, even inappropriate,
to assume that postindependence African constitutionalism is based on the
same assumptions.

The balance of this essay considers the five basic assumptions of Western constitutionalism in African contexts. I will examine whether African
states have adopted such assumptions and with what consequences,
whether apparent imitation of Western constitutional processes aids or im-
pedes African constitutionalism, and whether implicit or explicit departures
from Western constitutionalism signify a constitution's failure or the slow
emergence of distinctive, more appropriate, African processes of constitutionalism.

Most of the evidence is drawn from eastern and southern African countries: Tanzania, Kenya, Uganda, Ethiopia, and Zimbabwe.[6] These countries
represent an appropriate cross-section of the continent. They include an empire never formally or fully subject to colonial rule, countries that experienced significant European settlement (Kenya and Zimbabwe), and ones
that did not (Ethiopia, Uganda, and Tanzania). There are states that have
enjoyed a degree of regime stability (Kenya and Tanzania) and those which
have not (Ethiopia and Uganda). The sample includes a variety of ideological approaches to state building: ideological adherence to Marxist-Leninist
principles (Ethiopia), a cautious approach to scientific socialism without
Soviet inspiration (Zimbabwe), an exponent of African socialism (Tanzania),
a country that reformed rather than discarded Westminster's constitutional
principles (Kenya), and countries that are as preoccupied with preserving
the state itself as with shaping the direction of the state (Ethiopia and
Uganda).[7]

Assumption 1: Formalism

Constitutional structures in Western countries have, in general, been
specified and adopted formally. Great Britain is an apparent exception to
this generalization, yet even here the settlement of 1688 was explicit and
formal. How much formal constitutionalism has there been in African states
and what do the answers signify in terms of the extent and vitality of African
constitutional processes?

African states have experienced formal constitutions, but the *relation-*

ship of African states to those constitutions has been very different than in the case of the industrial democracies. African constitutional structures evolved over a period of decades, where Britain's evolved over centuries. Britain's constitution, however, evolved in response to the demands of emerging commercial and, later, industrial classes. The closest parallel in our African sample is Ethiopia where Emperor Haile Selassie established constitutional structures. Constitutional structures in Britain reflected concessions of power by kings and nobility, while those in Ethiopia created only the appearance of such concessions.[8] The gap between constitutional appearance and reality under the emperor appears to have been a factor in the apparent rejection of formal parliamentary democracy in postimperial Ethiopia.

Alien powers imposed formal constitutions in Germany after World Wars I and II and in Japan after World War II. Formal colonial constitutional structures were also imposed in Africa, but the purposes behind such impositions were different, as were the responses to them. Postwar formal constitutions in Japan and Germany were intended to change the political cultures and practices of established polities shattered by war. Colonial structures arbitrarily defined "national" political entities for the purpose of sustaining alien rule rather than preparing the way for a resumption of independent self-rule. A most important consequence was that African independence movements gave birth to, and nurtured the formation of, nation states within these formal, alien frameworks of governance unlike the situation in both Germany and Japan.[9] In Africa, therefore, the political distinction between embryonic African nation-states and the alien structures through which they were articulated was blurred. To what extent, in the minds of leaders and constituents alike, did articulation of nationhood within alien, formal colonial structures lead to the legitimation of such structures, and to what extent not? In most colonial circumstances, this question appears never to have been clearly answered. The ambivalent relationship between nation building and formal constitutional structures in the colonial period undermines the legitimacy of formal constitutionalism in the postindependence period.[10]

African states have varied in their colonial relationship to imposed, alien structures. The political dominance of formal constitutional structures by European settlers in Kenya and Zimbabwe may, on the one hand, have clarified in African minds the distinction between the processes of nation building and formal constitutional structures. Preindependence civil wars in both countries may have led to the alienation of nation-building movements from formal colonial structures in these countries. In Kenya, however, politically moderate European settlers and the colonial administration worked actively to encourage African acceptance of a Westminster-style constitutional structure. In Zimbabwe, Robert Mugabe, by contrast, has sought to use the inherited colonial structure as a framework—*after independ-*

ence—within which to build a Zimbabwean nation articulating scientific socialist values. In both cases, therefore, the basis for nation building after independence may have been more the inherited colonial constitutional structures than the nationalist movements alienated from them.

The relationship of state building and imposed colonial constitutional structures in Tanzania may be quite different. In a League of Nations Mandate territory and, later, a United Nations Trust territory, Tanzanian nationalism found expression outside the colonial framework to a greater extent than did other African colonies.[11] European settlers did not dominate colonial politics to the same extent as elsewhere in eastern and southern Africa. The alienation of the nationalist movement from formal colonial structures may, therefore, have been less profound. This combination of less alienation and a nationalist movement's somewhat greater independence possibly resulted in less blurring of the lines between informal African nation building and formal colonial constitutionalism. Nyerere's postindependence government thus gained greater freedom to employ formal constitutional changes to nurture the development of a Tanzanian nation. Tanzania, in short, may be among the states relatively fortunate in successfully steering between the shoals of cooptation by, and alienation from, formal processes of state building through colonially constituted structures.

Uganda represents another pattern of interaction between formal colonial constitutional structures and African preindependence nation building. Here, the effect of formal colonial structures appears to have reinforced rather than diminished antagonism among the traditional lacustrine kingdoms, as well as between them and less formal traditional communities to the north.[12] In many respects, the concept of Uganda was a product of those formal colonial structures; nationalist movements found expression more in regional terms. The problem for Uganda is not that formal constitutionalism was confused with Ugandan nation building; it is that it was used to undermine "subnational," and more independent, expressions of nationalism that were consonant with established, traditional state structures, such as Buganda.

Assumption 2: Comprehensive Constitution Building at a Point in Time

One of the characteristics of Western constitutionalism is the comprehensive formulation of constitutional principles at a point in time: the settlement of 1688 in England, the Fifth Republic in France, the imposition of constitutions by the allies after World War II in Germany and Japan, and, of course, in the United States in 1789 (a point frequently overlooked is the prevalence in the formation of these constitutions of "legislators"—in the Rousseauian sense of the term: e.g., allied powers in the cases of Germany and Japan, the Constitutional Convention in the United States, de Gaulle in France). By contrast, the constitutions of African states were, in a majority of cases, decided incrementally over a period of years because of nationalist pressures and imperial concessions.

The critical point here is that constitutionalism in the industrial democracies either reflected or decisively shaped political processes but was not employed to restrain or limit the practice of politics. Postwar German and Japanese constitutionalism imposed democratic politics in nations with a history of authoritarianism, substantially broadening rather than restricting political participation. De Gaulle sought to change the focus of French politics from parliament to the presidency, diminish party fragmentation, and increase the use of legislative and constitutional referenda—reshaping but not restricting the breadth and scope of political participation. The U.S. Constitution provided for more direct popular participation at the national level even as it restricted its scope.

The history of constitutionalism in Africa has been to restrict rather than enlarge the scope and extent of political participation. Colonial authorities had conferred broader suffrage and more political responsibility on African nationalist parties. Independent African countries, in short, inherited a working definition of constitutionalism as an obstacle rather than a means to political empowerment.

African political elites neither received nor took the opportunity to make a decisive, immediate break with preindependence constitutionalism. Kwame Nkrumah in Ghana transformed the inherited colonial constitution by stages over a period of several years.[13] Julius Nyerere in Tanzania and Milton Obote in Uganda waited more than five years before proposing decisive breaks with the colonial constitutional heritage, and only Nyerere was successful in doing so in political if not in developmental terms. Kenya continues to make incremental formal changes in its 1963 constitution to preserve the image of constitutional continuity, and Zimbabwe's Robert Mugabe appears to be following suit, his scientific, socialist rhetoric notwithstanding. The prevailing absence of comprehensive, telescoped constitutional change in postcolonial Africa has as one very important consequence the preservation of the idea of constitutionalism as an obstacle to political empowerment and, therefore, of tarnished political legitimacy.

Assumption 3: Constitutionalism as a Means of Creating Political Order

The operative word in the third assumption of Western constitutionalism is "creating." Each of the Western constitutions defined new political orders and represented sharp breaks with the past (the possible exception being the 1688 settlement in Britain, which should perhaps be understood as confirming an already evolved constitutional order). The manner in which constitutionalism evolved in colonial and postindependence Africa has seemed to preclude a similar creativity. The association of "constitutions" with alien rule, the ambivalent relationship between processes of nation building and formal constitutional development, and perpetuation of arbitrary colonial boundaries did not establish precedents for postcolonial "creative" constitutionalism.

African leaders, since independence, have in some instances used constitutional structures as means for the creation of new political realities. The *ujamaa* policies of Julius Nyerere and the redefining of regional boundaries in Uganda and Nigeria represent examples of such "creative" constitutionalism. Of these three, only Tanzania appears to have been successful in purely political terms in reshaping the polity by constitutional means.[14] Nigeria and Uganda do not appear to have moderated or decisively reshaped regional and ethnic conflict through redistricting. The relative ethnic homogeneity of Tanzania and its distinctive colonial constitutional history discussed above helped the Nyerere government to accomplish and survive postindependence constitutional change, though the results in political and economic terms have been disappointing. In short, the precedents for and the record of constitutional creativity in Africa have been limited. Each of the industrial country's constitutions was formulated and instituted decisively at moments of profound political crisis. The pattern of African pre- and postindependence political history, especially periods of transfer of power from colonial to African hands, appears to have deprived African countries of such moments of high constitutional opportunity.

Assumption 4: Constitutionalism at Any Stage of Development

This assumption questions whether there are socioeconomic, cultural, or historical prerequisites for successful design and institutionalization of constitutions as they are known in industrialized countries. Circumstances surrounding the formation of constitutions in industrial countries suggest that either of two sets of circumstances are preconditions for the successful introduction of new constitutional structures: the emergence of (1) a working consensus among relevant political actors on how to construct the political order so that constitutional processes and documents simply confirm what is already accepted, or (2) a working agreement among those same actors that the existing political order has collapsed beyond repair. England appears to exemplify the first set of circumstances; Germany, Japan, and France illustrate the second set.[15] Both sets of prerequisites appear to have been present in the formation of the U.S. Constitution.

The problem in African settings is that in many countries neither circumstance seems to obtain. Working consensuses among relevant political actors is common to both circumstances in European settings, yet nothing is more characteristic of regime change and political instability in Africa during the past quarter-century than the absence of such a working consensus on basic political principles or on the bankruptcy of existing political processes—or even agreement upon who are the relevant political actors.

Conquered in war, neither Germany nor Japan had need of further evidence that their preexisting political systems had collapsed completely. Having been subjected to a wartime occupation government, France's situation after World War II was similar. A later threat to the integrity of national institutions prompted the reappearance of de Gaulle and the promulgation of the Fifth Republic. Direct relationships between weaknesses in political structure and economic chaos prompted the establishment of the U.S. Constitution.

Ironically, instability in African regimes has been, perhaps in a majority of instances, more corrosive than sudden, more incremental than total, and more quiet than dramatic. Neocolonial practices and allegiances, the effects of international trade barriers, interethnic tensions, and balance of payments crises are more subtle if no less serious than those that prompted constitutional renewal in industrial countries.[16] Because the undermining of postcolonial institutions is less visible, the impetus for elites to recognize and unite in addressing it is rare. Moreover, the problems of development are not in every case easily attributable to the particular constitutional structures maintained by colonial states. Such elite consensus as does emerge, therefore, appears to center less upon structure than upon socioeconomic processes.

Two cases where problems of development may be attributed to structural failings are prerevolutionary Ethiopia and Tanzania with its promulgation of African socialism in 1967. In the Ethiopian case, the superficiality of imperial commitment to democracy meant that democratic practices may have been tarnished by association with the Emperor; but, the focus of the successor military regime has been upon the old regime per se, not the manner in which power was formally distributed within it. In Tanzania, too, a careful reading of the results of rural villagization and collectivization known as *ujamaa* suggests that the failure of such policies to bring about development was less a function of the structures themselves than of the manner in which the policies were in fact implemented.[17]

Assumption 5: Democracy and Constitutionalism

The study of constitutionalism in industrial countries is closely linked with the study of democracy. Given the well-rehearsed argument that preconditions for democracy include levels of economic, communications, and human resource development well beyond what African states have achieved, is there a case to be made that constitutionalism may be possible even if democracy is not one of its products?

By such logic, Emperor Haile Selassie in Ethiopia erred by concealing the reality of continued absolutism beneath the facade of democratic institutions. Kenya's problem may be that it has been too inundated with Western culture and investment to have evolved many Kenyan answers to Kenyan problems of political and economic development and social change. Perhaps Kenya has maintained for too long the somewhat misleading impression that the country is wholeheartedly oriented toward democracy.[18] In fact, underlying struggles for political and economic power appear to be modulated to only a limited extent by constitutional structures not greatly different from those inherited at independence.

This issue is closely related to the first one. The results of ambivalent relationships between nation building and constitutionalism in preindependence Africa may have included more than just the weakened legitimacy of formal constitutionalism. Such ambivalence may also have linked aspirations for democracy with legitimation of essentially alien structures that acted to restrain as much as to institutionalize such aspirations. One may argue that in acting to strengthen and sustain modified, inherited colonial structures, African governments have in fact sought to infuse legitimacy into constitutional structures per se rather than doing so by relating them more closely to democratic aspirations. One might hypothesize that constitutionalism in Africa, for many leaders, is not about institutionalizing democracy but strengthening institutions as such. The reason may be not simply that some African leaders reject democracy, but that they view the constitutional agenda of the day very differently in light of the historical evolution of the institutions through which they work.

Conclusion

Regime instability and change in postcolonial Africa has been associated with the discarding or decay of constitutional structures inherited from the ending colonial and transfer-of-power periods. Analysis of this apparent political deterioration suggests that it may have little to do with incapacity in maintaining the structures or disinterest in doing so. It may be more from delegitimation of formal constitutionalism in colonial times, the institution of incrementalism in constitutional development, and the use of constitutions to restrain rather than promote political development. It can also come from the character of the crises of African development and their implication for elite formation and consensus, and the association of inherited structures with aspirations for democracy rather than with their actual transformation with such ends in view.

A practical implication of this analysis is that failure to fashion processes of constitutionalism—as well as administration and technology—appropriate to African circumstances is to undermine rather than broaden constitutional practice as we know it. From this analysis, therefore, I propose the emergence of a field of comparative constitutionalism that will center on the relationship between processes of constitution building and the socioeconomic, political, and cultural environments with which they are interrelated over the long term. At the same time, increased appreciation of intricacies in the relationship between constitutionalism and other political processes may encourage the evolution of genuinely African constitutionalism. Such African constitutionalism may be an important step in stabilizing and enhancing the political as well as economic development of the African continent.

Notes

1. *Representative Government* (New York: Dutton, 1951).

2. Carl G. Rosberg and Robert H. Jackson, *Personal Rule in Black Africa* (Berkeley: University of California, 1982).

3. Samuel P. Huntington, "Political Development and Political Decay," *World Politics* 2 (1965):368–430.

4. Lucian Pye, *Aspects of Political Development* (Boston: Little Brown, 1966).

5. John W. Harbeson, "Structural Adjustment and Development Reform in Kenya—the Missing Dimension," *Universities Field Staff International Reports* 7 (Hanover, N.H.: USFI Inc., 1983).

6. Among the most pertinent recent studies on the countries in this region are Goren Hyden, *Beyond Ujamaa in Tanzania: Underdevelopment and an Uncaptured Peasantry* (Berkeley: University of California, 1980); Gavin Kitching, *Class and Economic Change in Kenya: The Making of an African Petite-Bourgeoisie* (New Haven: Yale University, 1980); John Markakis, *Ethiopia: Anatomy of a Traditional Polity* (London: Oxford University); R. M. A. van Zwanenberg, *An Economic History of Kenya and Uganda 1800–1970* (Atlantic Highlands, N.J.: Humanities Press, 1975); J. W. Harbeson "Land Policy and Politics in Zimbabwe," *Current History* 473 (1982): 121–5, 138.

7. *See* Crawford Young, *Ideology and Development in Africa* (New Haven: Yale University, 1982).

8. Markakis, *op. cit.*

9. Thomas Hodgkin, *Nationalism in Colonial Africa* (New York: New York University, 1958).

10. John W. Harbeson, *Nation Building in Kenya: The Role of Land Reform* (Evanston: Northwestern University, 1973).

11. B. T. G. Chidzero, *Tanzania and International Trusteeship* (London: Oxford University, 1961).

12. David Apter, *The Political Kingdom in Uganda*, 2nd ed. (Princeton, N.J.: Princeton University, 1967).

13. A. Zolberg, *Creating Political Order: The One-Party States of West Africa*

(Chicago: Rand McNally, 1966).

14. Hyden, *op. cit.*

15. The exception to the generalization is the "reverse course" movement that was influential in the ruling Liberal Democratic Party in the 1950s, but whose impact over the long term was limited to some recentralization of institutions that were decentralized under the MacArthur constitution. For a discussion, see J. A. A. Stockwin, *Japan: Divided Politics in a Growth Economy* (New York: Norton, 1982); Robert A. Scalapino and Junnosuke Masumi, *Parties and Politics in Contemporary Japan* (Berkeley: University of California, 1962).

16. The nature of the current development crisis in Africa is outlined in the World Banks's *Accelerated Development in Sub-Saharan Africa: An Agenda for Action* (Washington, 1981) and its *Toward Sustained Development in Sub-Saharan Africa: A Joint Program of Action* (Washington, 1984).

17. John W. Harbeson, "Tanzanian Socialism in Transition: Agricultural Crisis and Policy Reform," *University Field Staff International Reports* 30 (1983).

18. Kitching, *op. cit.*; Colin Leys, *Underdevelopment in Kenya: The Political Economy of Neo-Colonialism* (Berkeley: University of California Press, 1975).

3

John A. A. Ayoade

The African Search for Democracy: Hopes and Reality

Recent political developments in Africa have led a good number of observers to wonder whether democratic experiments can survive there.[1] This feeling summarizes the disappointment with the process of political leadership change and with tenure of political office-holders. By April 1985, twenty-four countries were under military rule and twenty-one under civilian administration (Table 3.1). However, among the twenty-one countries under civilian administration, two, Sierra Leone and Uganda, had previously experienced military rule. Sierra Leone was under various military administrations from 1964 to 1968, while Uganda experienced one of the most notorious military administrations from 1971 to 1979. Furthermore, two countries, Cape Verde and Chad, are under militarized civilian administrations. In the case of Cape Verde, the administration is under Aristides Pereira, who was a prominent member of the Party for the Liberation of Guinea and Cape Verde (PAIGC) and a member of the liberation forces, although he is not a regular soldier. Similarly, Hissène Habré of Chad is not a soldier by profession although he toppled General Félix Malloum from power in August 1978.[2] Habré was only a member of the National Front for the Liberation of Chad (FROLINAT) but, since 1982, has been president of an embattled Chad, whose government is military except in name.

Apart from direct military administrations in the twenty-five countries and the two militarized civilian governments, there are also two civilianized military governments, in Algeria and Egypt. These are countries in which the military has held political power for a long time and has transformed the military office-holders into civilians; therefore, they also enjoy military traditions. Thus a total of thirty countries, including Sierra Leone and Uganda, have military traditions; this makes up about sixty percent of all the African countries.

Among the remaining nineteen civilian administrations that have not

TABLE 3.1   Regime Types in Africa

Military	Militarized Civilian	Civilianized Military	Civilian
1. Angola	1. Cape Verde	1. Algeria	1. Botswana
2. Benin (Dahomey)	2. Chad	2. Egypt	2. Cameroon
3. Burundi			3. Comoros
4. Central African Republic			4. Djibouti
5. Congo-Brazzaville			5. Gabon
6. Equatorial Guinea			6. Gambia
7. Ethiopia			7. Ivory Coast
8. Ghana			8. Kenya
9. Guinea			9. Lesotho
10. Guinea-Bissau			10. Malawi
11. Liberia			11. Mauritius
12. Libya			12. Morocco
13. Malagasy Republic			13. St. Thomas & Prince Islands
14. Mali			14. Senegal
15. Mauritania			15. Sierra Leone
16. Mozambique			16. Swaziland
17. Niger			17. Tanzania
18. Nigeria			18. Uganda
19. Rwanda			19. Zambia
20. Somalia			20. Zanzibar
21. Sudan			21. Zimbabwe
22. Togo			
23. Tunisia			
24. Burkina Faso (Upper Volta)			
25. Zaire			

experienced military rule only Botswana, Gambia, Mauritius, Senegal, Swaziland, and Zimbabwe have competitive party systems; these nations compose only twelve percent of the African countries that offer electoral choice of some kind to the people. In the single-party states, periodic elections are held, but they are supposed to confirm the views of the political leaders rather than offer policy or political alternatives. Thus both military governments and a majority of civilian governments offer little electoral choice to the people. In specific terms, using 1981 projected population figures, only 16,180,000 Africans (0.03%) out of a total population of 493,720,000 exercise a democratic choice in the selection of their governments.[3]

In addition to the denial of political choice, or perhaps because of it, the African countries experience a large turnover in government in the countries under military rule and a near permanence of governments under some military and civilian administrations. Some of the countries that had the most frequent changes of government were Benin (1963, 1965, 1967, 1969, and 1972); Burundi with two coups in 1966; Chad with three coups in 1979; and Ethiopia, two coups in 1974 and another in 1977. The Malagasy Republic had three coups in 1975, while Mauritania had a coup each year from 1978 to 1980. These frequent changes of government mean a low political stability index (psi).[4] The psi for Benin is 0.51, including the thirteen-year rule of Matthew Kerekou, without which it would be 0.3. Similarly, the psi of Chad is 0.51; but, discounting the fifteen-year rule of François Tombalbaye, it would only be 0.25. Ghana, since independence, has a psi of 0.39 but only 0.3 since the coup that unseated Kwame Nkrumah in 1966.

By contrast, the psi of the single-party states and monarchies tends to exceed unity, thus resulting in a high/low political departicipation index (pdi).[5] The Ivory Coast has the highest pdi at 2.1, followed by Tanzania at 2.0, Malawi at 1.6, Zambia 1.6, and Gambia at 1.5. The tenure of office of some individual leaders shows the level of departicipation more glaringly than the political departicipation index itself. For example, William Tubman was president of Liberia for twenty-eight years, the same length of time that Habib Borguiba has been president of Tunisia (Table 3.2). Sékou Touré was president of Guinea-Conakry for twenty-six years and Félix Houphouet-Boigny president of the Ivory Coast for twenty-five. Although all these leaders can claim to have "constitutionally" held these positions in their respective countries, the constitutions, more often than not, were choreographed to suit the wishes of the leaders.

The two factors of political instability and political departicipation have combined to threaten democracy in Africa. They have also been responsible for the initiation of a search for the means of achieving a more democratic political process. The search has been complicated by the fact that the leaders of the various countries accept the privileges conferred by the Western political systems without the corresponding obligations. At other times, they

TABLE 3.2 Rate of Political Turnover in Africa Since Independence

Country	Average Tenure per Leader (years)	Leader with Longest Tenure	Number of Years
1. Algeria	7.7	Houari Boumedienne	14
2. Angola	5.0	Eduardo dos Santos	6
3. Benin	4.1	Matthew Kerekou	13
4. Botswana	9.5	Seretse Khama	14
5. Burundi	5.8	Jean-Baptiste Bagaza	9
6. Cameroon	12.5	Ahmadou Ahidjo	22
7. Cape Verde	10.0	Aristides Pereira	10
8. Central African Republic	6.3	Jean Bedel Bokassa	14
9. Chad	4.1	François Tombalbaye	15
10. Comoros	5.0	Ahmed Abdallah Abderemane	7
11. Congo-Brazzaville	5.0	Marien Ngouabi	9
12. Djibouti	8.0	Hassan Gouled Aptidon	8
13. Egypt	10.0	Gamal Abdel Nasser	16
14. Equatorial Guinea	8.5	Francisco Macias Nguema	11
15. Ethiopia	3.8	Mengistu Mariam	8
16. Gabon	12.5	Omar Bongo	18
17. Gambia	20.0	Duada Jawara	20
18. Ghana	3.1	Kwame Nkrumah	9
19. Guinea	13.5	Sékou Touré	26
20. Guinea-Bissau	5.5	Luiz Cabral	6
21. Ivory Coast	25.0	Félix Houphouet-Boigny	25
22. Kenya	11.0	Jomo Kenyatta	15
23. Lesotho	19.0	Lebua Jonathan	19
24. Liberia	13.7	William Tubman	28
25. Libya	17.0	King Idris	18
26. Malagasy Republic	5.0	Philibert Tsiranana	12
27. Malawi	21.0	Kamuzu Banda	21
28. Mali	12.5	Mousa Traore	17
29. Mauritania	6.3	Ould Daddah	18
30. Mauritius	8.5	Seewoosagur Ramgoolam	14
31. Morocco	14.5	King Hassan II	24
32. Mozambique	10.0	Samora Machel	10
33. Niger	12.5	Hamani Dioro	14
34. Nigeria	3.6	Yakubu Gowon	9

35.	Rwanda	11.5	Grégoire Kayibanda	11
36.	St. Thomas & Prince Islands	10.0	Manuel Pinto Da Costa	10
37.	Senegal	12.5	Léopold S. Senghor	21
38.	Seychelles	4.5	Frances Albert René	8
39.	Sierra Leone	6.0	Siaka Stevens	16
40.	Somalia	6.3	Siad Barre	15
41.	Sudan	4.1	Jafaar El Nimiery	16
42.	Swaziland^e	8.0	King Sobhuza II	14
43.	Tanzania	24.0	Julius K. Nyerere	24
44.	Togo	8.3	Gnassingbe Eyadema	18
45.	Tunisia	14.5	Habib Borguiba	28
46.	Uganda	3.8	Milton Obote	9
47.	Burkina Faso (Upper Volta)	5.0	Sangoulé Lamizana	14
48.	Zaire	5.0	Mobutu Sese Seko	20
49.	Zambia	21.0	Kenneth Kaunda	21
50.	Zimbabwe	5.0	Robert Mugabe	5

Notes

[a] Egypt became independent in 1922, but 1952 is used as the base year for this calculation because 1952 is the year of the Naguib coup.

[b] Ethiopia was not really colonized, and was a monarchy till 1974. 1974 is used as base for the calculation of the rate of political turnover.

[c] Liberia, like Ethiopia, was not really colonized, so 1944 is used as the base year for calculating political turnover.

[d] Morocco is still a monarchy. This explains why it enjoys long tenure of office.

[e] Swaziland is also still a monarchy.

have also indicated interest in a return to precolonial African political traditions.

These precolonial traditions have themselves undergone change because of colonial influence. The changes vary according to either the resilience of the traditional systems or the impact of the colonial administrations, which were of many varieties. Africa minus South Africa, which is under Afrikaner minority rule, has seven main colonial traditions. These are British, French, Portugese, Belgian, Spanish, Italian, and German. Liberia and Ethiopia did not have any significant colonial tradition except for the Americo-Liberian presence in Liberia and the Italian occupation of Ethiopia. Among the remaining seven political traditions, German political influence was of a very short duration, lasting from 1884 to 1919. After World War I, German territories were turned over to the League of Nations as trust territories and administered by Britain, France, and South Africa. German contributions to the political development of Africa were therefore limited, but assessment is complicated by the fact that these colonies underwent a double colonial experience *seriatim*. In this regard, the experiences of Cameroon may be the most interesting. Eastern Cameroon was part of the German colony of Cameroon and was later governed as a trust territory by France. On the other hand, western Cameroon, also part of the German colony, was governed by Britain. Both now form the Republic of the Cameroon, bringing with them differing colonial traditions. While eastern Cameroon has a colonial legacy of French republicanism, western Cameroon brought into the union the experiences of a parliamentary monarchy, thus creating problems of how to forge a mutually acceptable political system.

Italian colonialism lasted longer than the German, but Italy also lost some of her colonies after World War II. Eritrea, which for all practical purposes was administered by the Italians as a republic, was merged with the monarchy of Ethiopia to form a federation. It is no surprise that the two systems, which are opposed in principle, have not worked too well together since 1962.

The situation in Libya was very similar. In 1943, Libya was split between the French and the British to be administered under a United Nations trusteeship. The provinces of Tripolitania and Cyrenaica were administered by the British, while Fezzan was administered by the French till the independence of Libya in 1951. This meant that Libya, in addition to her varied precolonial tradition, at different stages and in different parts, experienced Italian, British, and French colonialism. Similarly, independent Somalia also has a bicolonial tradition, having been made up of British and Italian Somaliland.

Former German and Italian colonies, therefore, experienced multiple political traditions by having been transferred from one colonial power to another, or even split between them. These countries emerged from colonialism with a babel of political traditions that resulted in conflict. In postcolonial Libya and Cameroon, the dangers of conflicting political traditions were minimized through the adoption of federal political systems. These were based on the implicit assumption of the equivalence of anglophone and francophone political traditions. In both cases, federalism has been abandoned; Libya appears relatively quiet, but Cameroon still has problems securing her unity. Similarly, in the case of Ethiopia and Eritrea, the mistaken assumption of the equivalence and compatibility of political traditions resulted in the failure of the federal experiment and in fratricidal war.

It is not only in the colonial experiences that the African countries differ; their precolonial political traditions also demonstrate wide differences. In the search for viable political systems, therefore, the African countries now have to focus attention on political traditions that cut across the multiplicity of ethnic groups. The selection of appropriate political institutional arrangements must be based on widely accepted political philosophies with which the ethnic groups can identify. This is surely neither an easy task nor a panacea because there may not even be political consensus within single ethnic units.

Colonialism retarded the growth of traditional political institutions in order to prevent them from competing with the colonial institutions for the allegiance of the people. By undermining these traditional institutions, the philosophical bases of duties and obligations regulating the relationship between the governing and the governed were destroyed. Furthermore, the denigration of African traditional religions undermined political duties and obligations by neutralizing religion, which had provided effective cultic support for traditional political authority. Traditional deities were believed to punish swiftly and sternly; Protestantism taught that salvation can be gained through faith alone, and Roman Catholicism preached forgiveness of sin through confession.[6]

The secular religions that were substituted in the form of national flags, anthems, and pledges did not have the same depth of appeal and compulsion evoked by the traditional religions. These modern-day constitutional incantations are hardly established and do not fully inspire the people as effective substitutes. Perhaps it is because these secular religions are alien methodologies for mobilizing the people. Culture is a complex whole, and the recognition of the delicate balance between its parts is essential for the maintenance of cultural equilibrium. The ecclecticism that characterizes secular religions in the African countries today only makes them discordant ritual elements in the political system.

In this connection, it must be pointed out that the colonial apparatus also succeeded because it was not, by and large, a consensual hegemonic administration; it was, in most cases, a military government and, at best, a single-party system. Until shortly before their departure (and that was true only in the case of Britain), the colonial rulers had never tried to exemplify the practice of democracy; they were perfectly content with ruling in a strictly authoritarian manner.[7] While it is true that the colonial administrations created no foundations for government by consent, it is also true that most of them had not experienced democracy for long either. Full democracy dates back to only 1918 in Britain, while Germany had it for only fourteen years before World War II. France has enjoyed democracy longest, while Spain and Portugal smarted, until recently, under authoritarian regimes.

To varying degrees, the colonial administrations toned down autocracy by establishing local legislatures in the colonies. In the early stages, this took the form of a harmless dose of participation that ultimately resulted in legislative and executive independence. This approach to colonial development was taken by the British and appeared to have ensured a peaceful transition, except in Kenya and Zimbabwe.

The French and the Portugese adopted the ambitious and visionary approach of incorporating what they saw as their overseas provinces into the "metropolis." This geographical illusion created operational problems that, for instance, forced the French to change their policy to one of union, without unity, with their African colonies. Guinea, however, signalled that even the relationship of union was unacceptable, and France was persuaded to concede independence, albeit grudgingly. All in all, the relatively peaceful transition in the French colonies south of the Sahara can perhaps be explained by the failure of her intransigence in Algeria and Indo-China. The Portugese, on the other hand, were not persuaded against their visionary Lusitanian empire until, after two decades, attritional war threatened to rip apart even the metropolitan sociopolitical traditions.

It should be noted that independence obtained through wars of liberation often produced radical regimes. This is not because of an ideological conviction; it is because the nationalists believed that colonial capitalism could not be confronted by any variant of capitalism, but only by an equal and opposite ideology. The consequence of this is that the unassimilated democratic ideology is replaced by an equally unassimilated socialist ideology. The physical revolt against colonial rule is accompanied by an intellectual revolt that destroys faith in the learned political traditions of the colonial period. Examples of such places include Algeria, Guinea-Bissau, Angola, Mozambique, and Zimbabwe. The survival of radical regimes in those places depends on a combination of factors, including the kind of political leadership and whether or not the problems that necessitated the radical choice persist. In the case of the leadership, it is possible to assume that, when the generation which saw military action expires, the succeeding generation will be less committed to the raison d'être for the radical option. Also, the frustrations of operating a system in which the succeeding generation did not receive any practical training may force a retreat. But, whatever choice is made, political instability is the result.

The general picture of most of the African countries can be interpreted in terms of administrative experiments through which they have gone. First, there is the traditional political arrangement that the colonial system disrupted in varying degrees. In some places the colonial powers protected traditional cultures, as the British did with the system of indirect rule. Similarly, the French practiced indirect rule in strong centralized states like Morocco. The Portugese did the same among the Fula of Guinea-Bissau, while the Belgians played the Tutsi against the Hutu in Rwanda and Burundi. The effect of this was an uneven spread of colonial administrative education. This was complicated by the fact that, where the traditional rulers were incorporated into the administration, the educated elites were excluded. But, at independence, it was the educated elites that inherited political power; this created tension between them and the traditional rulers, who felt disempowered. This perceived status reversal generated conflicts in the postcolonial period. Such conflicts were often within the same ethnic group. Among ethnic groups the conflict was often between those accorded ad valorem treatment by the colonial powers and those that were less favored. The best example of this is Uganda, where the Kabaka sought to modernize their traditions in order to participate in competitive party politics.

Apart from the open conflicts resulting from the colonial experience, the perhaps farther-reaching effect is the mental ambivalence of the emergent African political class. At the individual level, there is a duality of values that results in an asymmetrical relationship between the normative and the legal order. This is the result of alienation from the state because most Africans have come to perceive government as distinct and different from society. The negative attitudes of the nationalist era toward government have persisted and, for a large number of the people, government remains the "enemy" of the people. Similarly, at the societal level, there is a cultural dualism because traditional political cultures remain side by side with the Western political cultures. The process of widening the political horizon only produced a moral disorientation, and people oscillated between incompatible patterns of behavior. This is principally because the dissolution of the old ethics and ethnic solidarity was not accompanied by the emergence of new norms, and thus it produced an anomie.[8]

The Western political cultures have not been able to absorb the traditional cultures perhaps because of the existence of the duality of values at the individual level. This often results in a syncretic articulation of values by political leaders, usually to camouflage their desire to remain in power. Solutions prescribed by the people and their leaders in these circumstances have varied widely, and have included: (1) integrative processes that recognize but deemphasize ethnic differences; (2) a return to a hierarchic but autochthonous hegemonic control; (3) authenticity; and (4) institutional integration or monolithization.

The different variants of integrative proposals recognize the disintegrative potential of ethnic differences. More often than not, they accord recognition to all ethnic groups by recognizing their right to participate in government. This was the underlying principle of the union government proposals of the late Colonel Acheampong of Ghana. It was believed that the arrangement would erase the feeling of departicipation among minorities, and among professionals, and therefore reduce unhealthy criticism of government; this was also the hope of the proposal of "election by selection through representation" by Siaka Stevens of Sierra Leone. The suggestions were admissions of problems, but they did not receive mass approval because they were seen as strategies for perpetuating the political leadership in office.

By contrast, proposals for hegemonic control often emphasize the right of the majority to rule. It develops an ethnic hierarchy that subordinates the minority to the majority and may, in the short run, produce an enforced ethnic harmony. Such systems are usually repressive because they tend to establish a vertical relationship between the ethnic groups dominated by the majority ethnic group. Chad provides a very good example of this under François Tombalbaye (1960–1975). Chad, with a population of about 4.5 million, has 192 ethnic groups "of which the most homogeneous are the 1,300,000 Sara and related groups living in the five southern prefectures. . . ."[9] In the precolonial period, the northern ethnic groups raided the Sara country for slaves; but, during the colonial period, the Sara welcomed the French and quickly acquired Western education of which the people of the north did not avail themselves. In the postcolonial period, power devolved on the Saras, who took that opportunity to avenge themselves on the northern ethnic groups. The people of the north, particularly the Toubou Arabs, saw Sara hegemony as a form of internal colonialism against which they then had to revolt.[10]

In order to achieve domination, institutional pluralism is abandoned in favor of institutional monism. Institutional checks and balances are neutralized and power is concentrated in the hands of the leader and his nominees. The rationale is that, in postcolonial plural societies, it is only institutional monoliths that produce national integration, while institutional pluralism in plural societies simply confirms social pluralism, which adversely affects the integrity of the postcolonial state. Consequently, single parties are established and people's political choices limited. Strangely enough, these are often claimed to accord with traditional political cultures and are usually accompanied by a deliberate creation of both the mystique of authority and charisma for the leaders. These messiah attributes develop into personality cults that usually isolate the heads of states from the people and produce a high political departicipation index (dpi). There is an inverse relationship between the personalization of office and the participation of the people in the political process: the spheres of political participation narrow as the spheres of government activities widen. The progressive shrinkage of citizen initiative (normally a countervailing force and a refuge against government) results in a monopolistic government. The most outstanding example of such a phenomenon was Francisco Macías Nguema, who appointed himself: "President for Life, Major General of the Army, Chief Educator of the Nation, Supreme Scientist, Master of Traditional Culture, Chairman of the Parti Unique National des Travailleurs," as well as the "only miracle that Equatorial Guinea ever produced."[11]

By definition, monopolistic governments often close all options to the people. Party membership counts as collateral for the enjoyment of civic rights, and governments become big and ubiquitous. It is therefore not possible to opt for Candide's option of aloofness because the wielders of power invade every citizen's privacy. Paradoxically, it is the impossibility of opting out that aggravates political competition because the stakes of defeat and victory are inordinately high. "The consequent further deflection of ambitions into politics aggravates strife and reinforces the predatory propensities of the rules and their henchmen."[12] This undemocratic situation seals all hopes of democratic development as long as privileges obtained through political influence are indispensable for decent living. Political speechifying replaces political action, and leaders emit political solutions that camouflage their Jacobin concept of power, in which an ultracentralized state makes all decisions.

The policy of *authenticité,* which lays claim to equality with traditional culture, has equally restricted political participation. This experimental policy was coined by Mobutu Sese Seko in Zaire as part of his effort to come to grips with the problem of building a virile, united country. In the 1970s, François Tombalbaye of Chad adopted the same policy of inculcating respect for tradition and obedience to elders.[13] More recently, Captain Thomas Sankara of Upper Volta (now Burkina Faso, "Land of Dignity") adopted the same policy in 1984.[14] In both Zaire and Burkina Faso, the adoption of the policy was accompanied by the adoption of a local name for the countries. Except for Burkina Faso, where it is too early to pass judgment, these changes in Chad and Zaire are no more than cosmetic; the governments are in no way better informed by traditions. The substantive problems in Chad under Tombalbaye and in Zaire under Mobutu are left unattended to. It is perhaps no coincidence that both states have a high pdi because of the long tenure in office of the protagonists of this policy.

It is true that all these approaches have failed, but each of them, in varying degrees, accepts that the solution to the African problems of governance perhaps lies somewhere in the cultures of the people. The main problem, however, is that, with the exception of Somalia and Basutoland, there is no monocultural African state in which culture means the same thing to all. A return to the cultures and traditions of the people therefore raises the problem of selecting the common aspects of those cultures. Perhaps, though, the cultural scene is not as complex as it may at first appear. Generally speaking, all traditional African governments were of two types—centralized vertical and noncentralized horizontal.[15] These two types often coexisted in almost all the African countries and have analogous social mechanisms through which their integration could be approached.

What are these principal common elements? They are unity of church and state, institutional pluralism, gerontocratic leadership with mass participation, and life tenure in office. These are the factors that characterize traditional democratic practice in Africa. In essence, the systems guarantee the accountability of the rulers as well as the governability of the people. I shall briefly discuss each of them to show how they collectively guarantee a participatory democratic process and political responsibility and responsiveness.

In precolonial Africa, there was no separation of church and state. The church was an instrument of administration. The political leader was, in theory, also the chief priest, and he determined the religious calendar of the society. The close tie between church and state produced a spiritual element that governed the actions of governors and subjects alike. The transcendence of the spiritual in all activities—social, political, and economic—had the significant effect of producing only a single moral code for all relations. Consequently, economic, political, and social relations, as well as private and public lives, were regulated by the same moral code. This avoided the pernicious duality of values that characterizes the contemporary African scene. Government was shrouded in mysticism, and the fear of sanctions elicited probity from leaders and obedience from subjects. There can be no complete return to that condition, but it brings attention to a vacuum that has not been filled by the alternative of Western secular religion.

The second characteristic of traditional African governments was institutional pluralism. Different political institutions performing different functions were established and guaranteed by the system. Each institution checked the powers of the other institutions so that a delicate balance was established between all of them. Excesses were checked because each institution served as the constitutional watchdog of the rights of the people. This arrangement therefore reinforced the mystique of government and the mystery surrounding traditional political leaders. The postcolonial phenomenon of single parties destroyed the traditional pluralism of political institutions and eliminated the usual check-and-balance role that these institutions had performed since time immemorial. The effect was an unusual inflation of the power of the leaders and a corresponding diminution of the people's control over their rulers. Rulers now often justify the narrowing of people's participation by arguing that institutional pluralism in the form of political parties is alien to Africa. However, legitimate dissent and participation were always present.

The third characteristic of traditional African governments was gerontocratic leadership balanced by mass participation. Africans have great respect for age, which is used interchangeably with authority; but, leaders had to continue to earn and deserve the respect of their subjects, failing which the traditional process of recall and impeachment were invoked. Respect for leaders and obedience to the laws were not forced; they evolved in response to the performance of the leaders and, subject to good behavior, leaders held offices for life.

Conclusion

Colonial political formulas are inappropriate to the postcolonial situations because the objectives of governments have changed. While the primary objective of colonial governments was the maintenance of law and order, the purpose of postcolonial governments is development and the consolidation of independence. But the leaders of the various states have failed to keep the promises of independence, which they have replaced with new promises. They first excited the people and then incited them. It is hardly surprising, therefore, that a group of Zambians complained "Those blokes from the Party came to see us and told us to 'vote the right way.' They made us all sorts of promises, but they haven't been back once since the elections." This is representative of reactions in many African states. The mystique and credibility of governments are thus gradually being eroded.

It is true that the manipulation of the system resulted from the inordinate ambitions of the leaders, but the vulnerability of ill-understood systems also made it possible. The leaders themselves have, strangely enough, confirmed the problems with foreign political systems by suggesting the import of optional political systems. However, they make no proposals for containing their own ambitions.

There are ways of curtailing the ambitions of the leaders by situating political systems within the mental horizon of the people; thus, manipulating the systems can no longer be seen as just honest mistakes. A widely understood system tends to narrow the power gap between leaders and followers. This will obstruct the growth of political monoliths by not only ensuring a division of authority, but also by what Mosca calls "the balance of social forces." Big and all-pervading governments have an inverse relationship to efficiency; they give the people the impression that they do not have to do anything because the government will do it all. The people are thus mobilized without their political participation, and the leadership is not accountable because checks and balances are neutralized. Only small-scale governments can restore political participation and bind the society to the state by recognizing the functions of both.

Notes

1. Stanislav Andreski, *The African Predicament: A Study in the Pathology of Modernization* (New York: Atherton Press, 1968), 123.

2. Virginia Thompson and Richard Adloff, *Conflict in Chad* (Berkeley: Institute of International Studies, 1981), 91.

3. Ieuan L. L. Griffiths, *Atlas of African Affairs* (New York: Methuen, 1984), 191–2.

4. The political stability index (psi) is an indicator of the rate of change in government. It is calculated on the widely accepted convention that a head of state like the American president serves only two terms of four years each in office, making a total of eight years. Thus eight years or two terms is taken as the maximum for the calculation of the psi. The psi is therefore a continuum from low (i.e., zero) to high (i.e., one). It is calculated with the year of independence as base. Thus the total number of years since independence is divided by the total number of governments to give the average per government. That average is divided by eight to obtain the psi. For example, Ghana, which became independent in 1957, and has had nine governments since, has a psi of

$$\{(1985 - 1957) \div 9\} \div 8 = \frac{28}{1} \times \frac{1}{9} \times \frac{1}{8} = \frac{28}{72} = 0.39$$

The general formula is $\frac{ys}{ng} \times \frac{1}{2t}$

where ys = years of sovereignty

ng = number of governments in years

and $2t$ = two terms

5. The political departicipation index (*dpi*) is the indicator of the lack of participation of the people in the political process. There are different forms of departicipation. These include military rule, and one-party regimes with or without elections. The frequency of change of such governments does not increase the political participation of people. The rate of political departicipation of these regimes is not quantifiable but absolute. The practice of mixed civilian-military executives under military regimes does not confer any participation on the people. Neither does the frequency of change of such governments increase political participation. In fact, in some cases it reduces political participation because it sometimes postpones the return to democratic civilian governments.

It is easy to calculate the *dpi* of governments only by longevity. The *dpi* of a government is the excess of tenure (*et*) over two terms (*2t*) divided by two terms: i.e., (*et* − *2t*)/*2t* where

et = excess of tenure over two terms
and $2t$ = two terms

Thus by 1985, since Dr. Kamuzu Banda has been president of Malawi since 1964, Malawi's *dpi* = (21 − 8)/8 = 1.6

6. Stanislav Andreski, *op. cit.* 42.

7. Joseph LaPalombara and Myron Weiner, eds., *Political Parties and Political Development* (Princeton: Princeton University Press, 1966), 8. Cf. Stanislav Andreski, *op. cit.* 111.

8. Stanislav, Andreski, *ibid.* 13.

9. Virginia Thompson and Richard Adloff, *op cit.* 3.

10. Benjamin Neuberger, *Involvement, Invasion and Withdrawal: Qaddafi's Libya and Chad 1969–1981* (Tel Aviv: Shiloam Centre for Middle Eastern and African Studies, 1982), 15.

11. Lanciné Sylla, "Succession of the Charismatic Leader: The Gordian Knot of African Politics," *Daedalus* 3 (1982):18.

12. Stanislav Andreski, *op. cit.* 119.

13. Virginia Thompson and Richard Adloff, *op. cit.* 26.

14. Yemi Ogunbiyi, "Burkina Faso: The Visions of a Future Country," *The Guardian Supplement,* 24 March 1985.

15. Lucy Mair, *Primitive Government* (Penguin Books, 1982); T. O. Elias, *Government and Politics in Africa* (New Delhi: Asia Publishing House, 1961); M. Fortes and E. E. Evans-Pritchard, eds., *African Political Systems* (Oxford University Press, 1948); and Lucy D. Mair, *African Kingdoms* (Oxford: Clarendon Press, 1977).

Ilunga Kabongo

Democracy in Africa: Hopes and Prospects

Democracy, that is the accountability of the rulers to their subjects, is not un-African, in spite of the current trends toward more or less totalitarian forms of rule in Africa. In many traditional systems in Africa, it was the political principle around which life revolved. In many segmentary societies in Zaire, for example, such as among the Baluba, the rulers had to be approved by a set of clans whose specific role was formally to hand power to the ruler chosen from within the ruling lineage, and to make sure his rule was in accordance with both the tradition and the expectations of his people.

In postcolonial Africa, modern forms of democracy were tried in many countries shortly after independence. With varying degrees of success, these forms have undergone basic transformations in some countries so that they look totally different from what they were in the immediate postindependence era; but in other countries—though very few—they have survived the challenges of time.

One can, therefore, safely say that since democratic systems have functioned in Africa both in the remote past and in the present era, democracy is not intrinsically alien to African people. A more pertinent question at this juncture to ask oneself is why the Western type of democracy has been so difficult to implement in the African context over the years, and what kind of democratic mechanisms are more suitable to the underdeveloped and dependent African state.

First, let me stress that democracy is not to be equated with just the ritual of voting and elections, but it is rather the coexistence of a plurality of opinions guaranteed by freedom of expression under the rule of the majority, the rulers being basically accountable for their action to this majority.

In this light, I would argue that if the forms of the Western type of democracy have been very largely subverted, the potential for democracy in African politics has remained largely intact. This is not so much because of

35

the will of the rulers, as it is because the societies' underdeveloped nature makes it difficult for one minority exclusively to appropriate power for a long time and to establish a truly totalitarian rule over the majority of the people.

The Western type of democracy has basically failed to be transplanted in African societies because it is expensive, artificial, and too sophisticated for what it gives in return.

The multiplicity of opinions entrenched in a multiplicity of permanent constituencies, called political parties, is just too costly, given the smallness of the elite groups and their ever-present readiness to turn to violence. For unknown reasons, multiparty democracy was brought to Africa along with a zero-sum game political culture. As a consequence, any gain on any issue by a group is seen by all the losers as a total loss on all issues. The energies involved in such a game are so intense for all parties involved that even the winner does not have the opportunity to enjoy fully his victory; the losers simply tend to withdraw from the game altogether and revert to extralegal means to reassert their points of view.

The sophistication entailed by the democratic process of the Western type also constitutes a barrier to its successful transplantation to African soil. Distinguishing between shades of opinions and subtleties of all kinds is not easily done by a peasantry and a working class that is still very much illiterate. Besides, politics in most African countries are conducted in non-African languages, which makes the matter even worse.

Faced with the basic dilemma of how to get rid of poverty, malnutrition and illiteracy, political issues about constitutional arrangements and ideological differences seem largely artificial to the African masses and a gimmick that keeps the tiny elite busy.

Finally, the cost of running all this democratic machinery is not replicable in most African states. It is reported, for example, that $400 million were spent on the 1983 Nigerian election. When there are so many priority programs that await funds to alleviate the fate of the people, one may wonder whether, for what it gives in return, that type of democracy is not too expensive for Africa.

The many variants of democracy that the African leaders have devised—"liberal," "guided," "social," or "participatory"—are all, to be sure, one form or another of dictatorship. Even Richard Sklar, who distinguishes these variant forms in spite of his optimism, acknowledges that "liberal democracy" is "democracy with tears and many reservations," that "guided democracy is, to be sure, a form of developmental dictatorship," and that in social democracy one finds "oligarchies" and "profound bias against opposition to leadership." As for participatory democracy, Sklar finds that the "party-state in Zambia abhors the very idea of political pluralism."[1]

Does this gloomy assessment mean that Africa is characterized by various forms of more or less disguised dictatorships; and, that except in those few states that still practice the imported form of democracy, such as Botswana or Mauritius, all African states are undemocratic?

I would argue that this is far from the truth. For one thing, the modern political arena in most African states remains very small; much of the society's political activity remains outside the modern sector. Even if the hegemonic group at the center is authoritarian, it may remain quite inefficient and ineffective in the larger realm of the periphery of the Periphery.[2]

Even though in this periphery, the peasants always have the exit option, the people nonetheless remain prey to bureaucratic disturbances by low echelon bureaucrats and soldiers who extort from them in various ways.[3] This does not make the system a dictatorship but, rather, an inefficient polity where democracy is negatively expressed: people withdraw from the system rather than become involved in it.

Even in the cities, where the impact of the undemocratic rule is more strongly felt, it seems to me that there is still a large area where laissez-faire is the motto and, provided people are careful not to involve themselves in activities disturbing to the system, they are largely left to themselves, unhindered in their activities and uninvolved in the political system.

One can argue that there exist in many African countries unspoken rules and mechanisms, which make the rulers responsive to the demands of the ruled. One such mechanism is *radio-trottoir* ("street radio"), which in many countries carries the message from the people to the hegemonic group. And in many instances, the latter takes into account the message of the former and tries to make its actions conform to the wishes of the people.

In a sense, "it would seem as [if] the rulers and the ruled lived face to face based on some mutually accepted rules, the chief being to never miscalculate one's action. Hence the hegemonic group has practically a free hand, on the condition that it does not disturb too much the people's freedom to enjoy access to some basic commodities: rice or beer prices may jump, but only within certain limits; and, certainly, there cannot be a shortage of rice and beer simultaneously. On the other hand, the people may take some liberties with the hegemonic group: a small and silent strike here and there, but not a general prolonged strike; more or less open criticism, provided they remain largely drowned in an anonymous current and sound like mumbling."[4]

In short, lack of genuine democratic practice in Africa does not automatically mean authoritarian dictatorship of an extended range. What we see, rather, is personal rule, more or less benevolent and more or less responsive to the African masses.[5]

Such a system is not, obviously, a healthy one. Elections tend to be replaced by coups d'etat, palace revolutions, or, at best, by popular uprisings. Social mobilization is smallest, and the freedom enjoyed by the people is at the price of a partial or total withdrawal from the political system. In the long run, this means that the likelihood of development through the involvement of the masses in projects devised by their leaders is very much diminished. I would argue that this will remain much the same for a long time, as long as development does not come to African societies. One needs some degree of development of the productive forces with its ensuing development of political consciousness in order to get some kind of democratic practice ingrained in people's behavior and expectations on a large scale and in modern terms.

Africa, it seems to me, has, by and large, successfully passed the stage of legitimating the political arena and political institutions established after independence. The next stage is to establish generally accepted rules and mechanisms for the democratic exercise of political power. This can come about only if there develop modern interest groups based on the successful modernization and development of the economy and its extension to the periphery of the Periphery. Only then, can a more elaborate and more active form of democracy be established and evolve as part of the local tradition. This process will take many decades since there are no quick solutions to the problem of modernization.

It is in this respect that the outside world can influence the establishment of democracy in Africa on a permanent basis. Working with a formal code of conduct to compel African states to turn democratic just will not do; the trend toward personal rule, which bridges modern and traditional Africa, is too deeply ingrained. It is by working on the conditions to bring about economic development that outside forces can promote the real conditions that will make modern democracy work on the African scene.

There is one major objection to my argument. What do African rulers do with the foreign aid that flows into their countries? Does not the absence of internal accountability and of democratic mechanisms allow the leaders to engage in the embezzlement of these funds and thus divert these funds from their intended national objectives? The objection is a sound one. It leads to the realization that if development can lay the ground for democracy, one needs some minimal democratic practice to ensure that resources, both internal and external, are put to the very furthering of development itself. This vicious circle can be broken only by African people themselves. It is up to them and to the most enlightened of their elites to make sure that changes—even drastic ones—are made within their politics to combat mismanagement and embezzlement of funds by corrupt autocrats and regimes. When this is done, outside forces should not interfere, as they often have in the past, to salvage corrupt regimes under the pretext of fighting communism.

In conclusion, I would say that, if a public moral stand on grounds of human rights by outside forces is acceptable, it should not lead to outside interference in the internal affairs of African countries, either in terms of democracy or antidemocracy. Instead, Africa should be left alone to find her own way, through trial and error, peacefully as well as violently, to make the rulers more accountable to the wishes of the majority of the people. In the process, only democracy can win in the long run.

Notes

1. Richard Sklar, "Democracy in Africa," *African Studies Review* 26, nos. 3/4 (September/December 1983), 11–24.

2. Aristide Zolberg, *Creating Political Order: The Party-States of West Africa* (Chicago: Rand McNally, 1966), 134.

3. Goran Hyden, *Beyond Ujamaa in Tanzania: Underdevelopment and an Uncaptured Peasantry* (Berkeley and Los Angeles: University of California Press), 25, 26.

4. Ilunga Kabongo, "Déroutante Afrique ou la syncope d'un discours," *Canadian Journal of African Studies* 18, 1, 1984, 17, 18.

5. Carl Rosberg and Robert Jackson, *Personal Rule in Africa* (Berkeley: University of California Press, 1983).

5

Austin Amissah

Constitutionalism and Law in Africa

Lawyers often discuss constitutionalism without reference to the economic and social conditions prevailing in the countries affected. The results are an imperfect appreciation of the actual causes of success or failure of the system. The exercise may be likened to a survey of faults in the superstructure without consideration of the foundation. In so far as that may fail to properly diagnose the cause of the disease, any remedy it proposes would have nothing except luck to recommend its success. Mahatma Gandhi was once supposed to have said that an empty stomach is not a good political adviser. The attribution is probably apocryphal, but the statement has a large measure of truth. The pressures created by the rapid political, economic, and social transformation which independence has brought cannot entirely be divorced from a discussion of constitutionalism and law.

Constitutionally elected governments that forget that the purpose of government is not only the establishment of law and order but also the promotion of the welfare of their people are bound, sooner or later, to be ousted from power. A constitutionally elected government does little for the system which gave it birth if its first consideration is not to understand its people and their difficulties and give priority to them. It is not unusual, for example, for members of a newly elected government in some of our newly independent countries to begin thinking first of pomp and circumstance of government; they secure their own personal comforts and perquisites while the country they are elected to govern faces a most serious economic crisis.

I recall that a newly elected government set the task of determining the emoluments of its key officers of state at a time when the conditions of the country required the taking of immediate initiatives to arrest the obvious and inevitable consequences of a rapidly deteriorating economy. Arguments that the emoluments should be set at high enough levels to match the dignity of the offices and to stop corruption were advanced to support some

41

demands, quite unreasonable in the context of the day. Leadership in sacrifice, at a time when the political slogan was the tightening of belts by everybody, was not mentioned by the members of the government during this debate. It came as a surprise to the government, after awarding themselves large salaries and allowances, that the workers in turn demanded massive wage increases. Forced to give in on this issue, the government never thereafter came to grips with the spiraling inflation that followed. It was overthrown less than two years later. That government operated under a constitution that carefully distributed powers between the executive, legislature, and judiciary; protected the independence of judges; and made the judiciary the guardian of the constitution. The constitution contained a bill of rights and had several provisions that were almost impossible to amend.

Contradictory imperatives in developing African societies often impose heavy strains on the constitutional evolution of government as practiced. An obvious example of this is found in the concept and treatment of corruption. The need to stamp out improper demands for gifts to influence the performance of official duties conflicts with a number of political and social phenomena. A political system depending on large sums of money for party organization and operation and for elections in poor societies leads to corrupt practices and a consequent diminution of confidence and respect for the probity of government based on that system. The custom of giving gifts in greeting or appreciation of service (to some extent recognized by the British colonial administration in excepting gifts from chiefs) is not strictly consistent with the notion of service without consideration that modern governmental mores postulate. The fact that some people basically regard a relationship of bribery and corruption in contractual terms means that, as long as the service is performed, or the consideration is refunded, evidence for prosecution will not be there. A social system that requires the more fortunate to take care of the less fortunate, and has an adopted political system that widens the concept of the extended family to include members of a whole supporting constituency, makes it difficult for those in positions of responsibility (and on fixed salaries) to match their obligations with their means; it thereby reduces their resistance to temptations to accept illegal considerations to supplement their salaries. Many persons elected or appointed to high political office have little to fall back on in private life and yet are most conscious of the limitations on their tenure of office and the liability to removal at any time without notice. Add to that plain human greed, and the problem of corruption in public office reaches unacceptable levels. The ridiculous spectacle of a government selectively enforcing corruption laws, when everybody knows that it practices the same evils, perhaps on a much grander scale, heightens tensions, and reinforces the desire for that government's overthrow.

The foregoing is not intended as a justification of corruption. It is raised as an illustration of the internal contradictions in modern African societies, and to ask whether traditional attitudes always coincide with the norms and requirements of our societies as presently organized. As with the inconsistencies in the perception of corruption, so with other inconsistencies. One such is the expectation of practicing a Westminster type of democracy in a society that sees as intolerable direct public insult, especially to elders; thereafter, friendly cooperation between the insulter and insulted is unacceptable. Another inconsistency is the difference in methods and qualifications for selection of traditional leaders as compared with the requirements for the leaders in the modern governments selected through the adopted political processes. There is inconsistency in the position of a society with a reputation for conciliation that takes the adversary procedure as practically the sole method of dispute resolution. Some thought has to be given to removing or at least reducing some of these contradictions between traditional characteristics of African societies and the forms of government they are presently expected to practice before a more solid foundation for constitutionalism can be built. The setting of a complex of political, economic, and social forces peculiar to the nations under discussion has to be kept in mind, especially when measured by standards fashioned by societies with other conditions.

At the time of independence, the political structures established were those of the colonial administrations, which were later replaced in the respective countries. In black Africa, these were mainly British, French, and, to a lesser extent, Portuguese, Belgian, and Spanish. It is true to say that, at the beginning, the independent nations followed as nearly as possible the institutions with which they had become familiar through association with their former colonial rulers. The U.S. presidential system was, because of residence and education of some of the nationalist leaders in that nation, so well known in the former British colonies that, when some found the Westminster model they had started off with, not quite satisfactory, they adopted elements from the U.S. system. It is also true to say that, with minor exceptions such as Botswana, nothing substantial in the independence constitutions was based on indigenous political institutions.

In the new systems of government, the parliament or the national assembly, which was supposed to enact legislation, was a representative body elected by universal adult suffrage. Such an institution was of relatively recent origin for most of the countries where it was adopted. Kings, chiefs, high priests, or other traditional leaders, who ruled the political entities before, had achieved their positions without the assistance of the ballot box. They stated what the law was and saw to its enforcement without the assistance of any body of representatives elected by such suffrage. Elders of the society, who advised political heads on the laws, administration, and enforcement, attained their positions through seniority and service to the community.

In these circumstances, it is remarkable that not much thought was given to the development of a system better understood by the majority of the people it was meant to serve. Reliance was placed on fashioning a constitutional system that would appeal to the educated and sophisticated town dweller, ignoring the fact that the overwhelming majority of the population were simple country folk. In newly independent societies with kings or chiefs, the tendency was to gradually emasculate these rulers or all powers, leaving them with only their ceremonial functions. The tenacity with which the institution of chieftaincy has persisted in some modern African states is largely due not to encouragement by either the colonial administration or its nationalist successor, but to the fact that the ordinary people refused to see it die. When judicial powers were taken from the chiefs, people still continued to take cases to them for settlement under an escape clause that allowed chiefs, like any ordinary person, to deal with arbitrations to which both parties voluntarily consented. When the right to grant or manage their lands was taken from them, various stratagems were devised to ensure their continued involvement in land allocation and the receipt by them of some of its proceeds.

It is also remarkable that much success should have been expected of the new constitutions when so short a time was given by the colonial administrations to the development of supporting democratic governmental institutions before independence. Universal adult suffrage, expressed in the slogan "one man, one vote," was so new that even some of the leaders who had experience of government through the limited form of representative elections that were allowed before, and who were therefore expected by the colonial administrators to take over the government of their people after independence, were unaware of its implications. Thinking that, because of their earlier prominence, they would be accepted as the natural successors of the colonial powers, they did little to cultivate the masses in whom now resided the power to make governments under the new dispensation. As a result, they were completely caught off guard when the results of the system they had all agreed to were announced. In some cases these supposed leaders never recovered from being outflanked; in others, their enjoyment of power was made possible at a later date only by the intervention of the military.

Relationships forged by the colonial linkages, whether through formal ties or informal and subtle influences, served to restrict the examination of alternative systems of representative government in the independent states. Thus, the ex-British colonies saw constitutions and constitutional government in terms of the structures and conventions obtaining in that former colonial power. The ex-French colonies, on the other hand, received and proceeded in the French tradition. As exceptions, some ex-British colonies turned to the constitution of the United States in the hope that it would supply answers to the defects they had experienced in the independence constitutions. Even now, when new constitutional forms are being devised by some African states, seldom is there any intellectual investigation or discussion amongst constitution makers of the comparative merits of particular African models. The commission appointed by the Liberian government to consider a new constitution tried to overcome this deficiency by visiting some other African countries. However, with the known exception of Mauritius, ex-British colonies have adopted the single-member constituency electoral system in which the winner takes all. They have either refused to investigate or to see anything useful in multiple-member constituencies or in proportional representation. That is surprising, considering the variety of interests, and differences in tribes, religions, and customs, that have to be catered to in the new states. This constitutional self-isolation still continues to a large extent.

To the majority of African peoples, therefore, the institutions of democratic government that were ushered in by independence were alien, and not much was done to educate them about the need for these institutions, nor time given to them to make the institutions their own. They had always been used to a different form of government in their own traditional societies. Except towards the end, and for only a short period of time, an autocratic form of government had prevailed under the colonial administrations. Without much practice, the new states were expected to operate under the most sophisticated modern democratic constitutions. If constitutionalism implies the practice of limited government, it seems that the limitations imposed upon the government must broadly be understood and accepted not only by those who operate the governmental machinery, but by the people to be governed. Otherwise, observing constitutional limitations can be wrongly construed by the public as weakness on the part of government, when government, as remembered from the colonial days, had never been weak. Faults in the operation of the system, such as delays caused by following the constitutional procedures, may be wrongly ascribed to incompetence, corruption, or evil motives on the part of those operating the system.

It was important, therefore, that the constitution be as simple as possible and be allowed to evolve with experience. When some of the constitution makers, on the other hand, came to enact the chief executive/presidential type of constitution, they did not think of enacting a constitution in broad basic terms; rather, they promulgated a detailed document that contained an elaborate bill of rights, together with other protections and rights, which can be found in amendments, judicial accretions, and academic commentaries over the past two hundred years of U.S. history. The more complicated the constitution, the more likely it is, in my opinion, to invite constitutional litigation. When this has followed the enactment of these complicated documents, the party in power that found itself as a defendant in court against opponents, who had lost elections, accused its challengers of using the courts as a means of reversing the people's decision. The courts themselves, so called upon, were sometimes steeped in the laws and procedures associated with the colonial power and had not had time to establish an independent reputation free from political controversy. When the courts, where necessary, had the duty to declare governmental action unlawful, they were themselves charged with being antigovernment.

A result of a multiplicity of constitutional cases is that matters may be held up while a case is *sub judice* and possible legislative or executive action to meet an urgent situation is unduly delayed. This creates disillusionment amongst ordinary people, who do not understand all the issues at stake. The degree of simplicity in a constitution can, however, be a difficult matter to judge. The constitution would be no better than any ordinary legislation if it did not cover the basic necessities of the establishment and allocation of state power, and give protection against hasty and ill-considered change. Making constitutional provisions unamendable or proscribing change by coups, as is sometimes done, has never been known to deter violent change.

The justification for the colonial governments was their efficiency in administration and, by and large, providing the people with their material needs. Independence movements captured the imagination of the colonial peoples by demonstrating the indignity and restrictiveness of life under colonial rule. The colonial powers were also relatively neutral in their balancing of the interests between the people governed. The people did not expect to lose these qualities upon attaining independence. What they then expected was a further enrichment of their lives by the addition of their lost dignity and a broadening of opportunities. Kwame Nkrumah's slogan, preferring independence in danger to servitude in tranquility, was inspiring not because the masses fired by it believed that independence would alter their lives for the worse, but because it offered them the opportunity to show that their lives could not be any worse. When the governments that followed actually demonstrated that self-government was nothing more than living the negative aspect of the slogan, disenchantment was complete; and, the justification for continuing with governments in the form they had when they achieved independence was impugned. The desire of the ordinary man, with whom (under the one man, one vote dispensation) rested the power to elect the government constitutionally, was for a body that could govern effectively, as he saw it: supplying his needs, catering to his aspirations, and providing him with leadership. How this body was constituted or how it achieved power, especially after his disappointment with elected politicians, and in some cases, a bewildering number of violent changes, was irrelevant to him. This is not necessarily a failure in a particular constitutional organization or form. It can come from factors outside the frame of a constitution.

Military government after military government has been hailed as liberator, redeemer, reformer, or savior, with the hope that it would correct the gross shortcomings of the discredited politicians. Not having any constituency except the troops to answer to, military governments have been congratulated when taking necessary but unpopular decisions, which politicians found themselves unable to take. But time has often shown that whatever their political philosophy, the military regimes had nothing better to offer. So, pressure is applied for the return of representative government.

When people lose confidence in their government, the problem is one of the mechanics of change. In countries with a well-established democratic tradition, the government is changed by a method preordained by the constitution. Where no such tradition exists, and that includes countries with constitutions but without a demonstrated democratic disposition over an extended period, other means are found to replace that government. The desire of African leaders and their political parties in general to perpetuate themselves in office is notorious. In the independent states, I believe only Presidents Léopold S. Senghor of Senegal and Ahmadou Ahidjo of Cameroon have left office without the intervention of death or violent overthrow. That is not saying that popular governments must go into voluntary liquidation from time to time just to establish a point on democratic disposition. On the contrary, some of the longest-serving heads of state are amongst the best-loved of their people. But the fact that there have been so many changes of an unconstitutional nature argues that at least some of the governments overstayed their welcome. Indeed, the problem of securing democracy in Africa has not so much been with how to ensure that a government representing the will of the people is elected. It is how to make sure that an elected government, which has lost the support of the people, will be changed according to law.

Laws by themselves may be insufficient to guarantee an orderly change. The ultimate sanction of government is power. And when the need for change comes, whether through effluxion of time or total incapacity to properly discharge the obligations of office, that change, according to law, can be effected only if there is an authority in position to enforce such orderly constitutional transition. By this I do not mean the courts, which are traditionally recognized as the law enforcement arm of the state; they have no more power than the backing political authority and effective public opinion are prepared to put behind their judgments. I mean an authority or body with power to ensure that its will is obeyed by the mass of people within the state. In the African countries, the most coherent and powerful force left by the colonial administration, once the momentum of the independence movement or its successor party had subsided, has been the military. Often that situation has been created by a government in power, through the steady repression of the opposition or the establishment of a one-party state.

A survey shows that of about fifty black African states, only sixteen, that is less than a third, have never had a successful military coup since independence. Some, like Botswana, Cameroon, Gabon, Ivory Coast, Kenya, and Zimbabwe are among the economically relatively better-off on the continent. But it is difficult to ascribe stability in all countries to economic soundness, as countries that are not so rich can be found among the sixteen, while some comparatively rich ones can be found among those prone to coups. Generalizations, therefore, have to be made with caution. One cannot help noticing, however, that some countries, especially in the western part of the continent, like Benin, Burkina Faso, Ghana, Nigeria, and Sierra Leone have each experienced several coups. In these countries, the absence of civilian constitutions has afforded no guarantee against further military intervention. What it is that makes these states in the West more susceptible to military coups than in eastern and southern black Africa I leave to the political scientists to explain. Perhaps there is some relationship between traditional forms of government and modern constitutional practice that provides an answer. Perhaps the awareness, in the southern states, of an external, destabilizing enemy has a salutory effect on the internal stability of those countries. Paradoxically, it is amongst the countries that have gone through the most coups that can be found those in which the indigenous people were given comparatively the longest experience of representative government before independence.

It is sufficient to say that Africa today has a variety of governmental organizations. No more than eight states continue with the multi-party democratic systems that they inherited at independence. A further dozen, all of which except Ethiopia are in the west of the continent, currently have military regimes. Of the nonmilitary states, Swaziland stands alone in being a monarchy in which no political party is permitted. The majority have, in the course of time, adopted a one-party system of government, which is supposed to better express the African political will. The concept of a loyal opposition, charged with a duty to publicly oppose the established government by methods including negative criticism and ridicule, is hardly one that commends itself to African sensitivities. For that and a variety of other reasons, some good (e.g., the desire to curtail the wastage of time and expense attendant to a multi-party system), and some bad (like the desire to perpetuate the party's rule), the independence constitutions were abandoned for one-party versions. One-party rule, however, is not the same in all the states in which it occurs. The nearest to the system of democratic choice known to the former colonial powers is the one that offers a choice of candidates within the one party, as in Tanzania. In others, the views of a select band, whether described as the central committee of the party or otherwise, prevails. The establishment of a one-party state has been no guarantee against coups. Benin (Dahomey) created a one-party state in 1964, had a coup shortly thereafter, and subsequently had no less than three others. Though still a one-party state now operating under a constitution, it has not had a coup for the past twelve years. It will also be recalled that Ghana's first coup occurred after President Nkrumah had declared the country a one-party state in 1964. Subsequent constitutions ruled out the possibility of the establishment of a one-party state. Ghana has had several more coups since.

Within the no-party, one-, or multiparty configurations, a wide spectrum of methods of constituting governments exists. Of course each must have executive, legislative, and judicial powers. How these powers are organized and distributed differs from state to state. A monarchy like Mauritius is the Westminster type of constitutional monarchy with a governor-general representing the Queen and a prime minister as head of the government. Swaziland's king, on the other hand, holds all power—executive, legislative, and judicial—although the judicial function has been delegated to the courts. Although most African presidents are elected directly by universal adult suffrage, some are elected indirectly, as in Benin, where the election is by the National Revolutionary Assembly, or in Sierra Leone, where the president is elected by members of the National Delegates Conference of the sole political party.

The election of legislatures by universal adult suffrage may mean different things in the different one-party states. Quite a number of them have, in addition, varying proportions of the legislature nominated—usually by the president—as in Burundi, Kenya, Malawi, and Sudan. Sudan's constitution provides for a high proportion of representatives nominated by workers' groups, aside from the president's appointees. Benin has an unusual arrangement whereby representation in its legislature is by special interest groups, instead of on a constituency basis; and, elections to the center are indirect, being on a multitiered basis. Mauritius operates a system with three member constituencies. Members of the national assembly in Guinea have to be between the ages of forty-five and sixty, an obvious demonstration of African traditional deference to age and experience. The degree of freedom that the legislatures have in enacting laws varies, of course, from country to country. But it is to be expected that one-party states in which representatives are chosen by the party executive have the least independence from the executive and party machine.

Judiciaries on the continent have ranged from the U.S. type—independent, separate, with a power of judicial review—as was the case of Ghana and Nigeria before their latest coups, and is so of Botswana today. There was Guinea, until this year, where, under the constitution, the president guaranteed the independence of the judges; and, Mozambique, which subordinates the judiciary to the people's assembly. Several of the constitutions guarantee human rights defined in various forms. One such country is Botswana, where its constitutional court was asked a year ago in the *State v. Selaolo* to rule on an act of the legislature. The act required that long-term prisoners be flogged at the beginning and the end of their sentences, and, in between, at regular six-month intervals. The court decided that the act was unconstitutional, taking the view that flogging on an installment basis, as the penalty seemed to indicate, was counter to constitutional protection against inhuman and degrading punishment. Lesotho has the interesting constitutional provision that, "if challenged, the government must establish in courts that, where there are several ways of achieving its objective, the means least restrictive of civil liberties have been chosen." In countries with guaranteed human rights, but without independent judiciaries in the accepted Anglo-American sense, it is difficult to imagine how such rights are enforced. One is reminded of the saying of Chief Justice Telford Georges that, "established countries with smoothly working institutions adapted to their needs tend to be critical when they do not see identical institutions in other places. It is tacitly assumed that since the institution is not there, the work it is intended to do is not being done." Before we rush to judgment on the models which have no obvious or known institutions for the enforcement of human rights, some empirical study has first to be done. However, there is a need to revive interest in the African Charter of Human and Peoples' Rights, which President Jawara of Gambia did so much to promote at the beginning of this decade.

It seems from the experiences of Ghana that if the law is to give some underpinning to constitutionalism, and the courts are made the guardians of the constitution, ruling impartially on the constitutionality of executive or legislative acts and enforcing human rights is best met when judges are given a measure of independence from both the executive and the legislature. Further, the greater the judges' security of tenure, the more independent they are in discharging their functions. In a different manner, this proposition is confirmed by the examples of countries like Botswana and Gambia, where appellate judges are drawn from lawyers beyond the borders and are free from the internal pressures of the particular country. Such a system may, however, carry its own inherent risks in producing judges without sensitivity to the problems of a nation to adjudicate on its most sensitive issues. However it is looked at, judges threatened with summary dismissal or other forms of prejudice, or even worse, faced with the prospect of abduction or murder, are unlikely to meet the criterion of giving judgment without fear or favor.

With this wide variety of forms, it would be illogical to conclude that African countries have continued to copy the constitutional practices of their past colonial masters. Some of the manifestations of African constitutionalism, for example the one-party democracy that is now prevalent, would be forcefully disowned by the colonial powers. The regularity with which new constitutional forms have been interfered with by the military, the introduction of new forms, and sometimes reversion to the old constitutional structures are evidence of the period of experimentation in government that the continent is going through.

When in power, even the military needs to operate (unless the regime is wholly autocratic) under some form of charter that shows the organization and distribution of power. Starting from the position of having no constituency and owing nobody but their soldiers any explanation, they often soon reach a point where they need to return the country to normal constitutional rule or clothe themselves with some form of constitutional rectitude. What is it then that places constitutionalism in a position of advantage when compared with arbitrary rule? It is the system of established rules of power allocation, rules by which responsibility can be determined and action judged, rules that declare beforehand the rights of citizens and the manner of their enforcement. It gives notice to all, in advance, of the framework within which everybody must operate.

Military or other forms of arbitrary governments may be enlightened, benevolent, efficient, orderly, or less corrupt. But their system, which often relies on retroactive punitive legislation (sometimes acted upon before publication and mostly enacted without popular discussion), their summary tribunals (often composed of people with no other qualification than a claim to revolutionary zeal) from whose decisions there is often no right of appeal, and their capacity to act without recognition of any legal checks soon outweigh whatever positive virtues they may have. There is hope for constitutionalism in Africa.

Pauline H. Baker

Reflections on the Economic Correlates of African Democracy

Introduction

A common assumption underlying both conventional wisdom about the Third World and professional analyses of political behavior in developing countries holds that there exists a critical linkage between democracy and economic performance. However, little research has been done to test the validity of that assumption or to examine the ways in which the association operates in practice. Moreover, as applied to the African environment, the assumption seems to apply only in selected cases or under selected conditions. Some regimes, such as Zaire, Sudan, or Zambia, appear remarkably resilient in spite of severe economic distress. Others, such as Benin, Nigeria, and Burkina Faso (Upper Volta) have fallen victim to a pattern of coups d'etat linked to economic difficulties. Still others exhibit trends that seem to defy generalization in this regard. Jerry Rawlings, for example, said he led his first coup in Ghana because the government was going to devalue the currency; he led his second coup, in part, because the government was not going to devalue; and, during his tenure, he has presided over a 1000% devaluation.

While these events have thrown many observers off balance, analysts persist in trying to establish empirical linkages between economic performance and political stability. The most recent comprehensive empirical examination of this issue was conducted by Johnson, Slater, and McGowan in an article published in the *American Political Science Review* in September 1984. The authors examine a wide range of factors involved in African political instability, noting that:

> After nearly ten years of economic crisis, it is entirely plausible to reason that economic deterioration and dependence in Black Africa has been a

major force behind the military interventions of the 1970s and 1980s . . . we find that three measures of positive economic performance are all highly stabilizing and, conversely, that African states whose economies have not performed well in the 1960s and 1970s are prone to coups.[1]

To support this conclusion, the authors cite the correlations they found between specific economic indicators and the frequency of coups:

States where the ratio of industrial jobs to all employment increased the most between 1960 and 1978 have been relatively stable, as have states whose economies grew in the late 1960s and whose mid-1960s export performance was superior. Finally, . . . states whose commodity exports became less diversified in the early 1960s have experienced more military interventions than those whose economic or market dependency lessened in the same period.[2]

Even if one accepts the validity of this analysis, it leaves the reader with a profound sense of dissatisfaction because it does not explain how the association between democracy and economic performance actually works. Though we have empirical evidence supporting a linkage that has been widely accepted, if not conclusively proven, we still lack an understanding of the process by which economic success or failure translates into political action.

In this discussion, I draw attention to two different experiences in which this linkage operates. Both are based on field research undertaken in Africa recently and both touch upon sensitive questions with which all African governments must deal.[3]

The Indigenous Private Sector

The first topic examines the role of indigenous entrepreneurs as an example of a key interest group. An entrepreneur is defined here as a person who organizes, operates, and assumes the risk of a profit-making business venture, one who is a manager or a producer. Setting aside the agricultural sector, which has special needs, the African entrepreneurial class consists of a world of mostly small operators including artisans, traders, craftsmen, and small-scale manufacturers. The indigenous commercial sector is probably the most neglected and least understood facet of economic development in Africa. Research is limited, data unreliable or non-existent, and a great many misperceptions continue to prevail about the size, structure, and motivations of the entrepreneurial class.

One reason for this lack of knowledge is the African historical bias in favor of the public sector as the leader in development. At the time of independence, most developing countries believed that rapid economic development could only come about through very strong intervention and leadership by the public sector. Indigenous entrepreneurs, it was thought, could not play a strong role in development because they lacked skilled manpower, resources, information, and organization. Due to the wide-spread view of government as paternalistic and protecting, an attitude encouraged by tradition and colonial rule, the ordinary person looked to government to lead the way. Thus, in Africa the public sector was far ahead of the private sector in bringing about development strategies—the reverse of the situation in most advanced market economies where the private sector led the pace for development.

The public sector is now coming under severe criticism for having failed to fulfill expectations for development. The majority of coup-makers cite economic reasons—such as mismanagement, corruption, coming to terms, or failing to come to terms, with the IMF—as justifications for their rebellions. Once in power, however, the soldiers often follow a similar path, lacking the ability to enhance productivity, increase government earnings, or instill greater economic management. Moreover, they do not seem to have any better notion of how to relate to the private sector whose economic performance, more and more, will affect the fate of governments.

In addition to a historical tradition weighted in favor of the public sector, entrepreneurs face many current constraints, not the least of which is the widespread belief that they don't really exist or, where they do exist, do not constitute a significant or legitimate economic force. This may be a debatable question, but if one adopts a broad definition of entrepreneurs as indicated above, and if one observes the reality of how goods and services are supplied and exchanged, then the private sector may be said to be very much alive in Africa—albeit not very healthy.

Limited by depressed economies, entrepreneurs must operate in an environment of overvalued currencies, foreign exchange shortages, and bureaucratic bottlenecks. Import licenses, credit facilities, and contracts are often disbursed as patronage. In addition, a maze of laws, regulations, and accepted practices exist to restrict both foreign private capital and local entrepreneurs, which are frequently lumped into the same category. Several African governments have castigated the role of foreign capital, criticized the acquisitive nature of indigenous entrepreneurs, and promulgated laws that restrict both—this in spite of an array of policy statements, investment codes, indigenization programs, and tax incentives that extend a welcoming hand to the private sector and theoretically encourage its development.

The gap between the principle of fostering economic pluralism and the actual commercial environment in which entrepreneurs have to operate is harmful to the economic growth and political stability of many societies. Entrepreneurs are either driven out of business through policy directives not based on economic rationality, or, with increasing frequency, are driven to extralegal activities. In their eyes, the state is not a partner, a regulator, or an arbiter but a competitor and powerful opponent to be avoided, evaded, and disregarded.

Smuggling, illegal currency exchanges, corruption, parallel markets, and other illegal or quasi-legal practices have appeared at an alarming rate as common features of the economies of postindependence Africa. These practices cannot be attributed simply to the dishonesty and avariciousness of a few individuals; the phenomenon is too widespread for that. Nor can they be written off as a temporary phase of development, although historical changes in the mores and ethics of developing nations play an important role. Rather, it should be recognized that there is an intimate connection between the practices of the business community—practices that, whatever their legal status, are fulfilling supply and distribution needs of societies facing economic deterioration—and the commercial environment that state policies help to shape. That relationship has political implications for the emergence of both democratic institutions and political processes.

A related problem for the entrepreneurial community is ambivalence in attitudes of government officials toward indigenous businessmen. One might naturally assume that African governments would prefer to favor their own nationals over foreign investors, but they are deeply divided on this issue. Even those governments which have sought to encourage private sector activities have done so with mixed emotions.

The reasons are complex. Some governments are reluctant to foster a new African capitalist class to replace the white capitalists they associate with colonial domination. Scarce resources and conservative economic preferences for qualified skills further complicate the matter, with some leaders, especially in francophone Africa, openly admitting that they favor a foreign investor, who can bring management, technology, and needed foreign exchange to a project, over a local partner. Governments are also concerned about losing manpower skills in state institutions. Parastatals, government agencies, and foreign corporations have absorbed most high-level manpower, and officials do not want to dilute the degree of Africanization already achieved in these agencies.

Political considerations, as always, enter the picture as well. Governments are concerned over the possible political and economic impact of a thriving entrepreneurial class. Military and bureaucratic elites profit from indigenization efforts and are reluctant to see a private business class emerge to rival their power and status. It is not clear how an independent business class will assert its influence in the next political generation, a development which appears to be of real concern in a few states, such as Nigeria and Kenya.

This leads to a wider problem—the negative attitudes of the general public toward entrepreneurs. In interviews conducted in Kenya, Sudan, Zimbabwe, and Nigeria, local entrepreneurs reported that they are perceived as "exploiters" taking advantage of society as a whole. Public bias against local businessmen is a product of several factors, including the colonial experience, postindependence disillusionment with political leadership, ethnic competition, and ideology. In some areas, it is a legacy of the identification of capitalism with racism and foreign domination. In others, it is a more recent identification of government with corruption, the public assuming that successful entrepreneurs must have been granted special privileges to get ahead.

These three major constraints—government policies that unwittingly drive the business community into extra-legal or illegal activities, the ambivalence in attitudes of many governments about encouraging indigenous entrepreneurs, and negative public perceptions about the business community—illustrate the difficulties of implementing pluralism in the economic sector.

Revenue Distribution

It is not only in the private sector that economic trends affect the development of pluralism; an example from the public sector can be seen in the Nigerian experience with the revenue allocation system adopted during the second republic. Here is a case in which an African democracy unknowingly planted the seeds of its own destruction by failing to include provisions for accountability in what was, in every other respect, a model of revenue distribution based on fairness and equity.

Following the Nigerian civil war, the Obasanjo military government attempted to deal seriously with the task of institutionalizing local interests in a federal system that was reflective of the heterogeneous nature of the society and, at the same time, was resistant to manipulation by one or more communal groups. More states were created, civilian rule was reinstituted, and a new constitution promulgated. By 1979, the country was poised on the threshold of what seemed to be a promising future, launching a new experiment in democracy strengthened, it was then thought, by a trend of unprecedented oil revenue. By 1980, Nigeria's income had reached a peak of over $22 billion and this was, in large part, passed on to the nineteen states, which increased their revenue by about 300%, from 1977 to 1981.

Although it was not part of the constitution, a new revenue allocation formula was adopted by the civilian regime of Prime Minister Shehu Shagari to avoid disproportionate windfalls to certain states or groups as a result of political considerations. In essence, what the new system tried to do was provide for financial equity among the various interest groups, ethnic communities and political constituencies whose competition had previously created unrest and violent upheaval. This system was to ensure that cultural pluralism would be reflected financially, by a formula in which all major parties, represented through the states, would be guaranteed fixed shares of public funds.

The revenue law enacted in January 1982 was the fairest system of income distribution Nigeria ever had had. It ensured, by statute, that federally-collected revenue went to all the states according to guidelines that were based on predetermined, quantitative criteria on which there had been broad consultation and consensus. Allocations to the states were guaranteed by law regardless of the party in power, the states' record of performance, their ethnic composition or their geographic location—issues which were widely believed to have affected patterns of revenue distribution in the past.

The hidden weaknesses of the system were twofold: (1) a legacy of diminished states' authority inherited from military rule, and (2) the absence of procedures by which the recipients of public funds could be held accountable for their expenditures.

The soldiers who had ruled Nigeria during the 1970s had stripped away the states' power, including revenue-raising authority, in order to thwart secessionist tendencies and strengthen central authority. The states accepted this loss of power because they were compensated by large ad hoc grants and because, at the time, prospects for continued high income from oil looked good. Hence, the new revenue allocation system adopted by the civilian government in the early 1980s looked like an extension of this good fortune, with the added features that no one state or ethnic group would be able to manipulate federal revenues to its own advantage and state governors would be free to spend the money as they wished.

Two things happened to erode confidence in the system. First, the states interpreted their automatic allocations as blank checks that they could use at their own discretion. High expectations, a lack of control over expenditures, and the freewheeling activities of state governors who felt the need to respond to pressures for patronage led to uncontrolled spending, rapidly mounting debts, widespread mismanagement, and—what is probably the most critical failing of all—a lack of accountability.

The second thing that happened was the collapse of the oil market. The drop in oil prices and the sharp decline in federal revenue meant that the new revenue allocation formula gave the states a larger share of a shrinking pie. Their powers to raise revenue had not been restored and their spending commitments had mushroomed. Between 1976, when the nineteen-state structure was created, and 1982, when the new revenue allocation system was enacted, recurrent expenditures of the states had risen by 250 percent, most of which went for salaries and benefits for state employees. Intense lobbying for distribution of patronage and largesse focused on state governors. These power lords dispensed jobs, contracts, and benefits to local supporters and party loyalists with little or no accounting for either their state or party finances. So recklessly extravagant had the states become during the second republic that gubernatorial office became the most coveted political post in Nigeria after the presidency.

The irony is that the system that engendered this behavior had, in principle, brought an unprecedented degree of financial security and ethnic/state equity to Nigeria. It might have worked if the country had continued to generate large oil revenues, although state budgets would have ballooned at a phenomenal rate. When Nigeria fell upon hard times, the states were burdened by deficit financing, austerity, and inadequate revenue-raising authority of their own. The result was precisely the opposite of what had been intended: financial insecurity, a loss of confidence in the system, and an erosion of the legitimacy of the leadership. Politicians were regarded either as exploiters taking advantage of the situation for personal gain or as weak bystanders who lacked the strength or courage to stop the corruption. This development contributed to the decline of public confidence in the democratic system as a whole. To the average person, the system was opening doors for the enrichment of the political class, rather than, as originally intended, closing them to enrichment of particular ethnic or regional groups.

The collapse of the second republic obviously occurred not only because of inadequacies in the revenue allocation formula, but because of weaknesses in the Nigerian economy and mismanagement and lack of public accountability by the leadership as a whole. Nevertheless, the revenue allocation system contributed to the upheaval, in no small measure because it highlighted the disparity between the principles and the practices of democracy.

Conclusion

These examples focus on some of the economic correlates of political pluralism in Africa. They underscore the linkages between democracy and economic productivity and show the importance of perceptions of equity, not only among ethnic and communal groups, but among social classes as well.

This discussion also suggests some of the political costs of economic failure. In the case of the first example, the difficulties encountered by entrepreneurs throughout Africa represent a set of circumstances that impede the progress of what may prove to be Africa's most economically productive class. In the second example, we saw how the distortion of a revenue-sharing formula based on equity into one that was seen to promote the growth of a venal ruling class had the effect of undermining one of Africa's most promising democracies.

Perhaps the real lesson to be learned from these experiences is one that needs to be constantly remembered: in Africa, a political system is measured not by the extent to which it measures up to abstract principles of democracy or conforms to institutional models imported from the West. Rather, it is measured by the way in which it operates in practice; in particular, it is the extent to which it represents the interests of key groups, balances competing claims on limited resources, improves the quality of life of the masses, and offers hope of widening opportunity. It is a matter of differentiating the form from the substance.

The economic indicators used by Johnson et al., cited above, to interpret and predict political instability, touch the surface of a subject in which far more data needs to be gathered and far more research needs to be conducted. The most valuable research would go beyond correlating quantitative economic and political variables to delve into the specific ways in which deeper social and economic processes actually work in a continent in great transformation.

Notes

1. Thomas H. Johnson, Robert O. Slater, and Pat McGowan, "Explaining African Military Coups d'Etat," *American Political Science Review* 78 (September 1984):633.

2. Ibid. 634–5.

3. See *Obstacles to Private Sector Activities in Africa* (Washington, D.C.: Battelle Memorial Institute, 1983), and *The Economics of Nigerian Federalism* (Washington, D.C.: Battelle Memorial Institute, 1984).

Elliott Abrams

7

Pluralism and Democracy

The great nineteenth-century German chancellor, Otto von Bismarck, is reported to have said, "He who speaks Europe speaks nonsense." Bismarck was referring to the fact that European traditions were so diverse, European nations so different from one another, that to speak of an entity called "Europe" was extremely misleading. Africa's cultural, political, and ethnic diversity makes it quite possible to paraphrase Bismarck and state that, "He who speaks Africa speaks nonsense." That diversity helps explain why, when it comes to questions like, "How do you promote democracy in Africa?" or "What social and economic conditions, if any, are necessary for democracy to take hold in Africa?" few precise, or empirically verifiable, answers present themselves.

Two fallacies must be avoided in thinking about democracy in Africa. The first is the notion that Africa is essentially similar to the United States, except perhaps that it is poorer and blacker. This may be called the "mirror image" fallacy. In this view, the reason democracy is not a widespread form of government in Africa is simply because African leaders are either ignorant, corrupt, or power-hungry. If only the African "people" were consulted, Africa would overwhelmingly opt for democracy. After all, if democracy works for Americans, why shouldn't it work for Africans? This view, of course, is grossly misleading. African problems are very different from American problems. African cultural and political traditions are often very different from American cultural and political traditions, and the African social and political context is very different from the American context. To view African reality as essentially a mirror image of American reality is to misunderstand fundamentally the nature of the African predicament.

The opposite fallacy, of course, is the notion that African politics is so different from typical democratic politics that the gap is simply unbridgeable. Sometimes it is said, for example, that democracy can never take root in Africa, that it is basically foreign to local ways of doing things. Quite apart from the fact that serious students of African history have demonstrated that among the various native African political traditions, there does exist a significant democratic tradition, this view presents problems on broadly philosophical grounds. Human beings are not simply the products of their environment and their culture. We do enjoy free will; we can, within limits, transform our historical situation. If one believes in free will, and if one believes that historical outcomes are not predetermined, then one also must believe that differences can be bridged over time, that political systems can be adopted, and adapted by different cultures and societies.

For this reason, on the question of democracy in Africa, it is possible to be a realistic optimist. On the one hand, we should strongly reject the view that democracy in Africa can be established overnight, that it is all a question of political will. On the other hand, we should equally reject the view that democracy has no prospect of success in Africa, and that the democratic experience is not relevant to Africa. In studying contemporary African problems, we must constantly ask ourselves: What policies are most likely to promote movement toward democracy in Africa over the long run? What are examples of the kinds of trends we ought to be encouraging, and conversely, what policies ought we to avoid?

I would advance a number of propositions which may help us to respond to these questions. First, the role of political elites in African countries is obviously crucial. In 1957, there were few observers who could have predicted how matters in most African countries would turn out after independence. Many developments hinged on the wisdom, or lack of wisdom, of a handful of leaders. African history and culture did not predetermine the outcome. Leaders had, and continue to have, a large margin for maneuver. One can never underestimate the degree to which democracy in Africa depends on choices that remain to be made.

Second, most observers would grant that few if any African leaders set out to repress human rights and create a reign of terror in their countries. Their aim, rather, was not only to secure their own positions, but also to promote economic development as quickly as possible. It seemed to them that a command economy, run by the state, was the best means of mobilizing the populace on behalf of economic growth. In this view they were supported by some of the leading Western theorists of development. In the event, these theorists were proven wrong. In retrospect it seems obvious that in multiethnic, multireligious, traditional societies, "mobilizing the population" can only be attained through coercion. Since coercion provokes resistance, which in turn leads to even greater coercion, a brutal dialectic of repression and resistance quickly develops. To use a Leninist phrase: "He who say *A* must say *B*." Governments that set out to mobilize highly pluralistic societies, as African societies generally are, inevitably end up becoming dictatorships.

Decisions about social and economic development may in large part determine the future of democracy in Africa, as elsewhere. The decision to push the country into an economic "forced march" will have dire political consequences, even if this is not intended. Democracy and pluralism in Africa, then, will not thrive unless leaders seek truly open societies and free economies; when a strait jacket is prepared for parts of the society, dissidents and opposition figures end up being tied into it.

The essential fact is that when the government assumes such extensive power and control over the economic life of a society, control of the state becomes the sole means of economic and social advance. This is almost guaranteed to exacerbate ethnic, religious, and tribal tensions. When the state decides where all significant investments will be made and allocates the wealth, then talent, initiative, and enterprise get channeled into a fight for political power. Thus in one African country after another tribes or their leaders battle over control of the government while economic development languishes.

There are obvious exceptions, of course, and one is the Ivory Coast. Given the poverty, illiteracy, and primitive level of development that characterized the Ivory Coast when it achieved independence, most would agree that a strong government, and a charismatic leader, were required to hold the various communities of Ivory Coast together. Yet a strong government and an oppressive government are not at all synonymous. Unlike Sékou Touré or Kwame Nkrumah, Félix Houphouet-Boigny did not set out to control the tribal councils, the unions, and the churches—the crucial mediating institutions that protect the individual from the state. He proved that rapid economic development did not imply the "mobilization" of society by a central government, but was compatible with a high degree of respect for pluralism and human rights.

Maintaining the autonomy of mediating institutions like unions, churches, and local councils is important not only from a human rights point of view, but also from a democratic point of view. For history suggests that mediating structures are the sociological soil from which political democracy, if absent today, may grow tomorrow. As Professor Peter Berger has pointed out:

> It is in itself good if the state does not seek to interfere in the family or religious life of its people, or if it allows them to band together for the pursuit of economic interests. But beyond this immediate good, there is also the strong possibility that this kind of participation will eventually lead to pressures for political participation—and, just as important, will accustom people to social practices that are indispensable to the workings of democracy.

Thus, while stable multiparty democracy may be difficult to maintain in some African states, its future development can nevertheless be fostered and encouraged through wise policies. I therefore strongly disagree with those who say that political democracy is unrealistic for Africa. The great fallacy of this so-called realistic school of thought is that its horizons are limited by its particular moment in history, which it wrongly assumes will continue indefinitely.

It is quite conceivable that one day ethnic, tribal, and religious factions will be transformed from agents that seek control of the state to mediating institutions that circumscribe the claims of the state on the individual and foster expanded economic opportunities and greater expression of individual freedom. In fact, democratic development in African countries will hinge in large part, I believe, on the degree to which tribal and other divisions are transformed from the battle lines over control of the state to ramparts of defense from state power.

My own view is that the actions that a political elite takes, or fails to take, can have a decisive impact on how history turns out. For this reason, I believe that a serious commitment to the promotion of democracy requires the United States to do at least two things. Economically, it should encourage African countries to foster market economies and avoid state control of the economy. Politically, it should encourage authoritarian governments to grant as much autonomy as possible to the mediating institutions of the society, in the realization that these institutions are the seedbeds of future democratic development.

This admittedly is a very "American" view, and rests, in large measure, on our leading political theorists—America's Founding Fathers. They faced a problem not foreign to Africa; that is, "in framing a government which is to be administered by men over men, the great difficulty lies in this: you must first enable the government to control the governed; and in the next place oblige it to control itself." The need for government strong enough to govern, yet still not oppressive, is not a new problem. One part of the solution is found in the rich tapestry of African life, the many ethnic, tribal, religious, and geographic loyalties that can underpin democratic life. These can be perverted into divisions that create rival teams in a fight to the death over state power. Democracy in Africa will not thrive where that battle is joined, where all of life becomes permeated with politics. When cultural, religious, and economic life are allowed to develop independently, when individual enterprise means betterment of one's self, family, village, or tribe without the need to control the state house, police, or army, the chances for democracy will be greatly advanced.

Pathé Diagne

8

Pluralism and Plurality in Africa

In the light of current crises, the notions of ethnicity and pluralism have prompted an increasing interest in the complex and heterogeneous societies of contemporary Africa, the developing Third World, and even in the great industrialized nations.

Pluralism is a term that has many different and often contradictory meanings. The concept which interests us here is one that contains many ambiguities.

Any discussion of plurality and pluralism involves wider and more essential questions which encompass the social sciences, particularly the fields of sociology and political science, as well as anthropology.

One question alludes to judicial, political, social (ethnic or racial), economic, and even ethical or epistomological pluralism.

Another refers to the various understandings and usages that the term has been given, notably in the United States and France. But, more recently, there are various understandings in the young nations of the Third World threatened by external domination or internal instability.

Furthermore, we can observe that the renewed theoretical interest increasingly reflects the fact that the concepts of *pluralism* and *plurality,* and a *plural* and *pluralistic society* have become the controversial subjects of debate. This debate has divided the important schools of thought. These differences are in themselves revealing and lend a further understanding of the concept. They contribute to heuristic, methodological, conceptual, and theoretical approaches, while expressing a doctrinal and philosophical foundation.

Like many researchers, I understand the term "plural society" to refer to a heterogeneous and complex society. This especially refers to the context of a society's racial or ethnic components and how they interact in the socioeconomic realities, territories, regions, ideologies and beliefs, and

Translated from the French by John R. Heilbrunn.

65

even its political institutions and class struggles. It is unimportant whether these parts be dominant or subordinate, in a state of permanent stability or instability, in conflict within themselves or with each other.

It is in this perspective that a great number of societies, which have been attempting for several centuries or decades to construct nation-states, are in varying degrees plural. This is true whether one is speaking of Nigeria, Zimbabwe, India, the United States, Yugoslavia, or even the Soviet Union. Cultural, ethnic, socioeconomic, historic, or regional differences are found in the core of the modern state. If the governing powers do not succeed in reducing these forces, they are forced to compromise. These differences are the echoes of plurality. This has been admirably described for the United States by Thomas Sowell in his book *Ethnic America*.

Pluralist claims, which explain the aspiration for individual liberties, for many political parties, or a state of democracy, are linked to plurality. Pluralism is also present in demands for social justice in the interior of the monocracies and single-party systems of Africa.

The plural society, whether stable or not, autonomous or dominated from the outside, is a universal phenomenon. The dominated society of a colonial empire is not an exclusive example. The system of apartheid in South Africa, among others, is a model. Apartheid as a nondemocratic pluralistic state adequately furnishes a model of a dominated system. The lack of democratic pluralism can be discerned in a number of totalitarian systems controlled by ethnic or ideological minorities. Plurality, as the expression of diverse factors, whether conflicting or not, constitutes an axiom.

Democratic pluralism and its antithetical forms constitute a major, universal debate. It is a controversy that is hidden in the heart of all relatively heterogeneous societies. It is one of the forces of social, ideological, and philosophical history.

Pluralism in this sense and in the understanding of a great number of theoreticians is linked to a conscious or unconscious agreement on organized heterogeneity. This means that pluralism is linked to a more or less explicit strategy of agreement on, or acceptance of, the plurality of racial, ethnic, ideological, political, and socioeconomic differences. This can be done through consensus and balanced relations; it can also be done from the worry that one of the components of the plural entity will be able to dominate the others.

It is my opinion that pluralism as an approach constitutes a latent tendency in the African vision. This is especially true in black African culture facing problems of differences and diversity of the "one" and the "many," and all the potential conflicts tied to heterogeneity.

Pluralism may have contradictory consequences of an unpleasant nature for the balance and equality between African communities. This is also true for other societies where there is oppression and the absence of freedom of expression. Therefore, the notions of a plural and pluralistic society of plurality and pluralism must always be qualified.

A modern philosophy professing pluralistic civilization and culture, monotheism, law, power, epistomology, or esthetics, is the opposite of segregationist, reductionist, and totalitarian pluralism. This places itself in contrast to ideologies which condone segregation and totalitarianism, thereby reducing pluralism. Pluralism as a philosophy and political practice has been the instrument to resolve at least two great problems. The first is that of the balance or imbalance between different communities. The second concerns the liberties of the individual with respect to the group and the state. Thus, there is an individual and a communal pluralism. They are each distinctive; and, moreover, they are not in opposition.

Modern times began with the intellectual and industrial changes of the fourteenth and fifteenth centuries. The political revolution against royal and ecclesiastic absolutism occurred in England. It continued in the American colonies, where the first decolonization occurred in 1776. The French Revolution was the first to confront the idea of pluralism and the relationship of the individual to the group and the state. Pluralism posed the problem of private interest in conflict with the interests of public order in the community.

Individual pluralism takes into consideration the diversity and the singularity of each man's destiny; it has contributed to modern political thought, liberal or conservative. It can be discerned in the philosophies of Africa, the Orient, and in Roman-Hellenic tradition. The sacred right of exile, or "gaddaay" (freedom of movement) of the seer, the myth of Prometheus, habeas corpus, and moral responsibility that is personally expressed before God are all illustrations of individual pluralism.

Communal pluralism is found in the dilemma posed by the coexistence of differentiated groups having diverse identities and interests. It is a problem encompassing a wide domain. Pluralism was certainly present in one form or another in the origins of the first contacts between different peoples, religions, and ideologies. One can see how plurality operated in Africa from the Nilotic and Saharan revolution between the eighth and the fifth millenniums B.C. until the protocolonial epoch. Pluralism can be seen in this sense as having influenced the heterogeneous empires of the medieval African states in the seventeenth and eighteenth centuries. The European nationalist movements, which led to the creation and dissolution of empires and states in the nineteenth century, had to confront the contradictions of genocide and the problems of a balanced communal pluralism.

In conclusion to these definitions, I will say that if plurality and a plural society are givens, then pluralism and the pluralistic society are the results of practice. This practice may be a philosophy that permits not only coexistence but also interdependence and solidarity between communities, individuals, or common modalities of freedom. Pluralism may also be the manipulation of oppression legitimated by taking into consideration all differences; apartheid is an example of such manipulation. The concepts and themes bound to the ideas of plurality and a plural society are buoyed by emotional and conflicting definitions, and these definitions sometimes have serious consequences.

Pluralism and Plurality in the African Sociopolitical Tradition

Plurality in African Tradition

African plurality can be traced to prehistory. It was clearly a fact in the origins of humanity and the first cultural revolution, which occurred around the eighth millennium B.C. in the Nilo-Atlantic regions between the tropics. It was thus that African history began in the central Sahara in a period of optimal climatic conditions. The climate contributed to innovations in agriculture, fishing, animal husbandry, and the beginning of a sedentary village life with its associated industries and artisans. The Nilo-Atlantic and Saharan civilizations rapidly expanded their settlements to such sites as Hoggar, Ennedi, and the Nile. Their apogee was in the Nubo-Pharonic culture of ancient Egypt during which they spread into the regions and sociocultural territories of the Sahara and the equatorial forest.

Plurality in Africa is a factor that has been present in the essential social, political, religious, epistomological, and technical heritage since the time of the artisan and mechanical civilization. The ethnic lands of Africa, those political and cultural names, which are the foundations of the later plural or pluralistic states, were built upon those autonomous communities that were present in the original and specific empires and periods.

Plurality is also a consequence of the geography of the continent, which has remained to this day underpopulated, vast, and open to migrations and new occupants. The groups and the African cultures had all the time and space to unite, break out, or scatter themselves in relatively homogeneous entities. Homogeneity of small populations is as much a primary notion as plurality of larger aggregations.

The African civilization north of the equator had built its powers uniquely on an assembly of diverse cultures and ethnic groups. In contrast, however, numerous ethnic groups and subgroups of native cultures in central Africa, the Bantu meridian, the Joola country of northern Senegal, and in the Niger delta, were seen, until recently, as stocks or subdivisions of an almost pure larger group. Each ethnic group and subgroup itself may, perhaps, have evolved through centuries in isolation.

Racial plurality arose when occidental and oriental Caucasians came in contact with the black autochthones at the peripheries of the Mediterranean, the Red Sea, and the Indian Ocean. It was already an important factor in the

Nubo-Pharonic, Saharan, and North African civilizations from at least the third millennium B.C..

It is thus possible to lay out maps of the development of racial, cultural, religious, and socioeconomic homogeneity and plurality on the continent.

Pluralism in African Tradition

African pluralism established a mode for taking into account the management of diversity and multiplicity, which was certainly a part of progressively forming internal physical and metaphysical practices.

The sheer abundance of space in Africa during its medieval period offered a propitious economic and physical life for the then flourishing civilizations. The continent did not experience the scarcity and demographic pressures of overpopulated Asia or the unfavorable climate of Western Europe. Competition for space was not necessarily a concern for the African seeking to settle or to begin economic activities. It will never be a problem in the sense of that which exists in the West. Land, therefore, will above all have a metaphysical quality—a space associated for all time with its first occupants, divinities and gods of the communities living on the land.

The ability to establish and conserve old and new lands has offered the permanent possibility of individual, family, or collective migration, and it has certainly influenced the proliferation of pluralist practices. In this fashion, great flexibility is given to groups to accommodate themselves or to go away. The Saharan and Nubo-Pharonic societies thereby had the space needed to make different ethnic groups, cultures, and even already established powers coexist. The Kikuyu, Lebu, Temne, Ibidio, Fang, and the hundreds of other peoples were thus able to preserve their cultural lands and identities. Moreover, they maintained their relatively homogeneous ethnic technologies. Some were even able to remain totally autonomous in the interior of an African state or empire. The state, the empire, and contact among nations created plurality and the need for pluralistic policy and philosophy in Africa. The intrusion of the modern nation-state made it all difficult.

Through anthropology and the ideology of African unity we have become habituated to an image of a communal African culture, in which the individual is subsumed to the benefit of the family, the group, and, finally, the omnipotent power. This is a somewhat distorting vision. There is a sense of multiple status for the individual person as a creator-hero, a model of reference, and a moral subject responsible for his behavior. The individual model of the Ibo or Joola is not like that of the hierarchies and castes of the Sudanese-Nigerian model.

The communal area retains a certain balance; this area permits the various components to live together and to find proof of their identities and their points of support. However, it is possibly in the historical dynamics of the generations' succession that the creator role of the individual and the role of the more or less marginal subgroups appear more obvious. It is often in the initiation into secret societies that sources of individual innovations are created. The scheme of change also affects the culture and community, and the personalities affirm them.

The generations who make the symbolic masks of revolution and change have gone beyond celebration of the rites of passage to use those occasions to reassert the cause of social order and the group. The occasions are the opportunity for the affirmation of individual personalities and elites. In this way the communal African society is also that of a pluralism of elites, of wise men, and of individuals.

Complex and hierarchic social structures have not developed in all African cultures. It is according to the historical periods and contexts that hierarchies of liberty, order, guilds, and castes were formed. Mythical and real kinship can also be found with their cleavages, associations, and domestic village units with open or closed economies. The Saharan cultures and their peripheries were the source of many developing heterogeneous societies. These contained communities of free and captive men, of royal and common lineages, of people bound to castes and guilds, and of secret societies. They were all more or less differentiated and hierarchic, and this social and communal pluralism was often institutionalized by an exact method of segregation. This all occurred in a pluralism that enabled sorting social categories by similarities, thereby each producing its correct means of accountability and its own elites acting within precise spheres.

A study of how the Sudanese-Nigerian societies functioned illustrates the role of castes and classes in the Hausa-Fulani, Yoruba, Bantu, and Wolof societies. At the center of this model, democracy, equality, and identity operate exclusively in the internal dynamics of each caste or class. The homogeneous society, which has neither slaves, castes, nor guilds, and which is individualist or egalitarian, will not have to confront major problems of social plurality. This type of democratic village is found among the Ibo, the Joola, and the Bantu; these homogeneous societies are often egalitarian. (For example, the Ibo society either assimilated strangers or simply eliminated them.) The place of the individual, the extent of his or her rights, liberties, and participation in the secret assemblies of age groups of adults and children could have been extensive.[1]

It is certainly one of the original aspects of African culture that oral expression, and even graphic and written works, left the field open for the coexistence of diverse systems of ideas and beliefs. The resulting epistemology led to greater pursuit of knowledge and scholarly activity, which generally assumed the speculative form of long and fecund discussions. Thus, dialogue is the mode of confrontation—in which ideas correct and reform themselves without reducing the dialectical opposition.

Religious Pluralism

In the realm of religion, which is internally vital to African societies, ideological pluralism has played a pivotal role. It is implausible that traditional African beliefs, in fact, cultivate a polytheism. This has been suggested by superficial observation, but as the ancient Egyptian pantheons of the Nubo-Pharonic civilization would indicate, Ra, Amon, and Atum are actually the same god of creation under different forms and images. This suggests a pluralist monotheism created according to the sensibilities and the perceptions of the subgroups who lived in the Nile Valley.

Each cultural power that conquered another land sought to be associated with or to accommodate the local deity. Pharonic religious thought produced a pluralist monotheism—which affirms the oneness of the God-Creator—through the coalescing of diverse deities and divinities. This avoided an exclusive, totalitarian monotheism, imposing one faith for all. It allowed in his name and his message a multiform god of vocation through whom the cultures and languages of many different peoples living in one empire were preserved. This Pharonic approach was common in many African societies where beliefs were not strongly held. It can be observed in the cultures of Egypt, the Yoruba, the Bantu, and the Wolof and Ibo with their *gods of the earth.*

African religious pluralism has its roots in a very ancient tradition, which was ignorant of evangelization. This tradition knew nothing of the reduction of the "other" and His faith, and rejected the *jihad* or a crusade in the image of God.

Artistic and Esthetic Pluralism

Artistic and esthetic pluralism draw on the same sources. William Fagg, a historian of Nigerian art, speaks of the tribal aspect of art to stress that the great diversity which characterizes the artistic expression in one culture may be present in another. It is Elsie Lewzinger, however, who has best understood the logical reasons of esthetic pluralism. She saw the tribal aspect of art as being reflected in the freedom of forms and the choice of materials. In *Ama, the Art of Negro People,* this great critic emphasizes that African art is a metaphysical expression of a subjective individual or collective vision. This is the vision that a mask or a sculptured head makes in an abstract or elaborated projection of the interior; it is a representation that rarely treats the objective and exterior reality. Fetishes and the masks, the products of a formal, occasionally figurative art, search to express the invisible, but it is not possible to have a unique perception of this unknown, metaphysical phenomenon. Each culture invents, in its own subjectivity and singularity, its own vision. It is from this enormous artistic and esthetic diversity that a culture's socioreligious function is displayed throughout space and time.

Therefore, it is from this denial of a unique canon or esthetic referent that inexhaustible freedom results from creative energies.

Ethical Pluralism

Ethical pluralism is obviously the immediate consequence of social pluralism. Ethical pluralism enables autonomous, and often coterminous, communities to create for themselves their own conditions, values, morals, and individual references. The Wolofs say, "Ada, bari, bokkul," "Cultures and customs are different; they vary."

There is one aspect in this that is rarely put forward as evidence: this is that the African ideologies and philosophies in the larger scheme of ideas are like a total system of successive records and pragmatic syntheses. They are never systematic totalizations that reduce or construct unitary, simplifying, or definitive dogmas.

Political Plurality and Pluralism

Power, like law, is one of the instruments of the privileged and the dominant organizations of society. It interprets the forms that social, economic, and ideological forces will give to their institutions and state. The homogeneous societies that were without a state, such as the *lamana* of the Bantu, the Ibo, or the Joola, did not know the contradictions of multiracial religious and ethnic societies. (The *lamana* were the first migrants; they created the religion of the land.) They would not have had to bring about a pluralistic state or empire. There was no need to regulate the equality of the rapport established between component parts. The early multiethnic African empires of the Mediterranean, east and west Africa, the lacustrine cities, and the port cities like Mogadishu and Sofala have had to confront plurality. They have generally been organized from the beginning into states that have taken diverse directions.

The pluralist state is distinguished by the identification of different socioeconomic, ideological, cultural, religious, and linguistic communities. These communities established laws defining equilibrium or disequilibrium, equality or inequality, whether groups would interact on a basis of one dominating, and what their respective rapport and degrees of autonomy would be.

The pluralist state is of variable form and it furnishes a variety of models, according to the techniques with which one chooses to analyze them. On the whole, it is communalism that is its central component. Through their established allegiances and sovereignties, each community is free to invent and exercise its own laws and institutions. It is this communalism that is translated into the judicial, cultural, religious, social, and linguistic pluralism that is present at the heart of every subsystem. One can almost always find a certain number of communities in a political state that partici-pate, to various degrees, in the use of power in the African pluralist tradition. These communities are present in the exercise of sovereignty and the ad-ministration of goods and services.

The states and empires that flourished during the period when the Sa-hara had an optimal climate were the result of a federation of states of differ-ent ethnic communities. The Egyptian Far I was the leader of an empire, which assembled many native kingdoms to its north and the south. The Ghanaian Tunkara, the Malian Mansa Mandeng, and Ashanti Omahene, to cite but a few examples, confederated the more or less subjugated and the autonomous political entities into empires and states.

Although the Mansa exercised the authority of the Kayta over the Malinke, Bambara, Wolof, and Fulani states, these groups were represented in the internal power structures. They were thus identifiable in the charac-teristics of the state; the Mansa did not impose a Pax Mandingo. There were similarities in the circumstances of the Ashanti, the Buur Wolof, and others.

In the kingdoms of the Sereer of Sinn, and the Wolof of Kayoor, the sovereign exercised power with the collaboration of the *jaraaf* (representa-tive) of free men, the Farba of the captive class, and the other leaders of the various communities present in the kingdoms. These are the Malaw of Laobe, the Biseet of the Moors, or the saintly, innocent Fakk Taal. It follows that those communities that controlled royal power maintained and exer-cised their preeminence. This was not only so of the lacustrine states of east Africa, but also in a great number of political structures across the African continent. For example, the royal lineage of the Mandingo Gelwar were the eligible carriers of the crown in the states of Sinn and Salum. They profited from autochthonous commoners in the same way as the Tutsi had of the Hutu, or the Hima in Bunyoro.

Any structure of political communalism, whether hierarchic or segrega-tive, finds itself back at the political issue of race and of racial differences. The black Africans have generally tolerated communities of whites and vari-ous minorities even in contemporary times. The Jews and the white Libyans held autochthonous positions during the Pharonic period. They had their own districts and institutions, and in some cases, even cities. Timbuktu, with its Muslim district and white district of Sankore, serves as an excellent illus-tration. Fatow Sow has pointed out that the African city was founded on the coexistence of a number of ethnic and cultural districts with fluid bound-aries.

The accession to power by the white minorities, who came from differ-ent cultural and, above all, political traditions, had the effect of upsetting the preexisting pluralistic balance. It introduced the concept of an ethnic state based on elected officials. This model was taken from occidental and Arab-Islamic influences.

This model was a state imposed on Africa, which inspired the *haratina* system of the Negro-Semitic Sahara and the black Islamic state built by the Alamia. They were in direct contrast with the pluralist, pluriethnic, and pluriracial states of traditional Africa. They were essentially worlds separated from each other. The black aristocracy of the Islamic Torobe of the Futa, the conquerors of Rwanda, imposed themselves on the ideological trends in much the same way as the warrior Hassan, who conquered the black populations and Berbers of the Sahara. They installed the hegemonic systems with which they were able to discriminate, and imposed a hierarchical order of communities and an ethnic pluralism and socioideological imbalance.

It is obviously in those zones, where there had been the greatest degree of contact and friction between the African and the Oriental and Occidental cultures that plurality resulted in models that have the most differentiated political organizations. It is in these examples that the conflict between the perspectives of a balanced pluralism based on a multiethnic, multicultural state, and a state split between ethnicity, culture, language, and religion, is most clearly revealed.

Pluralism in Crisis

The revolutions that occurred in Europe since the seventeenth century have provided the heritage for the egalitarian, segregated, and unbalanced pluralism of the modern period.

The colonization of Africa by the European powers was part of the profound crises, which were the result of the contradictions of industrial civilization and the experiences of liberal, socialist, and collectivist democracy. The colonial powers assembled cultures, which had had no prior contact before that time. Decolonization released the drive toward the nationalist, racial, and cultural hegemonies that had been forced to cross their original boundaries. Plurality is still an accepted fact at the base of the postcolonial societies with their poorly adapted states.

In effect, pluralism is a very difficult model because it decentralizes and disperses power and the institutions of social accounting. The modern African state has risen in a context of conflict, and competition has often produced a reaction in favor of centralization. The pluralist state does, however, accommodate itself more easily to the economies of the premodern, domestic, and artisan industries than to the liberal or collectivist macrotechnologies that presently dominate the industrial-mechanical revolution. It is this macrotechnology superimposed on the underdeveloped society that is at the base of the present evolution. The desire to return to past models is a movement that some would like to reverse in favor of more modern paradigms.

The pluralist state of traditional Africa had been able to create a certain stability by balancing the interests of its social and political components.

This allows a juridical and religious pluralism that is essential for the coexistence of cultures and individuals. Nevertheless, it has not, in all contexts, necessarily generated an egalitarian democracy with freedom for all communities and individuals.

The new postcolonial state has arbitrary borders and different communities based on an ethnic, religious, or cultural scheme. As pointed out earlier, it was most often the colonial empire that put such diverse groups together for the first time. The ethnic panorama of Nigeria with its Nupe, Yoruba, Hausa, and Ibo is as complex as that of the Ivory Coast, Ethiopia, Sudan, and even Egypt or Morocco. Regionalism and cultural and religious plurality were repressed under colonial domination and later exploded in the absence of balanced power. In the postcolonial period, ethnicity and tribalism are not perceived as manifestations of an acceptable and unconflicting plurality—they are seen to represent fundamental and destructive conflicts.

Cultural, racial, and ethnic pluralism have been invoked by liberation movements in southern Africa. This has contributed to a sense of segregation and inequality, which is not clearly seen in their apparent unity. However, the communities of captives, guilds, and castes have been imprisoned in their vocations and socioeconomic status by an endogenous power; they have been subjugated by the nature of their work. Even as the societies have evolved, their status as oppressed groups has continued. These groups are not able to take advantage of a social or political pluralism or segregation.

This pluralist philosophy is the result of stable intellectual, ideological, social, cultural, religious, and political relations. These relations perhaps include a system of discriminatory and separatist pluralism. The difference in this philosophy reveals, in effect, that in Africa the metaphysic condemns the individual to his hereditary essence. It demands that those who are born within an order of categories or castes be unable to emancipate themselves. It is this differential metaphysic that shows a similarity between the social, traditional pluralism of the Sudanese-Nigerian and the Hindu systems. It must be understood so that it can be challenged.

For all these reasons, pluralism in contemporary Africa is a modern controversy. It can be disassociated from the egalitarian, democratic state based on law. The modern democratic state attempts to direct the many and the different, the specific and the singular, as well as the groups and the individuals. Pluralism addresses the question of plurality and diversity, and also that of universal order. It would be an error to classify pluralism as merely a scheme or practice that has the exclusive status of a transformation with its beginnings in the period of colonial domination. Plurality and pluralism belong to a very ancient and oddly contemporary history that breaks through the borders of a still more prodigious diversity. The techniques of the communications revolution have touched its ideological and cultural humanity. Even the smallest and most hidden communities are henceforth going to be not only influenced, but will open themselves to expose their identities and originality. The most violent overflow of plurality is thus attributable to the evolution of communications and hidden potential conflicts, which only the pluralist approach to phenomena and the human condition would be able to reveal.

It is for this reason that the current theoretical debate merits being followed and reoriented. In my estimation, certain of its initiators have limited its import, especially in America. In this sense, it is reasonable to reexamine recent history to illustrate the argument. I now turn to developments in Europe, where this history finds its antecedents.

The European Contribution

European political thought and its conception of the state has had a profound and universal influence. It is not possible to understand the present sense of the debate on pluralism and plurality outside of that context and its axioms.

The Heritage of the Eurasian State

The pluralist state has been debated in Eurasian philosophy since its very beginnings. I do not wish to be peremptory and a simplifier of the Eurasian civilizations and their histories. My observations are certainly debatable. Nevertheless, they can contribute in spite of some errors in this new and perhaps more correct approach.

In my opinion, the Eurasian state was created easily because of its tenured land system and unified political entities, which assembled different provinces and areas with their respective customs and laws. These examples are well known and have existed since the time of Hammurabi and Babylon, Alexander, Rome, and the Christian and Islamic empires. The Eurasian state is characterized, above all, by a political, administrative, and territorial pluralism. Rarely is the distribution of power arranged to take into account all the racial, ethnic, cultural, or religious communities, other than in the hierarchical and oppressive rule over conquered minorities.

In this way, the tendency to reduce differences and autonomy has been very strong.

• The Babylonian empire organized itself from its beginnings as a centralized kingdom. It obliterated the Sumerians. Hammurabi was not content with merely subduing the conquered cities, he suppressed them. He imposed a state of law and the worship of the god Marduk on the population.

• The Hebrew kingdom initiated an ethnic, electoral state that federated ten tribes and raised Jehovah to the status of a national and exclusive god. This state has been highly influential in our own history.

• Athens destroyed the League of Delos in 447 B.C. This greatly benefited its development before the founding of the Alexandrian empire, which
was renowned for its generous governors and heirs.

• The Roman Empire has its roots in the Roman defeat of the Samnite
League. This prepared the way for the Judeo-Christian, as well as the Oriental-
Islamic empire.

There are similarities between the European monocentrist state and the
Chinese and Japanese empires. These influences were clearly present in the
African empires that came to exist during the Islamic-Christian expansions.
The modern nation-state reflects the history of the Oriental and Occidental
empires. It continued to develop similar institutions and philosophies of
power as the monarchies and the commercial republics that flourished from
the Crusades and the Renaissance to the period of great change between the
seventeenth and nineteenth centuries.

The Eurasian state encountered internal conflict quite early because it
was not overly pluralistic in its racial, cultural, ideological, or religious composition.

The European Philosophical Tradition

Natural claims for a balanced, pluralist communalism have been constantly
echoed by separatist movements—whether nationalist, religious, or cultural—which have existed throughout history. The tendency to polarize the
energies between the security and prosperity of the nation-state has given a
dignity to the revolt against the group, the religion, or the state. This has
been marked by a Promethean ideology and by a figure no less symbolic
than Socrates.

The prophecies of revolutions and the religious reforms of an epistomological or esthetic nature have come to be more and more within the
nation-state with a view toward increasing individual autonomy and responsibility. Modern individual pluralism undoubtedly has its more profound
roots in Western philosophy. Aristotle did not see a conflict between the individual and the society; he saw man as a social animal. Socrates did not see it
this way. His student, Plato, in *The Republic* and *The Dialogues,* theorized an
aristocracy and a meritocracy of individuals and people existing through the
quality of their relations in a hierarchy of preeminence. The relationship of
the individual to the state was reexamined throughout Western political
thought from the Renaissance on; Dante developed the idea of a "monarchy
by divine right" in *The Monarchy. The Prince* by Machiavelli is a sociological
and political study, and especially a strategy in the art of governing men.
Thomas Hobbes theorized in *Leviathan* that the nation-state seeks security
and prosperity in the context of a community in competition. Thomas More,
a neo-Platonist and the author of *Utopia,* theorized an idealized theocracy.
Martin Luther published *On Civil Authority* in 1523, and defended the tem-

porary authority of a monarch controlled by law and vulnerable to rebellion if he is seen to have betrayed the people's faith. Calvin, in *The Institution of Religion* and Theodore Beze, author of *On the Punishment of Heretics by Civil Magistrates,* strongly supported the idea of Protestant individualism, and were condemned for proclaiming religious pluralism in opposition to the monolith of church and state, which was predominantly Catholic. It is clearly John Locke, the resolved adversary of Hobbes, in whose books, *On Human Tolerance* and *Two Treatises on Government,* that the individual Socratic pluralism emerged in a new form. His theory was that anarchy has no place in free or plural societies.

Pluralism was a central concern of the authors writing at the beginning of the industrial revolution, such as Voltaire, Montesquieu in his *The Spirit of Laws* and especially in *Persian Letters.* Pluralism was also a theme in the works of David Hume, a partisan of free speech; Jean Jacques Rousseau, the author of *The Social Contract;* and Thomas Paine, author of the significant book, *The Rights of Man.* Communal pluralism can be found in the works of Abbé Raynal (1713) and Abbé Sieynes (1796). They were all writing at the time of the beginning of colonial domination and the ideas on "the noble savage."

These liberal tendencies provoked strong reactions. Edmund Burke, in his *Reflections on the French Revolution,* compared equality and pluralism and their roles in the three struggles of the period. He was the precursor of Joseph de Maistre, who in his *Contemplations on France and the Pope,* extolled a return of the monolithic theocracy. In part, the new theories inspired by Hegel were similar to this. They were philosophical centerpieces of the period when Proudhon and Fourier proclaimed themselves against all private or public constraints. This was the century of Marx and libertarian Marxists (including Bakunin, Herzen, and Trotsky; or nationalists like Lenin, Kautsky, and Tito), or the authoritative reducers (including Marx himself, Rosa Luxemburg, Stalin, Mao Tse Tung, and the leaders of the communist parties in the colonial metropoles).

European pluralism has always had aspects that are highly contradictory. This was so, regardless of the points of view and the terminologies employed, whether they were individual or communal, of the political right or left, liberal or conservative.

Conservative pluralist thought, has tended to push group singularity to the extreme right. This is what Hegel and Spencer and their rivals in African and Asian countries consciously theorized. Furthermore, it is that on which Hitlerian, Afrikaner, or Brahmin racism is based. However, they did not invent the idea of a chosen people, which they take as their model—this idea came from much earlier sources.

Radical, revolutionary, or Marxist liberal thought is itself normally distrustful of the possibility of excesses by the state. It professes to liberate the individual from the totalitarian oppression of the group; it recognizes differ-

ent communities, thereby protecting their right of separation, or, more simply, individual identity and specificity. There is nothing currently in Europe
that has been more assimilationist and thus more hegemonic in its real national interests, that are considered as *universals,* than the Communist and
radical parties of the colonialist countries.

Contemporary Interest

In the West there is a revival of interest in the problem of pluralism. The new
controversy has been rekindled in two remarkable books that merit attention. The first is D. Nichols's *The Pluralist State* (1975); with Michael Clark's
*Coherent Variety: The Idea of Diversity in British and American Conservative
Thought* (1983), these two books are at the center of a very rich literature.

Nichols, in his notable book on the pluralist state, explains that the European society had previously overcome most of the controversial aspects of
individual pluralism in its earlier history. He points out that the major problem revolves around the demands of the individual in the face of the group
and, ultimately, the government that embodies that group. He cites John
Donne, who sought to legitimate individual pluralism when he wrote in
1624, that, "God himself would admit a figure of society as there is a plurality
of person in God though there be but One God." He demonstrates how the
nationalist Italian, and especially German, states during the Bismarckian
period used the concept of *kulturkampf,* which appeared oppressive to the
individual in the view of liberal social pluralism.

English individualistic pluralism originated as a defense against this vision of the all-powerful state. It was that which in turn militated for the "voluntary groups" and for pluralism in a "society of societies" against coercive authority. Nichols points out that the idealist pluralists Harold Laski, G. D. H.
Cole, and Bertrand Russell, and even the conservative de Tocqueville and
the leftist Proudhon, subscribed to this view, holding individualist pluralism
to be against the state and the concentration of power.

Clark, in *Coherent Variety,* shows how Tiggi, the author of *Elements of
Politics: Voluntary Societies and State* and *Authority in the Church,* and even
Laski and Cole claimed that the pluralist state, which maximizes individual
liberty, prolonged a popular sentiment against the infallible church, or the
sovereign state invested with secular power. Pluralism does not function
well in the modern or liberal state, according to Marcuse, because there is
hostility in marginal and emerging groups. The spirit of political pluralism
is not to be confused with social and cultural pluralism. Analyzing the work
of William James, Clark notes that when defining his philosophy, James insisted on the necessity of breaking with "the idealist singularity of contemporary philosophy in consideration of the federal republic which is neither
empire nor kingdom."[2] The demand for true pluralism is in contrast to a
domination of interest groups. C. Wright Mills raises several aspects in his

analyses of the U.S. political society. In *The Power Elite* he writes that the United States is controlled by a coherent and sinister group, which, in his opinion, manipulates a relatively theoretical pluralism.[3] The departing warning of President Eisenhower on the role of "the military-industrial complex," is reflected in the question of R. Dahl, "Who Governs?"[4]

At the same time that there are demands for pluralism, the definitions vary greatly according to the authors. There also emerges a routine by which certain excesses are denounced. Today this is the case particularly when reexamining the philosophies of Jeremy Bentham, John Stuart Mill, Spencer in *Man Vs. State* or Maine in *Popular Government.* These are the inspiration of a school of thought that is precisely traditionalist, and in which there is a vision and a pluralism, which only reveals a fanatic individualism.

Michael Clark, in *Coherent Diversity,* recalls and renews this debate. His ideas are the more interesting because they are limited to Anglo-Saxon culture, which at least theorized, if not invented and put into practice, individualist pluralism in a contemporary liberal democracy. Clark was struck by the paradox that was raised in the defense of diversity, thereby bringing the theoreticians of the pluralist left, such as Montesquieu or von Humboldt, together with the conservative right and their counterparts in England and America.

He came back to the advice of Burke, who stressed that "Christianity was monotheist but not monistic." Burke was hostile to the place of "the uniformitarianism of the continental prophets," as he was to "the English wise diversities of custom and tradition." It was the principles of liberty, equality, and fraternity, which Burke upheld as having appeared like feminism, which is "the aversion of difference, the aversion of sexual inequality." He stressed that American federalism and diversity were based on the idea of a racial and religious variety in the land. (The demons of the South and the division between blacks and whites have obscured more complex diversities.)

George Harris, author of *Inequality and Progress,* combined Hegelian idealism with the more ancient vision of society as a "harmony of unequal ranks." For him, variety brings about inequality. Harris writes that, "inequality is the middle term which gives personal liberty on one side and social fraternity on the other side . . . for essential equality would destroy personal freedom and would leave as much fraternity as a man enjoys when he looks at himself in the mirror."[5]

Robert A. Nisbet was inspired by these same preoccupations. In his book, *The Quest for Community,* published in 1953, Nisbet lamented the destruction of the domains of associationism. He stressed "the intimacy and the security of these groups that provide the psychological context of individuality and the reinforcement of personal integrity."[6] He adds that, "it is the *diversity* of such groups that creates the possibility of the numerous cultural alternatives in a society."[7] In *The Twilight of Authority* (1975), Nisbet reasserted that tradition is an instrument for the conservation of diversity.[8]

In fact, a philosophy not of difference, but of segregation and inequality, is hidden behind these euphemisms.

Eric Vogelin, the author of *The Order in the Path of History* (1956), received very positive press in American conservative circles. He criticized Toynbee and Jaspers for their conception of the classification of civilizations that, in the face of cultural diversity, necessarily takes into account "an unmuddled sense of their hierarchical relationship."[9]

It can be noted that the problem of Anglo-Saxon or European pluralism remains, in that it is dominated by the place of the individual in the groups in conflict with the state. This is so despite the importance of the community in the plural society.

African Political Science and Anthropology, and the Debate on Pluralism

The debate on African pluralism has been obscured from its beginnings by the part played by anthropologists. This will be corrected by the contribution of political science, a limitless discipline.

J. S. Furnival, the colonial administrator and economist, invented the term "the plural society" in his excellent study devoted to the Dutch East Indies; he was describing a multiracial, colonial society, dominated by the interests of the white colonial community.[10] Quite simply, the plural society designated the colonial society and its pluralism—the circumstances or the analysis of its societal type. He wrote that the governing and the governed belong to two or more elements or social orders which live side by side without forming a political unity.[11] Furnival was interested in this case, however, without realizing that he was actually revealing the limits of anthropology. He showed that heterogeneous societies with dominant and dominating communities, destabilized by their conflicts, were relatively universal. This was so even if the models were colonial or noncolonial, racial, ethnic, cultural, or religious. They could be as different as those of southern or western Africa, southern Asia, nationalistic Europe, or multiracial, multireligious, and multicultured North America.

This perspective has dominated the debate on the plural society and pluralism. This has remained so even when it is analyzed by political science in a more universal perspective. The conflict between anthropologists and political scientists has revolved around this theme since its first presentation by three of its most brilliant protagonists: Leo Kuper, M. G. Smith, and Pierre van den Berghe. *Pluralism in Africa,* edited by Kuper and Smith, (1967) contains excellent articles by M. Lofchie, Ali Mazrui, M. G. Smith, and van den Berghe. It remains the closest to the work of Furnival in its presentation of the measures and the ideas of a plural society and pluralism. These ideas are presented by them and reviewed especially in the context of a society of diversity and more or less latent conflict between its component communities.

In his introduction to "Institutional and Political Conditions of Plurality," Smith writes that "Pluralism is a condition in which members of a common society are internally distinguished by fundamental differences in their institutional practices."[12] The plural society and pluralism would seem to be axiomatic variables in nation-states.

Pierre van den Berghe, in "Pluralism and the Polity: A Theoretical Explanation," is not too far from this definition. For him, societies are plural from the moment in which they put into evidence two fundamental facts on either a small or large scale: (1) the differentiation of associated groups, which are very often estimated to have different cultures or subcultures; (2) a compartmentalized social structure that is present in institutional norms, analogs, and uncomplementary but identifiable parallels.[13] He comments that these two criteria distinguish plural societies both from societies composed of related units (such as those based on lineage and clan) and from those societies that have a high degree of functional specialization and differentiation in their institutional structures. It follows that an additional characteristic, which is frequently associated with pluralism, is the relative absence of common values and a consensus. Therefore, the relative presence of cultural heterogeneity and conflicts between dominant and associated groups in their primary or segregative relations will not be affective and specific when their functions between such groups are along total utilitarian lines.

This is not the place to discuss the well-founded, structural-functionalist theories that attempt to describe and typify African societies in terms of lineage, segmentation, or clan. That approach has already been criticized in my *Traditional Political Power* (1967). We should note, however, that the ideas of pluralism and plurality explained here are like those of Furnival and Smith, who saw plurality as more or less institutionalized and conflictual. Van den Berghe has evoked the image of a pluralist African society in his writing; it is apparent to him that anthropology fails to see the relatively universal truth in plurality. He sees plurality in the light of its different zones and types, as found in North and South America, India, Great Britain, Iran, Lebanon, Nigeria, and Mexico.

Leo Kuper's approach is quite original. He makes a distinction between pluralism in the traditional sense and pluralism in a modern and limited sense. He confers a new approach to the concept that complements the arguments of Furnival, Smith, and van den Berghe. Even if Kuper is not always clear and does not contrast plurality and pluralism, or plural and pluralistic societies, his approach permits the concepts of pluralism and plurality to be returned to an understanding which is illuminating.

He describes plural societies as "characterized by cultural diversity and social cleavage arising from the contact of different peoples within a single political unit."[14] In this context the characteristic expression of pluralism takes the form of dissension and conflict between ethnic, religious, and regional groups, and the system that maintains itself through domination, regulation, and force. Here, a plural society and pluralism, in Kuper's terms, connote organized plurality. This sociological analysis and concept include the multiracial, multicultural, and multireligious, federalist America, as well as the societies of the federal states of Nigeria or Mexico, or those unitary nations like India, Guinea, Lebanon, Israel, Iran, the USSR, or Zimbabwe.

Kuper is equally correct in defining pluralism as a strategy of democratic relations and a balance between communities themselves, as well as between the group and the state. Plurality is universal, whether under colonial, neocolonial, or imperial forms. This is rightfully emphasized by Kuper when he writes that the plural society "includes the colonial societies that subjected most of the peoples of the world to the domination of rulers of different race and culture."[15] Kuper perceives "two quite antithetical traditions in regard to the nature of societies characterized by pluralism." These traditions, he writes, "derive from the opposition between two basic social philosophies expressed in the antithesis between equilibrium models of society [particularly consensual] and conflict models of society."[16] On the one hand, these balanced models tend to associate pluralism with democracy; on the other, models of instability exclude equality and democracy. It should further be understood that the critique which Kuper addresses in relation to the arguments of Furnival, Smith, and van den Berghe is highly pertinent.

Ali Mazrui has done a notable analysis of plurality apropos the multiethnic and multireligious state of Uganda. This country is relevant because of its ancient kingdoms and its present-day Indian and European minorities. In their article of 1983 on democracy in Africa, M. Lofchie and Richard Sklar also moved the problem of plurality and ethnicity to the area of political science rather than confining it to anthropological analysis. This very important evolution has perhaps helped make possible the general debate on a plural society, pluralism, and pluralistic philosophies and their roles in an increasingly complex world.

Conclusion

The technological revolutions have changed the boundaries of pluralism and have, paradoxically, multiplied the spheres of diversity and homogeneity. The individual exists precariously in a society held together by the intimate relations among cultures, which have developed over time and which are threatened with dissolution. At the same time the individual and the group reassert themselves by revolutions that endow them with the means to survive and that affirm their identity and specificity.

The debate on pluralism has its own momentum; it will continue to collide for a long time with prejudices raised against it that cite racial, ethnic, religious, or cultural differences. It is obvious that pluralism will have to invent its own modalities and strategies in each contest: in Zimbabwe, South Africa, multiracial America, in multiethnic Nigeria, or even in an India with its castes and segregative metaphysics. Pluralism does not have the primary objective of organizing or institutionalizing plurality as such. This would lead to tribalism, to apartheid, and to ethnocentrism. Pluralism must accept and integrate differences so as to go beyond plurality, thereby allowing individuals and communities to accept for themselves an identity as they need it. Pluralism has chiefly to make individuals and communities accept each other.

The main problem of plurality and pluralism in post-colonial Africa has been the inability to educate people so that they move from the *societas* to the *civitas*; so that they build a common destiny and citizenship beyond the primordial and psychological fears and reactionism that lead to racial, ethnic, or cultural differences.

Such a new political philosophy and state cannot avoid the economics and the role of class struggle in ethnicity or any other oppressive strategy used to manage plurality. Indeed, a number of crises in Africa arise from ethnic and tribal monopolies of the state and its resources. A socioeconomic strategy is needed to promote a system whereby individual and communal prosperity is achieved on the basis of individuals with merit competing in a context of equal opportunity. Most African and non-African political scientists presently agree on the necessity of having a strategy that goes beyond plurality and strives for pluralism. Many suggestions deal with the structure of the state and constitutional models that assure protection and integration of the individual and the community. Education and nonracial, nonreligious, and nonethnic party and social organizations are commonly suggested as the tools for the achievement of such a new state. It is certain that pluralism has to be a component of the ideological framework of an egalitarian state and society in Africa. All of this is in hopes of a transformation of institutions and a new approach that will turn from mechanical laws of numbers for the benefit of democratic ways and laws of a larger consensus.

Notes

1. Pathé Diagne, *Pouvoir politique traditionnel* (Paris, 1967).

2. Michael Clark, *Coherent Variety: The Idea of Diversity in British and American Conservative Thought* (Westport, Conn.: Greenwood Press, 1983).

3. C. Wright Mills, *The Power Elite* (New York: Oxford University Press, 1956).

4. R. Dahl, *Who Governs? Democracy and Power in an American City* (New Haven and London: Yale University Press, 1961).

5. George Harris, *Inequality and Progress* (Boston: Houghton, Mifflin, and Co.,

1897), 154.

6. Robert A. Nisbet, *The Quest for Community* (New York: Oxford University Press, 1953), 246–7.

7. Ibid.

8. Nisbet, *Twilight of Authority* (New York: Oxford University Press, 1975).

9. Eric Vogelin, *The Order in the Path of History* (1956).

10. J. S. Furnival, *Colonial Policy and Practice: A Comparative Study of Burma and the Netherlands Indies* (London: Cambridge University Press, 1948), 303ff.

11. Ibid.

12. M. G. Smith, "Institutional and Political Conditions of Plurality," *Pluralism in Africa*, eds. Leo Kuper and M. G. Smith (Los Angeles: UCLA Press, 1969), 27.

13. Pierre van den Berghe, "Pluralism and the Polity: A Theoretical Explanation," *Pluralism in Africa*, 67ff.

14. Leo Kuper, "Conflict and the Plural Society: Ideologies of Violence Among Subordinate Groups," *Pluralism in Africa*, 153.

15. Leo Kuper, "Plural Societies: Perspectives and Problems," *Pluralism in Africa*, 7.

16. Ibid., 7–8.

9

Bona Malwal

The African System of Pluralism

Both pluralism and democracy mean different things to different people and therefore are controversial terms. Academics have variously defined pluralism as: (1) a condition in which members of a common society are distinguished by fundamental differences;[1] (2) a word simultaneously connoting a social structure characterized by fundamental discontinuities and cleavages, and by cultural complexity based on systematic institutional diversity;[2] (3) a state that exists when the entire population, or at least the overwhelming majority, shares a common system of basic institutions, while being systematically differentiated at the secondary level of institutional organization in which occupationally political and religious or ethnic structures predominate.[3]

Using only these three definitions as samples, it would appear that every society in the world may be considered to be pluralistic.

My basic thesis is that Africa has failed to achieve democracy, and will continue to fail to govern itself well, as long as the African system of pluralism is not allowed to develop. I shall argue that true African pluralism is inconsistent neither with a good system of government nor with a peaceful and disciplined society, but rather is a form of democracy that has been denied the chance to develop. The outside world must allow African pluralism to develop as a system by refraining from their East–West ideological conflicts and contests on the continent. Furthermore, the African elite (to be more accurate, the ideologically "brainwashed," educated Africans, including the military) can no longer ignore that it is in their best interest to further the development of this pluralistic system by using the tools of modernity to make it a more complex, and functioning system of government. Strongly set traditional rules and regulations that relate to tribal lands, to grazing and watering rights, to social customs such as marriage and divorce, and to disputes and wars (and their settlement in tribal courts) can be refined into constitutions, laws and regulations.

After more than two decades, it is fairly clear that foreign systems of gov-

87

ernment that have been tried in Africa have failed. Yet how did these foreign systems come to be dominant in Africa? The answer is simple enough: Africa was a colony for a long time. Along with the search for raw materials, cheap labor, and trade, there was also the mission to "civilize." Africans were taught the European forms of religion, Western norms of civilized behavior, and the notion of rule of law. Although European administrators found that they could govern the tribes better by using the African system of kings, chiefs and headmen, Europeans still felt that Africans could be made to adopt European ways.

From the European desire to civilize came Africa's biggest problem: Christian missionaries, who were assigned by the colonial powers to provide cheap education in Africa and to convert Africans to Christianity. Unfortunately, apart from giving Christian religious instruction, missionaries spent the greater part of their time degrading African ways and systems. One can see the need of belittling another's ways in order to make one's own acceptable, but the missionaries might have gained more had they recognized and accepted even a handful of the good African practices. Many African practices were misconstrued. For instance, some missionaries and scholars erroneously maintained (as some do, even today) that non-Christian Africans were not believers in God because they believed in many little gods; in fact, Africans considered these little gods to be representatives of the one real God.

Blame for the decline of African pluralism cannot be placed solely with the European colonial administrators and the Christian missionaries. African pluralism as a system was betrayed primarily by the so-called African elite, who found in education and Christianity something that would set them apart from country folk. These elite were educated and were believers, who, accordingly, were slightly more acceptable within the colonial system. As education spread and feelings of nationalism prompted national independence movements all over Africa, this educated group tried to implement democracy the European way. "We will have a government 'by the people, of the people, and for the people,'" they preached. "We will abide by the 'one man, one vote' results." Common Africans did not know what was in store for them from their fellows.

Independence movements, under whatever names, brought with them greed for power among some educated Africans. Whether the movement was called the "National Liberation Movement" or the "Just Freedom," many thought that their countries could be free if they were at the helm. Naturally, they had to worry about colleagues, classmates, or others also wanting to become the leaders in their places. Power had become associated with personal fortune.

When Europeans left power in Africa, most of them were not interested in ensuring that an African system of government survived after them; in fact, what was done actually ensured that the political system had little chance to survive after independence. The fight for the spoils went on unabated among the African elites. Those who got to the top, whether by chance or by other means, generally had no concept of human rights—all they cared about was how to remain on top, and they were willing to use any means to stay there.

Army takeovers became fashionable in Africa. Western democratic- and Eastern socialist-based governments were replaced by military regimes, which showed little respect for the rule of law, and rarely for human life. Repression is now a way of life in Africa, and democracy and freedom are the things of yesterday. The first loser in this is the ordinary African, for no one looks out for the interests of the common person, whose traditional systems of rule have been tossed aside.

The second loser in this was possibly the Western European system of government. Many Europeans originally thought that Africans would continue to imitate European systems of democracy and of government long after they had gone. Their desire to impose their systems on the Africans rendered them blind to the failures inherent in exporting a system foreign to Africa.

In the late 1930s, the British sought to impose in the southern Sudan a centralized system of administration headed by the British district commissioner, once the administration thought that they had sufficiently pacified its tribes. The district commissioner possessed both executive and sole judicial powers. The idea was to apply the strict rule of law as a way of preventing crime among the tribes. However, European law did not always succeed, as one case from a Dinka tribal district illustrates.

A murder case was brought before the district commissioner of the Dinka region, in which it was proved beyond doubt that the accused was guilty. The district commissioner sentenced him to death, and the accused was hanged. A few days later, the relatives of the murdered man killed one of the relatives of the hanged man; the new murderer also confessed to his crime.

The British district commissioner was stunned by this. Before sitting again as judge to try the second case, he consulted the Dinka tribal leaders as to why this second murder had happened. The chiefs told him that, from the Dinka point of view, the first judgment was incomplete; the family of the murdered person had to avenge their relative because proper compensation, in the form of cattle, was not paid in accordance with tribal custom. The Dinka believe that if one receives cattle payment for his murdered relative, he can use that to marry a wife who will produce children in the name of the deceased. In that way, one has not completely lost his relative. The district commissioner's decision had ensured the victim's family's total loss. Now, with the second murder, the case had become complicated, and further murders or even a blood feud were likely to result.

The district commissioner then convened a court of chiefs with himself as the presiding judge, but he never uttered a word throughout the proceedings. The chiefs considered the evidence. Finally, they decreed that the family of the first murderer had to pay sixty cows, and the family of the revengers had to pay thirty cows; the man who had committed the second murder had to go to prison for life. The district commissioner accepted this judgment, as did the two families. Peace returned to the society.

In the Sudan, at least, the colonial authorities accepted the principle of indirect rule through tribal chiefs. Tribal laws became codified and were accepted as part of the legal system during the colonial period. They were used extensively to regulate conflicts within various groups in one tribe and between different tribes. Compensations, when required by tribal law, took into account the practices of other tribes involved, and payment was made in the commodities a tribe could afford. For instance, tribes that did not own cattle could pay in kind, grain, or money, which the Dinka, for instance, could convert into cattle if they so wished.

In postcolonial Africa, national authorities (which by now have become more military than civilian) insist on handing down orders that have nothing to do with their nations' societal norms. Since these leaders know that their orders are unacceptable and will not be obeyed voluntarily, they get their armies to impose them forcibly.

Had the system of African pluralism been allowed to develop, however, African democracy could have been one of the better forms of government today. Africans recognize that they live in many different tribes, and sometimes even recognize that they are divided among different peoples. They respect their similarities and connections among themselves more than do the various groups and nations in the "developed" and "civilized" societies. This respect is due to several factors.

First, Africans recognize that they and others belong together in this world, so they try to regulate themselves in such a way that no one has all resources to himself. However, European influence on the educated African has tried to change this recognition.

Second, Africans recognize the importance of collective security. If a family, a clan, or a tribe is united, it has less chance of being attacked or even of being provoked by neighboring communities.

Third, Africans recognize the importance of sharing with others both that which is public and that which is private. Water from the common river or well, land for cultivation, forests for firewood, and grazing and hunting areas are all recognized as being communally or collectively owned. Whenever one group or community tries to dominate these resources, problems arise and may lead to bloody conflicts. Unfairness is not acceptable and is therefore contested by those directly or indirectly aggrieved.

Fourth, Africans believe in leadership but do not necessarily believe in the wisdom of a single leader. That is why in an African society, even a powerful chief must still respect the view and opinions of even the humblest. No chief can retain the respect of his people (and therefore his authority over them) unless they feel that he is responsive to both their needs and opinions. It was common for an ordinary African to stand in the chief's court and say in the presence of multitudes, "Chief, what you have said is wrong or untrue." The critic fears no repercussions because, normally, repercussions did not occur. However, African leaders of the present day have learned repressive techniques from Europeans.

Last, Africans believe in democracy, not only as an ideal system, but also as a practical, daily reality. Therefore, in an election Africans wish to make known for whom they have voted. Traditional African ways of electing chiefs are still practiced in a few places, where the candidates stand with a line of their supporters behind them. Although these elections are completely open, no one fears reprisals for not supporting the elected candidate. Perhaps such open elections, in which the electorate lines up behind the candidates of choice, would eliminate the rampant vote-rigging in Africa today.

Pluralism does exist in Africa, not as something that prevents democratic institutions from functioning, but rather as a system that needs to be adapted to enable African democratic institutions to function better by employing traditional means.

Notes

1. Kuper and Smith, *Pluralism in Africa* (University of California Press, 1969).

2. W. Kornhauser, *The Politics of Man's Society* (London: Routledge and Kegan Paul, 1960).

3. Ibid.

Part 2

Practice
and
Problems

Lansiné Kaba # 10

Power and Democracy in African Tradition: The Case of Songhay, 1464–1591

Democracy in an Ambiguous World

Politics, like religion, is of vital importance to all countries and cultures because of its impact on people's life, behavior, and status. In the present, as well as in the past, individuals and groups have asked questions about the state: what it is and does and should be. Politics may thus appear as a reality or a myth. It is a system that can raise deep passions and can call forth a brutal and cold enactment of programs aimed at specific particularist or universalist goals. In other words, a people's relationship to the state is ambiguous because of the nature of politics. The state is both a source of material satisfaction and an institution of threat and coercion.[1] This ambiguity is associated with the view that society cannot function without authority, whether centralized or segmentary. The need for authority implies that people may agree, or often disagree in an orderly or violent way, on policies and politics. Broadly speaking, politics is an organizational and ideological system characterized by the existence (or coexistence) of compatible and contradictory tendencies; it is an arena of competition par excellence. In this dichotomy lies fertile ground for both political behavior and participation.

Political behavior and participation assume that groups may stand by either high principles or strong leadership against threats of political abuses by rulers, although, ideally, a strong leader is not a substitute for strong operative institutions. The ideal of all societies is to foster policies that do justice to all. If a given society highly values mass participation and a judicious sharing and control of power (that is, perhaps, democracy), it follows that it must seek and implement the structures compatible with these goals through the establishment of appropriate political settings, leadership, language, and administration. Political participation entails normative values.

The extent to which such participatory and controlled systems have been practiced in Africa, in the past or present, or will be practiced in the future, is an appropriate and timely question. To be fully appreciated, this question requires a balanced view of political mobilization and performance. Whether one speaks of people's democracy, national democracy or liberal democracy, as is now the case, one need not overlook the scope of responsibility and freedom of speech, the interplay of individual rights and collective needs, the degree of autonomy of bureaucratic institutions vis-à-vis the government, and the degree of collegiality in national leadership.

The concept of democracy is an ideal and a reality. As an ideal—that is, the consciousness we have of it—it implies that no system of government is perfect, and that a constant effort must be made to strengthen democratic structures and move closer to greater democratic practices. But as a reality, it calls forth the enactment of and respect for principles inherent in the concept. In other words, although any definition of democracy is arbitrary, the practice of democracy should include all or part of the following processes: free choice of leaders, free political participation and competition, fair election in the sense of adherence to the general idea of one person, one vote without fear of punishment, accountability of leadership, respect for minority rights, greater social justice, and equitable distribution of a country's wealth. To a degree, following de Tocqueville, modern societies tend to be all democratic in the sense that they progressively reduce ascribed ranks and status and establish the criteria of achievement and merit as a basis for social differentiation. Paradoxically, however, the same modern societies can lend themselves to authoritarian, autocratic or liberal systems of government. The nature of power and political organization thus becomes a determinant criterion. The manner in which power is held and organized indicates the nature of a society and a political system. Therefore, politics is a vital, ideological and social reality with definite parameters. Have the criteria implied in the notion of politics and democracy been met in contemporary Africa? Are these criteria found in precolonial Africa? My paper based on the Timbuktu chronicles answers the question through a study of the concrete examples of Songhay in the sixteenth century.

Historical Background

Centralized political rule, able to establish effective techniques for controlling large populations in peace and promoting economic activities, played a significant role in the history of west Africa from the fourth century A.D. The state of Songhay in the middle Niger River valley, a truly pluralistic kingdom including various groups and ways of life, belonged to this tradition.[2] A large and complex empire by any standard in the 1480s, it functioned with little strain between 1464 and 1591 despite the change of dynasty in 1493. The conquest of the kings Sonni Ali (1464–92) and Askiya Muhammad I (1493–1528) resulted in the creation of a vast political and economic unit, in which peace reigned due to such factors as the strength and speed of the security forces (including a large fleet), the officers' loyalty and competence and the administrative system, which sought an equilibrium between the methods of direct and indirect rule. The period from the overthrow of Askiya Muhammad I in 1528 to the battle of Tondibi against the Moroccan mercenary army in 1591 included eras of stability and instability. The latter is evidenced by bloody rivalries in the royal clan between 1528 and 1539 and between 1582 and 1592; the former by the long and peaceful reigns of Ishaq I (1539–1549) and Dawud (1549–82). Despite all, the policy of the Askiya Muhammad I, coupled with the efforts of his successors to expand the state and safeguard its borders, consolidated the power of the crown and reinforced the prerogatives of the Muslim intelligentsia.[3] Trade routes became secure; salt, copper, and gold were extracted and shipped; agriculture throve; and external threats were well controlled until 1591, when Moroccan mercenary forces, using firearms for the first time in this part of west Africa, crossed the Sahara and defeated the Askiya ruler and brought about the collapse of the Songhay state.[4]

Power and Participation in Songhay

A reflection on some broad issues is needed now. The evolution of the Songhay state from 1493 to 1592 reveals two contradictory tendencies: one, a strong move toward integration, and, the other, an irresistible drive toward anarchy because of a lack of succession rules. As stated above, the integrative policy of the Askiya Muhammad I and his successors resulted in greater unity and prosperity despite the years of drought. With the exception of the Kebbi kingdom and the Hausa cities, which regained their independence from Songhay, all the conquered chieftaincies continued to recognize the sovereignty of the Askiyas.[5] Tuareg, Dogon, and Fulah communities paid tribute. The powerful neighboring states of Mossi and Mali were driven back and kept quiet. With the expansion, new administrative initiatives were launched.

As soon as the Askiya Muhammad I came to power in 1493, he tried to reorganize Songhay and to equip it with functional institutions. For example, he appointed a Muslim judge (*qadi*) to each town, and sought the advice of Muslim scholars on major issues. A form of participation reserved to an oligarchy, this pattern of consultation had a political significance. He also made the office of the *kourmina-fari,* or *fari,* with its seat in Tendirma, the most important position after that of the askiya. The *kourmina-fari* became viceroy in charge of the administration of the large and rich northwestern province, including the Niger Bend. This office was reserved for outstanding members of the royal family. Such an individual, who could be the Askiya's brother or son, was expected to be heir to the throne. To substantiate this view, the *kanfari* Ammar Kumjago ruled Songhay between 1495 and 1497 during the pilgrimage of his brother, the Askiya Muhammad I, and assumed other important responsibilities afterward. The *fari* commanded a large number of dignitaries, including the commander of the western army (the *balama*). Because these high officials belonged to the ruling clan, one could argue that the administration of the vital northwestern province was a royal appanage and, therefore, a sign of social differentiation and inequality. Moreover, marriage between princesses and other dignitaries further reinforced political control by the royal family over the state.

At the same time, different institutions and ceremonials were introduced to the court. There was a special corps of palace officials that included eunuchs, the head of protocol, the senior bursar, the head of the household, and the "master of the speech," who was the public herald when the king held audiences, and the living repository of the state's oral tradition.[6] With the courtiers who frequented the palace, the aforementioned officials were the Askiya's closest servants. Another noticeable change was the increased responsibility and prestige of the imperial chancery. The head of this office, a quasi secretary of state (*alfa-askiya*), took charge of the royal correspondence and registry.

In creating a wise administration throughout the empire, the Askiya had to have an understanding of and respect for local political structures in order to secure greater cooperation at the regional level. Thus the Askiya rulers maintained and, in some cases, reinforced the prerogatives held by local rulers in the Niger Bend. For example, the ruler of the town of Jenne (*Jenne-koy*), who already enjoyed some autonomy, was the only dignitary allowed to sit on the same carpet as the Askiya; the chief of Dirma could ride his horse into the palace; and the ruler of Bara possessed a veto right almost binding on the king.[7] These functions and prestige survived during the first years of the empire; and, the way such dignitaries were treated was commensurate with their rank. But, as the crown grew stronger in the sixteenth century (that is, when the Askiya's image corresponded almost to that of an absolute, enlightened despot), these honorary considerations lost some of their political significance, although they retained value in relations between elites. Politically, the local traditional chiefs served as the normal links between the Crown and the masses; their service testified to a degree of local autonomy, and even collegiality, in imperial administration.

In the old Songhay proper, the region south of Gao, the governor of the Dendi province (*Dendi-fari*) appeared to be the first dignitary. Before 1493, this office ranked as the most prestigious in Songhay; but, it dwindled in importance after the creation of the empire and the establishment of the office of *kourmina-fari*. As proof, no *Dendi-fari* ever competed for the throne between 1493 and 1591, whereas the *kanfari* were always among the candidates and the most likely choices. Yet the *Dendi-fari* had many important officers under his command, including the commander of the fleet (*hi-koy*). In general, the office of *Dendi-fari* was reserved to the old nobility, although some *hi-koy* or competent loyal officers of lower origins were at times promoted to it. In other words, all this organization encouraged individual achievement; it was aimed at promoting greater administrative efficiency and uniformity, as well as political unity.

There were critical problems, however. The very institutions that had evolved were plagued by an inherent weakness. Despite their attempts, the Askiyas failed to adapt Songhay's structures to the emerging 16th-century conditions.[8] They did little to initiate innovative policies in such areas as international relations, defense and monetary self-reliance. Each administration, with the exception of Dawud's, also experienced tension between the crown and the high officials who belonged to the royal family. Furthermore, the death of an Askiya was generally followed by a period of serious rivalry and violence, which literally weakened the system. Born of frustrated ambitions, these tensions easily degenerated into mutinies and wars. In order to understand these conflicts, one must analyze the rules of succession, which were vague and confusing. Although the right of primogeniture played an important role in the succession, it was not a determinant factor. Consanguinity through the father line was a decisive criterion; when an Askiya died, all of his sons and brothers could compete for the throne because of their belonging to the lineage of the Askiya founder of the dynasty. After the death of Dawud in 1582, however, succession was limited to his own progeny, but the great number of children still remained a permanent cause of instability. Every time the throne was vacant, a civil war would follow and paralyze the government.

The coronation itself raised serious problems. It generally took place in Gao immediately after the death or the overthrow of a monarch. Far from being a race in vanity, as Jean Rouch has claimed, it involved pledges of loyalty by all the members of the high administration, including the army and the members of the court.[9] It also involved the handing over of the treasury and the insignia of kingship. These included the crown's twelve banners, drum and saddle horses, the Askiya's own sword, turban and ring, and, finally, the *din-turi*—the burning cinders from the first fire lit in the kingdom, which symbolized the royal power. In theory, this solemn but brief investiture was designed, as Levtzion has noted, to reduce the risks involved in a long and drawn-out political campaign.[10] When Songhay was small and limited to the confines of Gao, the ceremony was appropriate and functional; but, when a large empire emerged, it outlived part of its usefulness. It certainly corresponded little to a context in which the *fari,* the second official, resided far away in Tendirma in the Niger Bend. This archaic rule of succession was another example of a lack of innovation in the Askiya regime.

In this frenetic and dangerous race for the throne, time was a decisive element. In general, the successful candidates were those who met the political requirements and who were present in Gao at the time of the succession crisis; the losers were those who were absent, regardless of their popularity and other qualities. Distance from Gao was the major drawback of the office of *kourmina-fari*. To complicate the situation further, the election was not a guarantee of stability as long as brothers and cousins could pose a threat to the power of a weak Askiya. With the exception of the reigns of Dawud, Ismail and Ishaq I, the political climate was one of endless intrigues, revolts and gloom. In this respect, the Askiya era was, to a degree, a century of political crises.[11] The greed for power, the lack of sufficient and direct contact between the crown and the masses, the tension between the Muslim elite and the more traditional officials, the dynasty's illegitimate origin, and the lack of a definite political consensus in the king's inner circle all fostered conflicts. Finally the lack of a policy for military renovation and fiscal sovereignty deprived Songhay of the means to ward off Morocco's threats.

Because of its cultural achievement, Songhay is considered the high point of medieval west African civilization, even though the Askiya dynasty was unable to deal effectively with the twin issues of stability and free and full participation. The civil wars stemmed from the fear of political consolidation in the hands of one man and misuse of power.

The lesson is that a fair and long-term effective political system requires autonomous institutions. Without making value judgments, one can argue that all forms of government are not good, that is, not beneficial to the majority of the citizenry. "Good rule" implies minimal tension and violence for maximum peace and security. This concern for good government calls forth a search for standards to determine what is beneficial. Related to this concern are the issues of political legitimacy, equality, and consent.

In this context, an emphasis on the influence held by Songhay's Muslim scholars is in order. They participated in the 1493 war, which empowered the Askiya dynasty and they gave it a religious legitimacy. Then they suggested a land reform which, although reinforcing the owners' rights, also benefited the laborers. Their involvement in the post 1493 politics showed that knowledge and power, when associated with integrity and compassion for the common good, could improve justice, as evidenced by their roles as critics and conciliators. Two examples illustrate this point. The first involved the Askiya Ishaq I (1539–1549) in Jenne in a situation reminiscent of the Biblical story about the poor man's sheep and King David's repentance. Confronted by the theologian and jurist Mahmud Baghayo on the issue of oppression and injustice, the Askiya repented and obliged his challenger to assume the function of chief judge in the city.[12] The second story shows how the scholars of Timbuktu made themselves the defenders of tolerance for the minority rights of Saharan Jews against the arbitrary policy proposed to the Askiya Muhammad I by the sufi master al-Maghili.[13]

By placing some important legal matters in the hands of the Muslim courts, and therefore outside the legal authority of the imperial government, the Askiyas established for the Muslim intelligentsia the right to express their views, and to criticize the acts of the crown without fear of punishment. This practice made the Muslim elite not the voice of opposition but the defenders of an intelligent use of power for general betterment (although this type of participation did not extend to all). Despite these examples, the issue of general consent remained crucial in Songhay to a significant degree. Rule without consent and legitimacy, as evidenced by the fratricidal wars, is not stable and is not good for the people. In every society, be it pluralistic or homogeneous, the heart of the problem remains the elaboration of policies that work and satisfy most, and that minimize conflicts and permit people to fulfill their aspirations.

One may argue that the elite in Songhay had an idea of what democracy was and how it could function. Under the Askiyas, the privileged Muslim elite enjoyed almost completely the benefits of a wise and democratic use of power.[14] This practice, although it was limited, can be an example for contemporary states because it involved an association between the intelligentsia and the military for the common good or, metaphorically, the power of the pen and the sword, which are two essential sources of prestige and authority. It also implies that the ideal of democracy is neither foreign to African history nor superfluous in an Africa confronted today with major natural calamities and sociopolitical crises. To promote true development requires freedom and democracy, that is, fair distribution of opportunities, wealth and power, to unleash people's creative energy with responsibility and dignity.

Notes

1. For a discussion of the ambivalent nature of politics, *see* Harold Lasswell, *Psychopathology and Politics* (New York, 1930).

2. Pluralism may refer to societies with cleavages between the different population groups in terms of ethnicity, religions, and values. Force is needed in this context to maintain the system. Pluralism may also refer to a dispersion of authority among the groups bound together by common values and crosscutting loyalties to one another and to the system. This type of pluralism may foster democracy rather than coercion and conflicts. *See* Leo Kuper and M. G. Smith, eds. *Pluralism in Africa,* (Los Angeles, 1971).

3. *See* Lansiné Kaba, "The Pen, the Sword and the Crown: Islam and Revolution in Songhay Reconsidered, 1464–1493," *Journal of African History* 25 (1984), 241–56.

4. See Lansiné Kaba, "Archers, Musketeers and Mosquitoes: The Moroccan Invasion of the Sudan and the Songhay Resistance, 1591–1613," *Journal of African History* 11 (1981), 457–75.

5. *See* Nehemia Levtzion, "The Western Maghrib and Sudan," *The Cambridge History of Africa,* J. D. Fage and R. Oliver, eds. (London, 1971), 331–462.

6. There were many more officials in the immediate entourage of the Askiya rulers. Centralization reached a very high level in Songhay.

7. *See* Mahmud Kati, *Tarikh al Fattash,* (Paris, 1964).

8. To appreciate how the sixteenth century heralded the modern era, *see* Fernand Braudel, *La Méditerranée et le monde méditerranéen au temps de Philippe II* (Paris, 1949) and Immanuel Wallerstein, *The Modern World System: Capitalist Agriculture and the Origins of the European World-Economy in the 16th Century* (New York, 1974).

9. Jean Rouch, *Contribution à l'histoire du Songhay* (Dakar, 1953), 202.

10. N. Levtzion, "The Western Maghrib and Sudan," 443–45.

11. *See* Z. Dramani-Issifou: *L'Afrique noire dans les relations internationales au XVIe siècle* (Paris, 1982).

12. M. Kati, *Tarikh,* 167–69; and Abderrahman al-Sadi, *Takrikh al Sudan* (Paris, 1964), 159–60.

13. *See* Leo Africanus. *Description de l'Afrique, Vol. II* (Paris: Maisonneuve, 1956), 468; R. M. Hiskett, "An Islamic Tradition of Reform in the Western Sudan from the 16th Century to the 18th Century," *Bulletin of the School of Oriental and African Studies* 25, 3 (1962); and A. Batran, "Biography of Shaikh Muhammad al Magili," *Journal of African History,* 14 (1977), 381–94.

14. The Muslim scholars received different kinds of benefits because of their skills and moral influence. To have an idea of their social position in Songhay, *see* L. Kaba, "Power, Prosperity and Inequality in Songhay, 1464–1592" in Earl P. Scott, ed., *Life Before the Drought* (London, 1984), 29–48.

David N. Magang

11

Democracy in African Tradition: The Case of Botswana

The topic, democracy in African tradition, does not permit any textbook analysis or ideological stereotyping. This should be clear from the heterogeneous nature of traditional African society. It is true that many scholars have identified a common African concept of humanity or humanness enshrined in such words as "botho" or "ubuntu." But in terms of political or administrative arrangements, there was traditionally a wide variety of forms in Africa.

There were highly centralized kingdoms, such as Ashanti or Buganda. These kingdoms had an elaborate system of government that reached into every part of the country, with local, regional and national authorities; at the apex there was a supreme king known as the asantehene in Ashanti or the kabaka in Uganda. In Southern Africa, a totally different arrangement was found in the military-political system of the Zulu kingdom, which reached its pinnacle in the reign of King Chaka. This kingdom's political system could be likened to that of Sparta in ancient Greece. Of great interest were the segmented political systems based on clan or age groups, such as those found among the Ibo and the Kikuyu, where government was by consultation and consensus, and the great Islamic sultanates of Nigeria or present-day Mali.

The list is not exhaustive but I merely wish to show that there were, and still are, some traditional governmental systems in Africa, that in some cases existed for centuries before the white man came to Africa. When I speak of democracy in African tradition, therefore, it should not be assumed that this was a tradition uniformly observed and practiced in the whole continent of Africa. We must accept that the traditional systems existed in different varieties to suit people's history, culture, economic and social conditions.

At the risk of introducing some controversy into what is already a complicated subject, I wish to state that the existence of democracy in Africa is currently being questioned in Western political thought. As a result of the rise of military dictatorships, Marxist states and one-party states, it is being argued that Africa has rejected Western democracy or has never had democratic traditions. I would say that the new states that have emerged in Africa, to the extent that they are undemocratic, have borrowed such undemocratic practices from outside the continent in many instances. It can hardly be said that a military coup d'etat is in the African tradition, and certainly no Marxist state can be said to be traditionally African in character. In other words, the often violent criticisms of African governments on the basis that they have departed from Western democratic tradition are somewhat ironic, since the systems that are allegedly undemocratic are also Western in origin. Even those states modeled on Eastern European examples have come to Africa by way of English or French literature. I would argue that many of the state models being criticized are just as much a departure from Western as from African democratic tradition. I would argue further that, in fact, democracy does exist in present-day Africa and that it has always found expression in African tradition. The real issue is how to extend and enlarge the scope of African democratic tradition so that it eventually permeates the whole continent. This is not to suggest that there can be total uniformity in the application of African democratic tradition because there will always be critical factors such as cultural, economic, and social pressures, which affect different societies in different ways, depending upon their historical and cultural traditions.

I would now like to turn to my country, Botswana, where I believe there has been right up to the present day a very strong democratic tradition. The political system among the Batswana was, curiously enough, very highly centralized around the chief or ruler. In fact, in terms of centralization, the Botswana political systems were comparable to those of Ashanti. Yet, this was based on a system of consultation and free discussion on matters of public interest in the assembly known as the "lekgotla." These traditional assemblies in Botswana are basic to our democratic traditions and have been preserved to this day. Like the Greeks and the Romans, who conducted their public affairs at the agora and the forum, Batswana still conduct their public affairs and discuss issues of national interest on a nonpartisan basis in these assemblies, and the chief or subchief or headman, as the case may be, is always the chairman. Not surprisingly, these assemblies are still used extensively by politicians under the modern constitutional arrangement.

The chief symbolized the body politic. He held all the main resources of the people in trust for the people; he owned everything and, at the same time, owned nothing in the land. The chief derived his awesome powers from the people. This is expressed in Setswana as, "Kgosi ke kgosi ka batho," meaning the chief is chief by the will of the people. The chief was the apex of a pyramidical structure. Below him were regional and local chiefs, reaching right down to the smallest community. Like the chief, all these regional chiefs and headmen had executive and judicial functions and exercised their powers at the local level in the manner and on behalf of the chief at the national level.

One peculiarity of the Tswana political system is that the people did not live in small villages scattered all over the land. Indeed, the Batswana were organized, as they still are, in huge traditional villages, divided into wards governed by ward subchiefs or headmen, who also derive their authority from the chief who administered the central *lekgotla*. Thus, there was centralization at the village level and also at the territorial level throughout the country. Central to this organization was the *lekgotla* to which all inhabitants had access, and was the heart of day-to-day administration and decision making. In addition, the *kgotla* (*lekgotla* forum used as a court), tried disputes and issued judgments; any person with a grievance of whatever nature could go to the *kgotla*. This procedure still obtains in Botswana. It is therefore not surprising that in Botswana today, 80 percent of civil and criminal disputes are settled in these traditional courts, and only about 20 percent of such disputes find their way to modern Western-style common law courts.

In the discharge of his responsibility as a ruler, the chief clearly did not work alone. He was assisted by men of standing and experience in the tribe, called "counselors," mainly uncles. At the regional and local levels, this system was reproduced and thus provided effective government at all levels. This pattern of government has been preserved and operates side by side with the modern district administration within the present constitutional framework.

The arrival of colonial authorities superimposed on the traditional system a European administrative structure headed by a resident commissioner or governor. In political terms, the governor was an autocrat, who was sometimes assisted by an executive council. Basically, the system was based on decisions taken by the resident commissioner or governor, who, in turn, carried out the instructions of the colonial secretary in London. Thus, throughout the colonial period, the final decisions were taken undemocratically. The so-called Westminster system was never practiced anywhere in Africa throughout the colonial period. It is not surprising, therefore, that when the Europeans came to colonize Africa, those who earned the description of successful administrators employed a system of "indirect rule," that is, administering their colonial subjects through the existing traditional institutions and systems. This was the case in Botswana, though it was never a colony. Every public initiative, be it a tax collection matter, laws or policies, or dispensation to go to the arable lands to plough crops, required members of the tribe to gather at the *lekgotla* for a debate if the initiative were new, or to have it newly authorized, if it were routine. This process of government by consultation and consensus was the hallmark in most African countries during the colonial era.

What is often forgotten is that, before independence, a constitution was negotiated by the colonial power and the African political leaders, based on a system that existed in the metropolitan country and which had never been practiced during the colonial period. No wonder that, in most African countries, the Westminster system collapsed almost immediately after independence. Such constitutions were, more often than not, totally unfamiliar and not based on the experiences of the people either traditionally or during the colonial period. There is the instance of Swaziland, which accepted the Westminster type of constitution at independence for convenience; immediately after independence, the constitution was torn up in preference for the traditional type of government peculiar to that country for centuries—a monarchy with executive powers. Zimbabwe is already considering its present constitutional arrangement, which is based on the Westminster system of government.

In Botswana, several factors operated that were conducive to the establishment of a multiparty democracy of the kind familiar in the West. Paramount in these are that the main resources of the country—land and cattle—are largely owned by the indigenous population. The population is small and the country very large. The vast majority of the people are of the same stock and largely speak the same language, Setswana. The constitution of the republic is, in the main, a modern version of the traditional system of government, incorporating a president with extensive powers resting on a very democratic base. There is an elected parliament, which is subject to reelection every five years (Botswana has just had its fifth election since independence in 1966). In addition to the elected members of Parliament, there is the House of Chiefs, which forms part of Parliament; the latter house is, however, subordinate to the National Assembly as it acts in an advisory capacity in matters affecting traditions, customs or alteration of certain parts of the Botswana constitution.

I wish to show that the concept and practice of democracy in Africa has not remained static, but has evolved with time. Instead of adopting democracy from Western civilization, I assert that democracy in the African tradition has to be adapted because our societies have to be responsive to new developments and new concepts. Africans are now part of the international community and cannot afford to be insular or parochial. In this process of modernization, we have to introduce constitutionalism without discarding the basic concepts of democracy in an African traditional system of government; the danger is always the destruction of the traditional system in favor of foreign and unfamiliar systems of government.

In the case of Botswana Western democracy in the Westminster style was easily adaptable to the traditional system. In the minds of many people in Botswana, the image of the executive president is that of a chief, supported by a *lekgotla*—the parliament—which discusses matters of national interest and makes new laws as the traditional *lekgotla* did. Dissent is reflected in the existence of many opposition parties in Botswana, who generally express their opinions, some would say, too vociferously. Traditionally, the Batswana believe in freedom of speech; there are not, and never have been, political prisoners.

I believe that a society's particular type of political system must be determined by its values, traditions, norms, and preferences. Botswana has a political system of multiparty democracy because of its belief that freedom of expression and organization are fundamental human rights, safeguarded by the constitutional and institutional political framework. The Batswana believe traditionally in the determination of public policies through open discussions and participation of individuals or sections of the community, however limited this participation might be due to historical and social realities. Disagreement or dissent are fundamental ingredients of politics and inherent to human nature. A political system that seeks unanimity or restricted competition tends to become intolerant of criticism and opposition. Such intolerance often manifests itself in repression with coercion, conformity and loyalty as its characteristics.

No one in Botswana is so arrogant to assume that multiparty democracy, which is so successful in Botswana, is necessarily suited to most African countries. This system's main strength lies in the fact that an institutional framework, rooted in tradition, exists that allows opportunities for criticism, dissent, discussion, and participation. Within it certain fundamental rights and freedoms can be enjoyed by all equally under constitutional protection.

It may be said that Botswana, in many ways, is a de facto one-party state; the ruling party has held a very dominant position, since independence, in terms of the total number of seats held in parliament, or in the total number of votes polled in past general elections. In the main, the strength of the opposition parties is limited, as is their capacity to present before the electorate constructive and viable policy alternatives. It is not because of a constitutional constraint, because there is no fear of persecution or detention for expressing open disagreement with the ruling party. The rule of law and the independence of the judiciary guarantee freedoms to all citizens without favor. In other words, the political system that was adopted is suitable for the country and is undoubtedly connected with the spectacular economic development in an atmosphere of peace, stability, and democracy.

The question that arises is whether such a system as Botswana's is suitable for countries where there are numerous and powerful groups speaking different languages or in which there are strong vested interests held by competing groups. Is it not possible that the one-party states in Africa are an attempt to create one common forum within which all can express their interests? Whether or not the attempt will succeed in accommodating every interest within the system and foster a larger loyalty to the country is to be seen. The key question is whether or not dissent is permitted within any system. In my view, if a one-party state is used to stifle dissent or to protect the privileges and power of vested interest, then it will fail.

I must say that there is a tendency of scholars to study government in Africa, but not the role played by opposition groups or parties. It is necessary for political scientists to make a more comprehensive study of political development in Africa, to include not only the action and behavior of governments but also the corresponding, and often contrary, actions of opposition groups. For instance, the most serious revolts in Africa were those begun with military coups in Nigeria, Ghana and others; these countries have not known sustained stability since then. The same applies to Gambia, where the opposition attempted to destroy the democratically elected government. This makes African governments apprehensive of opposition groups who use the democratic apparatus to destroy democracy. This may well be the reason that some governments have opted for a one-party state; often, some African opposition parties are disloyal to the incumbent government, even to the point of soliciting financial and military assistance from foreign governments so as to take power by force and not by ballot.

There is a tendency of African leaders to hang on to power indefinitely. One might think that many political leaders in Africa are not inclined towards multiparty democracy because they are not prepared to leave power, and that they have little respect for the will of the people they claim to represent. The system adopted in Botswana may not be perfect, but it works because it is based upon the traditional values of tolerance and freedom of speech. There is a saying in Setswana: "Mafoko a lekgotla a mantle otlhe," meaning that every man is entitled by right to have his say. This system could succeed in other African countries on the condition that the ruling party leaders would be prepared to relinquish power and to share it with others who could receive the mandate of the masses if given the opportunity.

12

Pluralism, Constitutionalism, and Law in Africa: A Liberian View

On April 12, 1980, shortly after Liberia's nineteenth president, William Tolbert, had been killed in a military coup and his government overthrown, the Liberian constitution was suspended. This constitution had been the country's basic law without interruption since its independence on July 26, 1847. In April 1980, serious consideration was given by the ruling military council to the views of some Liberians, who were demanding a change of the country's name, flag and other symbols, because, in their view, nothing short of a new nation had come into being. The People's Redemption Council, as the new military government called itself, ultimately rejected such sweeping changes, but the country would never be the same again.

Because the circumstances that led to the startling collapse of the oldest republic in Africa were uncommon, almost as soon as the guns fell silent, the most far-reaching postmortem of the first republic, particularly of the suspended constitution, became an urgent national undertaking. This soul-searching by the Liberian people, which led to the preparation and adoption of a new constitution, provides unique material for an examination of how constitutional government, which is government under law, has dealt with pluralism in Africa.

Pluralism in Africa as a whole connotes numerous diversities. In the eastern and southern portions of the continent, where Europeans and Asians settled in appreciable numbers, racial diversity is a pronounced feature of the political landscape. In contrast, in West Africa the dominance of the Negro race is almost exclusive. A distinct feature of Liberia's 1847 Constitution was a provision restricting citizenship to persons of Negro descent. In 1984, more than a century later, despite many calls for change to reflect current norms of racial equality, this clause has been restated in the new constitution.

If racial diversity is not countenanced in Liberia's constitutional order, many other diversities are. This is a country of two million people, which has more than sixteen tribal and ethnic groups, among whom are Christians,

Moslems, and animists. The presence of so many groups in one of the smallest countries of Africa is in part explained by the migrations that took place from, and following the break up of, the Sudanic empires of Mali and Songhay. Later came Christian missionaries and the spread of Islam. Climate also played a part, in that dense equatorial forests restricted the movement of people while the unfavorable health conditions and frequent tribal wars gave the region a very sparse population. It seems, also, that whenever disputes arose among inhabitants of the area, there being no developed dispute settlement mechanisms available, the only way such disputes could be resolved was for the parties in conflict to withdraw into or to be assigned separate geographical areas. For centuries, bands of hunters strayed farther into dense forests away from settled communities. With the passage of years many divided and distinct tribal communities emerged.

In 1821, when black settlers began returning in West Africa from the United States to establish Liberia, the areas they settled were peopled by numerous tribal groups, which were not much more than large family units. Under the rule of chiefs in a polygamous culture, everyone was related to almost everyone else and the same structure of governance and officials regulated all community activities, whether private or public.

Founded in 1821 by the American Colonization Society, Liberia, from its beginning, was governed by laws promulgated by the Society through its agents. This state of affairs did not conform with the law of nations, which did not permit colonization except by sovereign nations. Objecting to what was considered unlawful interference with legitimate trade being carried out in Liberia by its nationals, the British government insisted that only laws enacted by a sovereign state could command the obedience of British subjects. Meanwhile, in the United States, where the storms of civil war were beginning to gather, interest in African colonization dimmed and, in 1846, the American Colonization Society engaged the services of the noted American jurist and Harvard professor Simon Greenleaf to draft a constitution which, in 1847, launched Liberia into independent nationhood.

The Liberian constitution of 1847 was modeled after that of the state of Massachusetts. It created a republican form of government with the powers of state divided on Montesquieuan lines into three coequal branches of government—legislative, judicial, and executive. The provisions setting out the governmental structure were preceeded by a declaration of rights, which set forth the basic rights of citizens and placed precise limitations on the exercise of governmental powers. The society thus envisioned was pluralistic.

Unlike the situation in the tribal communities over which the new Republic of Liberia now extended its sway, emphasis was placed by the Liberian constitution on individual rights and civil liberties. The individual was recognized as the source, creator, and chief beneficiary of governmental authority. "All power," the Constitution stated, "is inherent in the people; all free governments are instituted by their authority and for their benefit and they have the right to alter and reform the same when their safety and happiness require it."

Liberia's intentions to operate a pluralistic society embracing the tribes in one common body politic with the settlers were, at best, ambiguous. Even had such intentions been explicitly entertained, consistent with the ideals of pluralism in the constitution, Liberia lacked the resources with which to implement them. Only after resources became available to the government in appreciable quantities, one hundred years later, was it possible to weld all ethnic and tribal groups into one pluralistic society as envisioned by the constitution.

As Liberia's pluralistic society became a reality, the presidency came to overshadow and dominate the two other branches of government. The institution of the tribal chief, hereditary and powerful, was grafted into the constitutional system. A chief executive vested with autocratic powers beyond anything the constitution allowed sprang up. It was perhaps no coincidence that this dynamic constitutional development reached its peak during the country's longest administration, an administration of nearly thirty years. It was during this period that the Liberian people—tribal people and the descendants of the settlers—were finally united under the political order of a common constitution. This period also coincided with the first time in the country's history when manpower and material resources were available in proportions that enabled the government to undertake serious nation-building.

Nothing depicted more clearly the president as chief than his frequent convening of executive councils in the hinterland. At these large gatherings, which had the air of a political convention, the separation between the three branches of government, so painstakingly established in the constitution, were swept aside. The president in his role as the "big African chief" laid down law in one instant, in another interpreted law and ultimately enforced, often with swift rigor, that which a moment earlier he had himself decreed and judged.

Whatever the shortcomings of this chieftancy-presidency from a legal and constitutional standpoint, it made possible harmony and unity among Liberia's tribal people and allowed their incorporation into the mainstream of the country's political life. But it did more than this. If what the President decreed became law for tribal people in the hinterland, comprising as they did the overwhelming bulk of the country's population, it was only a matter of time before that same style and method of governing would become common to the whole country. This happened and, in the view of many Liberians, the country was never more effectively governed, before or since.

But this intermingling of the traditional with the modern in Liberia, as in many developing African countries, has had, by creating hybrid systems, very far reaching effects. It explains the people's attitude to law and their expectations of their leaders and of the state. Straddling different worlds, attempting to raise nation-states out of previously warring factions, African countries have made frantic exertions to acquire in the space of a few years what countries in other areas of the world took centuries to achieve. The consensus, patience, and discipline required to nurture national institutions and the determination needed to guard against foreign exploitation have been almost impossible to achieve. Thus, too many African countries have found themselves in a state of upheaval, confusion, and drift. Against this background, the Liberian republic collapsed, and the stage was set for a new attempt at nation-building.

One year after the Liberian military government came to power, it set up a National Constitution Commission composed of twenty-five persons chosen to reflect the country's political and social realities. Because of their education, the commissioners were more able than most Liberians to visualize concrete responses to the dual character of the society. The commission's specific mandate was to undertake a systematic review of the suspended constitution, to explain its provisions to the people of Liberia, and to seek their reaction and input for the preparation of a new constitution with which they would be proud to identify and which would be responsive to their needs. The commission felt, from the outset, that research into Liberia's dual legal and socio-political system had to be undertaken, and that the findings must be reflected in the new constitution.

Conducting nationwide consultations, also called hearings, was the commission's first major endeavor. The first hearings were held at the University of Liberia. The students' concerns focused on the causes of the 1980 military coup; they attributed the coup to departures by the previous civilian government from the constitutional system of checks and balances then in effect. In the up-country areas, the concerns expressed at the hearings were more practical. Complaints were heard about the lack of basic social services and infrastructure, the uneven burden and harsh methods of tax collection among tribal citizens and the failure by the government in Monrovia to respond speedily, if at all, to the needs of the interior. The hearings provided the commission with many valuable insights, but their greatest impact by far was the sense of participation in the historic remaking of a nation which they made possible for Liberians from all over the country and from all walks of life.

With the hearings completed and the standing committees' research work done, drafting began. The drafters had access to many resources; studies undertaken by the research arm of the constitution commission were available, as were results from visits made by some members of the commission to Ghana, Nigeria, and Sierra Leone. These countries had had recent experience in making constitutions and in staging elections. Experts on constitutional law, provided by the governments of the United States and the United Kingdom, also provided comments and information to the drafting committee.

The drafting committee sought to accommodate the desires of the Liberian people as expressed in the hearings. They also felt, however, that in areas where those desires were out of tune with modern trends, their task required them to lead in new directions rather than slavishly to follow public sentiments. For example, the people in the counties had insisted throughout the hearings that the chief administrative officers of the counties—called "superintendents"—be elected by citizens of the respective counties rather than be appointed by the president. This view was not accommodated in the draft; the commission felt that a national cohesion and efficiency derived from a common administration of the country was preferable to whatever benefits decentralization in a country of two million inhabitants would achieve. Also, many drafters felt that whatever the justification for the controversial racial test for citizenship in the 1847 constitution, it would be unfortunate in the closing decades of the twentieth century to carry a racial discrimination clause in the new constitution. In spite of these misgivings, however, the commissioners felt compelled to respect the strongly expressed insistence of the Liberian people that only blacks should be eligible for Liberian citizenship, as was the case in the constitution of one hundred and thirty seven years earlier.

The commission promised much research into various aspects of dualism in the Liberian social and political setting. Preliminary investigation of the topics considered appropriate showed that the work needed to conduct a meaningful enquiry would exceed the less-than-three-years time limit to the commission's mandate. Moreover, it was thought that the expected conclusions would not go well in a constitution. For example, especially in the tribal areas, the hearings received numerous pleas from some tribal citizens that the constitutions explicitly state that trial by ordeal was allowed; other citizens argued that polygamous marriage, the traditional African form of marriage, should be constitutionally endorsed. Some tribal chiefs argued that order would not be restored in the hinterland until the hereditary status of chiefs was restored and the chiefs were permitted to function in the traditional style outside the framework of the written constitution.

On these and other aspects of dualism in Liberian life the new constitution, just like the one of 1847, maintains a calculated silence. Even though a new chapter entitled "General Principles of National Policy" provides guidelines for governmental actions such as strengthening national integration, preserving and promoting positive Liberian cultural values and eliminating sectionalism and tribalism from Liberian life, these do not mean much.

The constitution-making exercise in Liberia reflects a conscious and deliberate effort at fostering pluralism, within a legal and constitutional framework, based on the country's own experience and aspirations. These efforts went forward at a time when there was no constitution in force and the country was ruled by military decrees. Initially, some Liberians saw the breakdown of the old order as an opportunity for retributive justice and the replacement of one set of rulers by another. Very quickly, however, the determination to preserve Liberia's historical continuity prevailed and law and order were restored. There were no prolonged departures from constitutional norms and the military council exercised power, for the most part, in a manner consistent with the spirit, if not always the letter, of the suspended constitution.

At the end of 1984, with the end of military rule in sight and the restoration of constitutional civilian rule set for January 1986, there were still areas where important diversities and concerns had not been properly addressed by the proposed new order. This failure could threaten Liberia's return to constitutional rule, as it has threatened elected civilian democratic governments elsewhere in Africa.

If constitutional pluralistic democracy and the rule of law are to have a future in Africa, at least three important concerns must be dealt with: first, the role of the military establishment; second, the role of the educational establishment, particularly institutions of higher learning, in the political arena; and last, how to minimize corruption and ensure a more equitable distribution of the national wealth.

With an ever increasing number of the states of Africa falling under military rule, it is obvious that soldiers will continue to demand and play a political role in African countries. Once having wielded the full powers of state, they remain aware of what, in many countries, is a short route to power and fortune.

During the drafting of Liberia's new constitution, some people called for a constitutional provision that would make military seizure of power unconstitutional. In the end, this clause (and another that would make it impossible to amend the constitution to extend the presidential term beyond two terms), was rejected. The new constitution, in fact, appears more tolerant of soldiers in politics than that of 1847, which stated that: "The people have a right to keep and bear arms for the common defense and as in time of peace, armies are dangerous to liberty, they ought not be maintained without the consent of the legislature; and the military power shall always be held in exact subordination of civil authority, and be governed by it."

Nothing like this language appears in the new constitution, but in the provisions where emergency powers are granted to the president, it is provided that: "All military power or authority shall at all times, however, be held in subordination to the civil authority and the constitution."

Attempts to curtail the powers of the military within a constitution are good only as long as the constitutional order stands. To guard against the threats that a politicized military could pose to constitutional democracy in Africa, the political role of soldiers must be squarely faced. The key questions are: Should soldiers be active in politics, and should soldiers have the right to vote? It seems urgent that a distinction be made between the army as an institution and the individual citizen-soldiers who make up the army. Like all other citizens, including those who are members of the state institutions like the civil service, soldiers are entitled to and must be allowed to exercise the right of franchise. Similarly, just as it is inappropriate and dangerous for, say, the legislature or civil service as bodies to engage in partisan politics, so too for the army. The constitution of any African country today must address this issue squarely and must bar the army from partisan politics in order to prevent the rise of a soldier's party or the endorsement of political parties by the army as a body. Beyond that, however, soldiers being voters, it is just as permissible for political parties to seek votes among citizens who live in military barracks as among other citizens.

In many respects the army and the educational establishments in developing countries have important national duties to perform. Given that few African armies ever engage in protecting the state against external aggression, the function they might usefully serve in developing countries needs reassessment. The diminution of the army in many African countries and the shift of their activities away from military combat-preparedness to economic development roles would do much to safeguard constitutional democracy in Africa.

The role of students in politics in a developing country like Liberia differs from the role of their counterparts in the more developed countries. Education in developed countries equips and prepares youths to follow in the footsteps of their elders. In a typical developing African country, education sets young people apart from their elders and, because of their education, young people are expected to assume the task of leading society to development and progress. Through education, citizens of any background may enter the mainsteam of the nation's modern social and political life. When, therefore, unlettered up-country citizens in Liberia educate their children, at considerable sacrifice, to the point where those children enroll at the national university or a foreign one, those parents expect their children—even while they are still students—to guide their thinking and to help them make decisions on national issues. Given this situation, the impatience that university students experience when excluded from participation in national politics is no surprise. At a time when soldiers, often younger than university students and with little education, have seized and wielded state power in many African countries, the need to find a political role for students within the political system assumes great urgency. It may not be necessary to create special seats in the legislature for college students, though the idea merits study; but, certainly, political canvassing can and should be permissible at institutions of higher learning. The students of these institutions, being leaders of thought for a great segment of the population, will be forced to resort to clandestine and confrontational methods of political expression if the normal channels are blocked to them.

The problem of what is commonly called corruption in developing societies is, in part, a consequence of dualism in the society. In traditional communities where the extended family system prevailed and economic assets were communally owned, there was not much scope for the appropriation of property belonging to others since there was precious little such property and, moreover, the need did not commonly exist in a family-based welfare system. People don't typically steal what is readily available, nor do they steal from themselves. With the spread of a private property-owning society, with the decline of the extended family, with the entry of foreign private investment, and with government involvement in virtually every facet of the national economy, fierce competition, even cheating and stealing in order to acquire unearned slices of the nation's wealth, have come to plague modern African society. The more some African governments have tried to stop corruption, the more it seems corruption has expanded—the potential curbers of corruption have themselves become corrupt. In some countries draconian forms of punishment, including the death penalty and public floggings of mere suspects, have been used in efforts to stamp out corruption. But the corruption problem continues to grow. In fact, there appears to be a strong correlation between the level of corruption and the extent to which the economy of a given country is regulated and controlled by the state. For this reason, the framers of Liberia's new constitution prudently stressed that individual initiative and private enterprise would be the system by which the economy of the country would be developed. Under the new constitution, the state would not control or dominate economic activities in the country; citizens could benefit from the powerful and natural incentive of protecting best that which is theirs.

Framers of recent constitutions in Africa have sought to deal with the corruption problem by setting out codes of conduct for public officials as part of the constitution, or else have called for the later passage of appropriate legislation. Nowhere have these enactments had any marked success. It has been said that a certain African government, which was overthrown in 1983, was perhaps the most corrupt government in Africa's recent history. Corruption on an immense scale flourished under a constitution that went to great lengths to try to stamp it out, and this in a country whose vibrant free press was unsurpassed at the time anywhere else in Africa. With such a background, why was corruption not checked? Perhaps it was because dualism in African society existed there in a very pernicious form. In some societies a free press, by exposing corruption, scares those practicing it and thereby checks corruption. In many African settings, however, in areas of high illiteracy and great inequality of wealth and incomes, the oft-repeated and oft-exaggerated stories of official corruption are soon taken by the populace to mean that all officials are corrupt.

In fact, officials in many African countries could not meet the society's expectation of them unless they were corrupt. How can an African "big man" discharge his responsibilities to his extended family or to the needy of the community, as is expected of him, on his miniscule government salary? If some officials are not corrupt, but strive to serve the public interests at great sacrifice, they will not be effective public servants for long. Almost everyone not in the government invariably brands all those in it as corrupt. In such an atmosphere essential ingredients for national unity and development—a people's sense of self worth, pride and mutual trust—are missing. Sensing the public frustration, demagogues arise to mouth slogans and promise a swift end to corruption. As a result of these onslaughts, democratically elected governments are soon overthrown, sometimes amid scenes of violence and barbarism. Overnight, new and unheard-of figures masquerading as saviors emerge and are greeted by public euphoria, all in the cause of ending corruption. Corruption doesn't end; soon, the new liberators, like others before them, will deservedly or not be branded corrupt and overthrown.

Corruption is a great evil, particularly in a developing country where the community's needs are great and its resources to meet them are few. The misuse of public funds is only one form of corruption; developing countries face many dangers greater even than this. When the bonds of a common national destiny and citizenship, and even the sanctity of human life itself, are deemed almost as of no moment, while the so-called fight against corruption, real or imagined, is made out to be the noblest crusade in whose pursuit any means whatever are justified, then every social malady, including rampant corruption in all forms, can become the inescapable order of the day.

Liberia's experience as the oldest republic of Africa shows that the growth of a pluralistic society is a positive advance in nation building. It ought to be and can successfully be fostered within the framework of law and constitutionalism. Given the peculiarities of Africa's history and the desire to cram the stuff of centuries into a few years, pluralism results in the commingling of cultures at different stages of civilization, where vastly different values, traditions, and laws inform behavior in society. The bewildering diversities thus created have already raised new dangers for democratic order in Africa. They therefore ought, with the greatest urgency, to be recognized, studied, and tackled within the framework of law and constitutionalism.

Victor A. Olorunsola

13

Questions on Constitutionalism and Democracy: Nigeria and Africa

The problem of constitution and law cannot be addressed in a vacuum. Indeed, if a constitution is to succeed it is absolutely essential that it be grounded in the sociocultural and political realities of the particular society. Consequently, within the parameters of our concern, the sociocultural and political realities of Africa are important. Here are some of the specific questions that are germane.

What are the traditional sociocultural realities in various African states? How compatible and heterogeneous are they? Under what conditions have various sections and subcultural groupings been brought together into the state framework? What are the frameworks and the histories of the interactive processes among the units, principal actors, and institutions? What are the ramifications of these interactions, processes, traditions, and the history of the democratic processes and behavior? Where democracy has been a declared goal of the polity, what various constitutional forms have they taken? Why have they had such battered lives?

The answers to these questions are important because, to a large extent, they are probably deterministic. At least we should ask these questions as we seek to assess prospects for constitution and democracy in Africa. On the whole, I am a little bit pessimistic regarding prospects for African democracies in the near future. I am convinced that it is no longer treasonable to ask whether, for example, in the case of Nigeria, structural realignment and solutions may not have gone as far as they can go. Has constitutional engineering of a democracy gone as far as it can go? Perhaps behavior modification and value reorientation are more in order and should now command greater effort and attention. We are compelled to ask two questions of these new constitutions: (1) Do these constitutions solve the problems or do they raise more problems and solve precious little of the old ones? (2) Do they generate internal contradictions of their own, which, ultimately, are likely to sabotage the democratic goals that they were devised to engender? Unfortunately, it appears that they often raise more problems and generate enormous internal contradictions. To say this, however, is not to say that in all cases such problems should constitute a significant disincentive.

Several years ago, following the demise of Nigeria's first republic[1] and its structural Westminster model, I had the opportunity to outline and discuss what I regarded as the fundamental problems that Nigeria must face squarely in the interest of national survival and political stability.[2] Briefly then, let me outline them:

1. The problem of differing political cultures among the various ethnic groupings in the country, as well as the inability of those in authority to reconcile differing norms with one another

2. The problem of the differing impact of colonialism that manifests itself in uneven educational opportunities, which, in turn, results in sharp differences in the rate of growth and uneven development among various components of the country

3. The problem of ethnic-based political parties, which, for the selfish interest of maintaining themselves in power, accentuate sectional feelings and intensify primordial attachments

4. The problem of the loss of idealism, the reckless pursuit of personal wealth by the fortunate few, and the widening of the gap between the haves and the have-nots

5. The problem of a sense of frustration by citizens regarding their future and fortune in the political order (the issue of rigged elections and the citizen's absence of freedom to pursue economic activity everywhere in the Federation)

6. The problem of politics of cultural subnationalism and the politics of regional security (the case of a part being greater than the whole Federal-State relations)

7. The problem of an apparent unwillingness to attack Nigerian problems at their foundation, i.e., the preferences for patchwork leading the country to develop a vicious cycle of crises

8. The problem of making national institutions behave in truly national fashion.[3]

Since I made these observations, two additional military regimes have come and gone; the second republic has come and gone; a new military regime has asserted itself.[4] The search for acceptable formulas is seemingly on again. Did we go or did we come?

Of primary importance then is analyzing the more recent attempt to cope with these problems and the consequences of the attempt. The most thorough and far-reaching effort to date is embodied in the 1979 constitution. It is particularly germane that this Nigerian attempt was resolutely rooted in a federal democratic framework and it sought a democratic goal. How did the 1979 constitution attempt to deal with the malaise? What were the results, and why?

The preparations for the process involved in the constitution for the second republic suggest that, for once, the leaders were seriously interested in attacking Nigerian problems at the foundation. There were comprehensive consultations. The constitution that emerged shows a number of radical departures from previous ones: the Westminster model was dropped in favor of what, on the face of things, looks like the American model of democracy; there were structural realignment and fundamental changes in federal-state relations.[5] The changes in the federal-state relations were devices to ensure that "the tail does not wag the dog." The introduction of the exclusive and concurrent legislative list is a careful definition of the parameters of authority between the states and the federation; indeed, even the authority and conditions for the creation of more states were defined.

In order to avoid the emergence of parochially-based political parties, sections 201 through 209 of the 1979 constitution provided for, among other things: the formation of national parties that must reflect the "federal character" of Nigeria and which must be opened to "every citizen of Nigeria regardless of his/her place of origin, religion or ethnic groupings"; the mandatory location of each party's headquarters at the capital of the Federation (perhaps recognizing environmental impact on political institutions and behavior).[6] In order to minimize the suspicion and fears of domination of the public services by one section, region, or ethnic group the constitution stipulates in Section 14 (3) that:

> The composition of the government of the Federation or any of its agencies and the conduct of its affairs shall be carried out in such manner as to reflect federal character of Nigeria and the need to promote national unity and also to command national loyalty, thereby ensuring that there shall be no predominance of persons from a few states or from a few ethnic or other sectional groups in that government or in any of its agencies.

Further, the content of Section 14 (3) in the 1979 constitution made it imperative for any presidential incumbent to appoint people from various states in order to meet the requirement of reflecting the "federal character" in appointments; this included ministers, board chairs, and ambassadors. In addition to the possibility that this could contribute to the creation of truly national institutions, it probably occurred to some of the framers that it would reduce the sense of frustration by citizens regarding their future and fortune in the political order. Moreover, the constitution mandated the same clause for the governments of various states—as part of the fundamental obligation of all governments of the federation.

These were designed to absorb the impact of the policies of cultural and regional subnationalism, curb the dual bogeys of tyranny of skills and tyranny of population, and create the nuclei of national institutions that will behave in truly national fashion.

Historically, the north-south conflict has been accentuated by the imbalance in the federal structure. General Gowon, the Nigerian head of state after the fall of the first republic, attempted to rectify this imbalance by creating twelve states. The former secretary to the federal military government under Gowon declared: "The most sensitive potential threat to the stability of Nigerian federation was a north-south confrontation; and, it was of strategic importance that the number of states in the 'northern' parts of the country should be seen as equal to the number in 'southern' states." Be that as it may, ultimately the number of states was increased. In effect, the 1979 constitution enshrined the breakup of the north, west, and east, although the old north was divided into ten states, as opposed to nine states for the old south. Section 126 (2–6), as well as the amendment to 126, stipulate that a candidate is elected president only if, in addition to the number of votes acquired, he or she has not less than one-quarter of the votes cast at the election in each of at least two-thirds of all states in the federation.

The so-called two-thirds rule was a measure to broaden the power of the president, and ensure the emergence of a truly national figure acceptable to most sections of the country. The provision for an executive presidency is meant to be an insurance against the paradox of 1965 in the first republic when, as some believed, the president was only a figurehead and the federal prime minister was politically impotent and unable to take decisive action. The president's authority to appoint a cabinet outside of the elected officials was a device to strengthen his executive capacity and put into operation a check and balance system not much unlike that in the United States.

Although not a part of the constitution itself, elected public officials were required to declare their assets prior to the assumption of public office.

With the constitution came the 1979 elections and the establishment of Shehu Shagari as the president of the second federal republic. In 1983, there was another series of elections that culminated in Shagari being declared president. On December 31, 1983, the military took power once again.

Why is it that, in spite of all the rituals, preparations, and care, things should come to a military takeover once again? What went wrong? Can this instruct us about the limitation of constitutions in guaranteeing democracy?

First, what did the partial architects of the constitution say caused the demise of the second republic? Lieutenant General Danjuma, a member of the federal military government of General Obasanjo, immediately after the Buhari coup remarked, "Democracy had been in jeopardy for the past four years. It died with the elections. The army buried it, they didn't kill it. All the parties were involved, but the greatest offender was the NPN. The NPN (National Party of Nigeria) had the largest gathering of the worst human beings that Nigeria could produce."[7]

If he is right, the problem seemingly is to be found in political recruitment and political socialization. In short, the system did not recruit people who could operate the system in the way the constitution envisaged it. Danjuma blamed the kind of people who operated the constitution. Furthermore, he expressed acute disappointment in the performance of the political parties; apparently the system did not socialize political actors in a way that would make their behavior consistent with expectant political behavior in a society such as the one conceived in the 1979 constitution.

General Obasanjo, after lamenting the demise of the system he worked so hard to put in place, declared that what Nigeria needs now is "a system that gives us: direction; decisive and purposeful leadership; and leadership that will galvanize us together as a nation."[8] By implication, the political leadership and political actors of the second republic, in the opinion of these men, lacked decisive and purposeful leadership ability and failed to give direction to the nation. There is more, too, perhaps; a loss of faith in the appropriateness of democracy.

What did those, who, according to Danjuma, "buried the second republic," have to say? They seem to have felt that the second republic and its enabling act died because of the performance of the political leaders who operated the political system. In a speech, General Buhari asserted that "little did the military realize that the political leadership of the second republic would sacrifice most of the checks and balances in the constitution and bring us to the present situation of general insecurity." Continuing his explanation of the demise of the second republic, he said, "The premium of political power became so exceedingly high that political contestants regarded victory in election as a matter of life and death . . . they were determined to capture or retain power by all means."[9] General Buhari, the post-1983 coup leader, granted that the worldwide economic recession was a liability, but he asserted that the impact of this recession was grossly aggravated by mismanagement. He went on:

> We believe the appropriate government agencies give good advice, but their advice was disregarded by the leadership. The situation could have been saved if the legislators were alive to their constitutional responsibilities. Instead, the legislators were preoccupied with determining their salary scale, fringe benefits, unnecessary foreign travels, etc., which took no account of the state of the economy and the welfare of the people they represented. As a result of their inability to cultivate financial discipline and

stringent management of the economy we have come to depend largely on internal and external borrowing to execute government projects with attendant domestic price pressure and soaring external debt.[10]

General Buhari lamented the situation in the country in which there was heavy budget deficit, weak balance of payment posture, and little prospect of building a virile and viable economy. On the other hand, he did not consider the last election a legitimate election. In fact, he said, "The last general election could be anything but free and fair. There is ample evidence that rigging and thuggery were related to the resources available to the political parties. This conclusively proves to us that the political parties have not developed confidence in the presidential system of government on which the nation invested so much material resources."[11]

Finally General Buhari added:

> While corruption and indiscipline had been associated with our state of underdevelopment, these twin evils in our politics have attained unprecedented height over the past four years. The corrupt, inept, and insensitive leadership in the last four years has been the source of immorality and impropriety in our society, since what happens in any society is largely a reflection of the leadership of that society. With no corruption in all its processes, this government will not tolerate kickback, inflation of contracts and overinvoicing of imports, etc. Nor will it condone forgery, fraud, embezzlement, misuse and abuse of profit and illegal dealing in foreign exchange and smuggling. Arson has been used to cover up fraudulent acts in public institutions.[12]

In sum, from General Buhari's point of view, poor leadership, political and economic mismanagement, political party irresponsibilities, political corruption, personal power, and other selfish interests sabotaged the lofty aims and hopes embodied in the 1979 constitution. By implication, these forces aborted democracy. Is that all of it?

Let me return now to the set of troublesome thoughts. Could it be that the 1979 constitution contained the seeds of its own destruction? Like most medical prescriptions, the 1979 constitution too, as a remedy for the country's ills, may have had its side effects. For example: Is the tendency towards greater rigging in the last election related to the desperate attempts to achieve a two-thirds majority rule? If so, to what extent? Is the tendency towards rigging elections related to the requirement of federal character and orientational focus, which could have forced various political parties to devise avoidance mechanisms? Thus, to what extent is the NPN's "landslide" victory related to the Zone strategy?[13] In short, if candidate Akinloye wants to become the next president at the end of Shagari's term must he deliver Oyo State at all costs? Must presidential aspirant Ojukwu from Anambara State deliver Anambara State by hook or crook?

Could it be that the faithful operation of the 1979 constitution required high-profile political leadership in a system dominated by political compromise? It is an open question whether or not a high-profile president can survive in Nigeria for a long time. Could it be that the attempt to curb the power of the regions by creating a lot of states has led to a dependency syndrome that inflated the power and authority of the federal government?

Another Troublesome Thought About the Future

As early as August 20, 1983, some Nigerians were quietly raising an intriguing and vexing question: Does the creation and existence of democratic institutions and structures raise unrealistic participatory expectations? One might ask a number of questions subsumed under the first one.

Does a high level of participatory expectations, when not matched by system performance, lead to rising frustration? Can such frustration lead to loss of faith in democracy? Do political participants, who feel helpless and disenchanted because of this participation hiatus, engage in actions not sanctioned by democratic theory? Does the conduct of elections in such a system—contrary to providing an avenue for political stability and peaceful change of personnel in the echelons of power—unwittingly contribute to, accentuate, or institutionalize political instability?

In short, political recruitment, political socialization, political corruption, unrealized high participatory expectations, unrealized economic expectations, and the paradox of high-profile political leadership in what may be essentially a low-profile system, may have contributed in varying proportions to the demise of the second republic.

Equally troublesome are the more subtle notes; for example, there is the remarkably increased confidence of the Nigerian military establishment in spite of itself. Do we have a feeling of déjà vu both on the part of the Nigerian citizenry and the Nigerian military, which may mean greater impatience? To many, these seem to be an Africa-wide phenomena.

How about the future? Is it time for despair? After all, political recruitment seems to have failed. Political socialization seems not to have worked, democracy not to have been operated properly. Hope for a high-profile political leadership would seem inappropriate in a fragile state like Nigeria.

All in all, I think there is no need to be discouraged—at least not yet. Nigerians love political discourse, and they like to organize. The press loves its freedom; and, the Nigerian military, in the long run, may prove not to be without blemish. There is ample evidence that in these aspects, African states may be more similar than dissimilar.

The point is that structural realignment and solutions may have gone as far as they can go in some African countries. Perhaps constitution making has gone about as far as it should or can go in such countries. A significant part of the problem may well stem from the continuation of value dualism and the anomic character of the state. The Nigerian case demonstrates that perhaps behavior modification and value reorientation are more in order now. They should command greater efforts and attention in the interest of good government to assure majority rule, minority rights, and the rule of law.

Notes

1. The first republic was brought to an end by a group of young army officers in a coup d'etat on January 15, 1966.

2. Victor A. Olorunsola, *The Politics of Cultural Subnationalism in Africa* (New York: Doubleday, 1972).

3. A more detailed exposition is in Victor Olorunsola's *Societal Reconstruction in Two Different States* (Washington: University Press of America, 1977).

4. The second republic was ushered in by the 1979 constitution. A few months after the election of 1983, on December 31, 1983, a military *coup d'état* ended the second republic and installed General Buhari as the head of a new military regime.

5. Federal Republic of Nigeria, *The Constitution of the Federal Republic of Nigeria, 1979* (Lagos: Government Printer, 1978).

6. Ibid.

7. Reported in *West Africa* (30 June 1984), 197.

8. Ibid., 198.

9. Quoted in *West Africa* (7 January 1984), 58.

10. Ibid.

12. Ibid.

13. The Zone strategy was an understanding designed to accommodate the non-Northern (particularly Ibo and Yoruba) members of the NPN, who feared that the leadership of the party would forever be dominated by the northerners. It was an understanding that the principle of rotation would be allowed in the decision of the party's presidential candidate. Akinloye was the Yoruba member of the party that would have benefited from such a strategy.

Ali Khalif Galaydh

14

Democratic Practice and Breakdown in Somalia

The successful voluntary integration, after independence, of British Somaliland and the Italian-administered trusteeship of Somalia was unique in Africa. For the average Somali that was only natural and the next step was to bring together the rest of the family members. The robust multiparty parliamentary system that was installed and maintained for almost a decade was, if not unique, a rarity in the African political landscape. There was no song and dance about the merits of the single-party doctrine, nor was there a serious aspirant for the position of president for life. On the contrary, Somalia's first president, Adan Abdulleh Osman, who maintained a dignified distance from factional politics and provided an astute and stabilizing leadership, was voted out of office in July 1967. The transfer of power was peaceful and it had to be according to the then rules of the political process.

However, significant deviations from democratic standards were occurring, especially during and after the last general elections, but there was a measure of legitimacy in the exercise of power, and certain salient features of democracy—consultation, consent, respect for human dignity, and rule of law—were present. This was pushed aside when, contrary to conventional wisdom, Somalia supposedly immune to African coup fever was smitten in October 1969.

Democratic Practice in Africa

Very simply put, democracy is a method in the exercise of freedom. There are no absolute attributes of democracy, but there are essential parts in the exercise of freedom: individual freedom, as in participation and in the exercise of choice, particularly of leaders; freedom of access to valued resources, be they economic or social; and, freedom from the arbitrary application of law. Democracy in practice, over time, is bound to be democracy in parts, but the crucial issue is whether the essential parts of the exercise of freedom

127

are in place. Democratic practice, to be self-sustaining, must also have expanding boundaries for the exercise of freedom: an inclusionary perception in participation and choice and increased access to valued resources are requisites for the unfolding of democratic ideals and spirit. I submit there is nothing un-African, let alone un-Somali, about this. The essential, and unfolding, parts of democratic practice are universal aspirations despite the self-inflicted myopia of some Africans and the prevalent skepticism of some students of African politics.

Aspirations aside, democratic practice in Africa has not flowered profusely in tropical Africa. Famine, drought, and economic mismanagement have brought in their train stagnation, destruction, and economic crisis, which is enveloping the bulk of Africa. Land, labor, capital, and personal rule are the factors of production in Africa's blighted political economy. Political instability has blossomed and coup begets coup; where there is respite from coup-making, authoritarianism is ensconced. There are a few exceptions. Botswana, Gambia, Mauritius, Senegal, Djibouti, Zimbabwe, Egypt, Morocco, Tunisia, and Uganda possess, in varying degrees, the essential parts of democratic practice. However, shrill voices in praise of a single-party system coming out of Zimbabwe do not augur well for the unfolding of democracy. In Uganda, despite the tentative achievements, one can hardly talk of human rights and the rule of law when the carnage continues and national reconciliation disappears distantly into the future. The democratic experiments in Senegal and Egypt are encouraging and, if successful, will have positive effects beyond the borders of these two important countries.

Here are a group of African countries who possess, presently, the necessary aspects of democratic attributes. Rather than delve into the sterile discourse of whether Western democracy is appropriate for Africa or not, a more productive enterprise is a closer examination of the experiments in these countries. No presumption is made that the process of transplanting successful "exercises" will be any easier among African countries. The examination of the relevant and significant factors that have contributed to their democratic practice will help in debunking single-party-system doctrine and in demystifying the demands of democratic rule.

The Somali Case

The traditional Somali system of self-government has evolved through the centuries. While the Somali people share a fairly homogeneous political culture (a common language, history, segmentary lineage system, and Islam), there were neither centralized social nor political institutions. The system of self-government was characterized by a marked degree of decentralization; it was direct democracy in which typically all the male adults—or their ad hoc representatives—participated in decision-making with no mediating organs. The harsh environment set limits to the carrying capacity of the land and militated against the establishment of large permanent settlements, except in the coastal areas. Seasonal transhumance enabled the pastoralists to master the environment and their decentralized system of self-government facilitated the structuring of their individual and group activities.

The accordionlike segmentary lineage system was the vehicle for mobilization purposes and determining the level at which decisions were to be made. The self-governing arrangements of the lineage system were augmented by a system of political contracts, which guided policy-making and conflict resolution. Power was exercised in a moral framework, and the structures of pastoral democracy were valued for their efficacy and legitimation.

The colonial interlude had multiple effects on the traditional self-governing system. First and foremost, whatever possibilities the system had to evolve were arrested, and an authoritarian system of government was introduced in which power was exercised in a moral vacuum, at least in the eyes of the colonized. Elaborate administrative structures were imposed on the body politic without regard to appropriateness or efficiency. The colonial interlude, on the other hand, helped in nationalizing the traditional political culture. Increased urbanization, access to modern education, and the aftereffects of the Second World War enhanced the centripetal forces affecting the social structure. The exercise of freedom for the Somali nation was twice-hobbled by the colonial negation of self-governing rights and responsibilities and the division of the land into five distinct colonial parts. In the main, the quest for self-rule was to be forged separately except during the British military administration, which controlled four of the five territories. It was during this period that the first modern political organization, the Somali Youth league (SYL) was formed. Its aims and organization were pan-Somali, but it was soon frustrated by the dismantling of the British military administration and the reverting of the territories to their erstwhile rulers.

The SYL led the independence movement in the Italian-administered trusteeship. Its constituency was territorywide, and it was the dominant force in the creation of the nationalist agenda. It easily won the first municipal election of 1954 and repeated its success in another municipal and, prior to independence, the two general elections for the national assembly. (HDM, Benadir Youth and other transitory parties were much wedded to clan-based politics and were therefore parochial in character.) The SYL itself was not divorced from the convoluted clan politics either in the "balancing act" that was to be performed or in the decentralized nature of its decision-making processes. With respect to the British-administered territory, party representation was not allowed until shortly prior to independence. When it was allowed, the Somali National League (SNL), though lacking a territorywide following, emerged as the dominant party in the February 1960 elections. It joined forces with the United Somali Party (USP), which complemented its power base. Independence movement politics in British Somaliland was even more prone to clan politics and manifested extreme pastoral-democracy attributes.

Immediately after independence and union, a coalition government was formed by the SYL and the SNL-USP. This coalition formally commanded 115 seats in a parliament of 123 seats, but that did not insure automatic support for the government of the day. Party discipline, even prior to the multiple coalition-building schemes, was problematic. Ideological cleavages were absent and the antiauthoritarian streak that permeated the traditional political system of self-government, was reflected in party politics and in the spirited parliamentary debates. Municipal and parliamentary elections (1959 to 1960, 1964, and 1969), as the instruments of organized political participation, were held with the regularity stipulated by the constitution. Choice, in terms of parties, which mushroomed during the campaign periods, and of candidates was abundant. Democratic practice and spirit were also portrayed in the vigorous and free press (DALKA is a most eloquent testimony to that) and in the lack of human rights violations.

The Somali political system of the 1960s typified democracy in parts. Ironically, it suffered from certain excesses in the exercise and in the inordinate fluidity of organized political behavior. The highly individualistic and decentralized political intercourse was not tempered by the evolution of mediating sociopolitical structures, which were supportive of change and development. Though blessed by a fairly homogeneous traditional political culture, the new state lacked a similarly homogeneous political elite. It possessed a miniscule, but fragmented, intelligentsia and professional class; almost all postsecondary education was obtained overseas in diverse countries. The relatively low level of urbanization and socioeconomic development and the fragmented intelligentisia and professional classes contributed to the absence of mediating structures and viable alternatives to the ponderous and fraction-ridden SYL governments.

Yet the task at hand, in terms of integrating disparate administrative systems bequeathed by the colonial regimes, liberation of the still-colonized Somalilands, and effective management of the desired socioeconomic development was enormous, by any measure. Added to that was the slender resource base of the country.

The apparent delegitimation of the system may, in part, have been attributable to undue excesses in expediency: the violence and chicanery associated with the general elections of 1969, the attempted taming of parliamentary debates, and the naked effort to preempt the presidential election (after the assassination of the president) all smacked of a drift to a tightened single-party system and the curbing of a meaningful exercise of freedom. The resignation of General Abshir, the much respected commander of the police force, was symptomatic of the ominous gathering clouds. Ultimately, however, the delegitimation of the system was grounded in efficacy and efficiency considerations. The perception was that it was unable to deliver the goods: social and economic demands were hardly being met, the securing of the liberation of the still-colonized Somalilands was at an impasse, and the designing and maintaining of an effective and responsive administrative machinery was palpably missing. It was, and still is, a tall order for both Somalia and other African nations.

Part 3

Prospects

15

Richard L. Sklar

Reds and Rights: Zimbabwe's Experiment

In this day and age, Marxism-Leninism is the leading and least parochial theory of social revolution in Africa, Asia, and Latin America. It strongly appeals to intellectuals who believe that capitalist imperialism in "neocolonial" forms perpetuates social injustice on a world scale; and, that a "conscious minority" or vanguard of the downtrodden should establish a "developmental dictatorship" dedicated to the pursuit of economic and social progress.[1] Since the death of Mao Zedong and the subsequent repudiation of his economic theories in China, collectivism is an economic strategy has been reassessed and found wanting in other countries whose leaders are disposed to learn from China.[2] For example, in the People's Republic of the Congo, where collectivist methods, inspired by Marxism-Leninism have been discarded in favor of entrepreneurial methods, the minister of agriculture has said simply, "Marxism without revenue is Marxism without a future."[3]

Opportune shifts from doctrinaire collectivism to pragmatism by the rulers of Marxist-Leninist regimes do not, of course, signify political conversions from dictatorial to democratic beliefs. Yet the ability of a ruling group or political party to change course in response to national needs, despite doctrinal rigidities, should not be underappreciated. At the very least, evidence of ideological flexibility can be used to counteract a Manichaean tendency in American political thought that tends to pit "our" good intentions against "their" evil designs in the minds of prominent national leaders and influential persons. To illustrate such rock-bottom reliance upon negative ideological stereotypes by architects of American foreign policy, this assertion by the National Bipartisan Commission on Central America can be cited:

> Regimes created by the victory of Marxist-Leninist guerrillas become totalitarian. That is their purpose, their nature, their doctrine, and their record.[4]

That language leaves little room for principled political cooperation between the governments of liberal democracies and those of Angola, Mozambique, or Zimbabwe, not to speak of Nicaragua, Vietnam, or China. Apart from the practical political effects of anathematization, this particular analytical effect should also be recognized: it virtually precludes any serious assessment of democratic practices in Marxist-Leninist regimes. The very idea of democratic development under Marxist-Leninist auspices has been excluded from consideration by an ideological edict—hence the value of evidence that appears to disconfirm a notoriously prejudicial opinion.

It is often alleged that in Marxist-Leninist systems the rule of law is illusory, while the rights of citizens are routinely violated for reasons of state. Such fears have surfaced in Zimbabwe with the determination of Prime Minister Robert Mugabe and other national leaders to establish a one-party state based on avowed Marxist-Leninist principles.[5] In August 1984, the ruling party's first congress since Zimbabwe became independent, in 1980, adopted a new, communist type of organization: there is now a politburo; Mr. Mugabe's office of party president has been combined with that of first secretary; and, democratic centralism has been proclaimed as the party's operational code. Furthermore, the congress also resolved to establish a college of Marxism-Leninism.

In Zimbabwe, as elsewhere, Marxist-Leninists believe in the necessity of a vanguard party, one that is dedicated to a theory of society that they believe to be scientifically correct. In power, the vanguard party undertakes to enforce *its* political truth as an official orthodoxy; dissent becomes dangerous and subversive, verging on treason—at the discretion of the authorities. Normally, ideological criteria are applied for appointments to all positions that come under the jurisdiction of government. These include courts, administrative positions, university appointments, and others.

Against that background, I wish to assess the durability of pluralistic defenses for liberty in Zimbabwe—the potential for their survival and growth under the aegis of a regime that is deeply committed to the establishment of a monopolitical order. I shall rely upon evidence produced mainly by Zimbabwe's courts, both because it is strikingly consistent and because the role of courts is often overlooked or underestimated by students of political economy. I shall briefly describe a few selected judgments involving constitutional rights in Zimbabwe and reflect upon their implications for the evolution of government in that country.[6]

Courts and Rights

The first of these judgments, *The State v. Slatter and Others,* was widely noted outside of Zimbabwe.[7] In July 1982, undetected saboteurs destroyed or damaged thirteen Zimbabwean military aircraft, various buildings at the main air base, and other equipment. Despite the fact that no eyewitnesses were produced, eleven air force officers, all whites, were arrested. Six of them, including the chief of staff and chief of operations, were tried and convicted for sabotage-related offenses on the basis of confessions that were subsequently alleged to have been extracted under torture. In July 1983, their convictions were reversed by the high court. The judgment, by then Judge-President Enoch Dumbutshena, is remarkable for its detailed description of the methods of interrogation, including intimidation and torture, employed by the police. Furthermore, he established that the accused were denied access to counsel, beaten, and repeatedly moved at night to forestall discovery of their whereabouts until they had confessed. Dumbutshena's judgment is unequivocal in its condemnation of police conduct that violated both the constitution and the Criminal Procedure and Evidence Act; it was contrary to general principles of police procedure in constitutional democracies, particularly those enunciated by Chief Justice Earl Warren in the famous American case, *Miranda v. Arizona.*[8]

Immediately following their acquittal, the six appellants were rearrested under preventive detention regulations by order of an angered minister of Home Affairs. However, the high court's judgment eventually prevailed: the officers were released at intervals over a five-month period. Moreover, the judgment in *Slatter* powerfully reinforced the effect of several previous decisions in which constitutional rights had been vindicated in the face of administrative abuse. At issue in those cases were the rights of persons who were subject to preventive detention, meaning imprisonment by executive action without trial and beyond the normal jurisdiction of courts. The constitution of Zimbabwe confers upon detainees rights to appoint and consult with counsel, and to timely, periodic reviews of the detention by an administrative tribunal.[9] Preventative detention in Zimbabwe is authorized by regulations under the Emergency Powers Act, which Parliament has renewed every six months, continuing a practice begun by its Rhodesian predecessor in 1965. This act has been used frequently and routinely by Mugabe's government to circumvent the normal legislative process; hence, regulations have been issued for numerous purposes that bear little relation to emergency matters.

The second judgment to which I shall refer involved regulations under the Emergency Powers Act concerning the forfeiture of enemy property. In this case, *Minister of Home Affairs v. Bickle,* a white citizen of Zimbabwe had divided his property, including a ranch and other business interests, among his three children.[10] He did so while he was in custody on charges of having violated the law by flying a private airplane to and from South Africa; these flights had bypassed the legal ports of exit and entry. On one such flight, he carried a South African intelligence agent into Zimbabwe, although he denied having had knowledge of the fact that the individual was a foreign agent. Fined and released from custody, Bickle fled Zimbabwe for South Africa, fearing rearrest for violation of security laws; the minister of Home Affairs seized his property under the Forfeiture of Enemy Property Regulations. Bickle and his children then sought legal redress on the ground that the regulations, themselves, were contrary to the declaration of rights in Chapter III of the constitution of Zimbabwe, particularly Section 16, which prohibits compulsory acquisition of private property by the state except for specified reasons and in accordance with prescribed procedures and safeguards.

In the Bulawayo high court, Judge Roger Korsah ruled that the regulations were unconstitutional and that the properties taken should be restored to their rightful owners. Fundamental rights, he declared, should be given a "generous interpretation" so that individuals can enjoy them in their "full measure." The constitution, he observed, had been designed for

> a reconciliationist era after a prolonged civil war and with a view to the accession to power of a postrevolutionary government. And that is why private property and due process of law are not only spelt out in minute detail, but are entrenched by s 52. Once tempers had cooled a bit and the reconciliation had progressed for ten years, then the citizens of Zimbabwe can look again to see whether they still need these protections enshrined.[11]

The implications of this judgment are far-reaching. Not only would the constitution prevail over acts of Parliament that are inconsistent with it, but the entrenched clauses of the constitution, including the entire declaration of rights, would also appear to have a special or preferred status. Section 52 provides that for ten years from the date of independence—until 1990—entrenched clauses cannot be amended save by the affirmative votes of *all* members of the House of Assembly. Since freedom of association and the right to form political parties is guaranteed (Section 21) and entrenched, the ruling party—Zimbabwe African National Union (ZANU)—would not be able to create a one-party state before 1990, unless it could control all 100 votes in the House of Assembly. Moreover, the prime minister has often declared that, as a matter of principle, the constitution will be respected by his government.

The high court's judgment in *Bickle* was affirmed by the supreme court on appeal without, however, reaching the question of constitutionality with respect to the regulations on forfeiture of enemy property. The supreme court was satisfied to say that Bickle was not properly identified as an "enemy" according to law, since Zimbabwe was not at war with South Africa; hence, his property should not have been seized in the first place.[12] However, in August 1984, the supreme court met the question of incompatibility between the constitution and a statutory law directly; and, its decision was rendered without equivocation.

In that case, a lawyer took photographs at the scene of an automobile accident and was arrested by security policemen—members of the Central Intelligence Organization—and charged with having deliberately photographed their passing vehicle.[13] In custody, he was beaten by the police and threatened with prosecution under the Official Secrets Act, which could result in a sentence of twenty-five years imprisonment. In response to the aggrieved lawyer's suit, the minister of Home Affairs asserted that members of the intelligence police were rendered immune to prosecution by regulations under the Emergency Powers Act that indemnify the security forces. Since Section 13 of the constitution protects personal liberty, and specifies that "any person who is unlawfully arrested or detained" shall be entitled to compensation from the responsible person or authority, the constitution could not be upheld without declaring the regulations (a statutory instrument) unconstitutional.[14] A unanimous court found for the plaintiff and awarded damages with costs. In addition to its importance as a landmark of constitutional law and liberty in Zimbabwe, this judgment may have a salutory effect in western Zimbabwe (Matabeleland), where security forces have repressed armed dissidents with apparent disregard for the rights of citizens.[15]

Feasible Pluralism

The constitution of Zimbabwe embodies a political compromise, accepted with reluctance by the confident leaders of an irrepressible liberation movement at the Lancaster House (London) conference of 1979.[16] Mugabe and his associates did not, and still do not, like various key provisions, including the reservation of twenty seats in the House of Assembly for whites (who then comprised under 3 percent of the population), the entrenchment of pension rights for senior civil servants, and the entrenched protection against expropriation of land and other forms of private property. Yet there has been strict and principled compliance with the letter of the constitution and few flagrant departures from its spirit—for example, not an inch of land has been acquired in violation of the constitution. In cases decided by the high and supreme courts, which have involved infringements of the constitution by executive authorities, the judges have regularly insisted upon corrective action and, where appropriate, restitution.

Three features of the Zimbabwean judicial process to date are especially noteworthy. First, there is an absence of political criteria in appointments to the "bench," i.e., judges of the high court and the supreme court. Judges are appointed by the president (a titular head of state) upon recommendation of the Judicial Service Commission; however, the chief justice of Zimbabwe is appointed by the president, "acting on the advice of the prime minister,"[17] who must consult with the Judicial Service Commission but is not bound by its advice. It is not to be overlooked that Judge Enoch Dumbutshena was elevated to the supreme court and appointed chief justice shortly after his forthright and highly controversial judgment in the airmen case. Second, there is no political calculation in assigning judges to cases, and this appears to be a matter of pride for those engaged in the administration of justice. Last, despite occasional outbursts of bad temper,[18] the Government has usually evinced respect for judicial decisions. In January 1984, a staunch advocate of judicial independence, former minister of justice and professor of law, Dr. Simbi Mubako, was appointed minister of Home Affairs. In August, he made this characteristic statement in an address to officers at the Army Staff College:

> A judge must be loyal to the state yet be impartial even in a case involving the state. This means even in a highly sensitive political case he may have to pronounce judgment against the state if the facts and the evidence lead inevitably to that conclusion. In the last two years, we saw several examples of such cases which could be interpreted as a sign of impartiality and independence of the judiciary or as a sign of disloyalty and sabotage of the state. It should be remembered that the independence of the judiciary is entrenched in the constitution and we want it so; we pay our judges to be independent and they are.[19]

Not only the courts, but administrative tribunals too have been protected against overbearing political pressure. The most important example is the Detainee Review Tribunal for cases of preventative detention, prescribed by the constitution and established under Emergency Powers Regulations.[20] I have been informed by knowledgable persons that appointments to this tribunal have been made without regard to political criteria. Indeed the tribunal was, at first, chaired by the strictly nonpolitical national ombudsman, who is also a judge of the high court. Only a person who is qualified for appointment as a high court judge can serve as chair of this tribunal. According to the constitution, the case of every detainee must be reviewed at least once every six months. Although the proceedings and evidence are confidential, I was told by competent persons during July and August 1984, that the government had thus far complied with all recommendations of the tribunal. Why then, I asked, had Bishop Abel Muzorewa, a former prime minister, currently a member of Parliament and leader of an opposition political party, not been released? The only answers I could elicit were speculative, since the accusations against Bishop Muzorewa were secret. He had been arrested on November 1, 1983, on vague charges involving alleged collusion with South African elements.[21] Eventually, in September 1984, he was released, presumably on the recommendation of this tribunal.

In constitutional democracies, political pluralism is manifest in various forms. Of prime importance is the right of citizens to organize political associations or parties, and to compete for control of the government. No less significance should be attached to the autonomy of courts and those administrative tribunals, which act to restrain the exercise of political power and administrative authority. Pluralism within the structures of government itself exemplifies the idea of divided power, a concept that lies at the heart of the theory of constitutional government.[22] The true test of constitutional government will always reveal the presence or, as negative evidence, the absence, of built-in mechanisms for governmental self-control.

Strictly speaking, there is no theory of constitutional government in Marxism-Leninism, which is not to say that Marxism-Leninism and constitutional government are necessarily incompatible. Indeed, the Eurocommunist movement of Italy, Spain and (belatedly) France, seeks to reconcile Marxism-Leninism with democratic pluralism. However, the rationale for constitutional government, based upon the precept of divided power as an end in itself, does not emerge from Marxist-Leninist teachings. A theory and practice of divided, as opposed to consolidated power, embracing judicial independence and judicial review, would enrich and alter the practice of "scientific socialism" as we know it today. In the universe of Marxist-Leninist states, a practice of government based on the idea of divided power would be new and different. While it was envisioned by Czechoslovakian communists under Alexander Dubcek in 1968, as it is in Eurocommunist thought today, it has yet to be experienced in the communist state sector. A fusion of constitutionally limited government with Marxism-Leninism is not logically impossible; but its accomplishment would be both unprecedented and a distinctive contribution to Marxist-Leninist practice.

In the event of a one-party state in Zimbabwe, other forms of pluralism would assume degrees of political importance reminiscent of intellectual, religious, and trade union opposition to white supremacy in Rhodesia. Religious pluralism is deeply rooted; the contributions of church-based groups to democratic causes in Zimbabwe have been substantial—witness the watchdog reports of The Catholic Commission for Justice and Peace in Zimbabwe, which have monitored and criticized the government's exceedingly repressive and often brutal campaign against armed dissidents in Matabeleland.[23] One of the Commission's "main aims" is stated thus: "to get information on actual acts of injustice and violations of human rights in order to help the victims in any way we can."[24]

Similarly, artists and writers in Zimbabwe are prone to resist intrusions upon their creative activities. Thus, the Zimbabwe Writers' Union has protested the prohibition of both publication and performance of a play with political overtones by the minister of Home Affairs under Emergency Powers Regulations.[25] Concerning freedom of the press, an independent Catholic monthly journal of public affairs, *Moto,* and an emphatically liberal weekly newspaper, *The Financial Gazette,* are widely read by the intelligentsia. Two government-owned newspapers, the daily *Herald* and *Sunday Mail,* frequently public liberal and democratic socialist viewpoints, especially letters to the editor, that criticize ZANU party policies. When *The Herald* published the prime minister's extended defense of the one-party, Marxist-Leninist state, it featured a cogent rebuttal in the form of a letter to the editor on the same page.[26] Furthermore, the national university is robustly pluralistic and will probably so remain regardless of the form of government that emerges when all portions of the constitution of Zimbabwe become amendable by normal procedures.

In the sphere of economic activities, pluralism is grounded in the existence of a prosperous business and commercial farming sector that supplies the revenue required to finance social services on a grand scale, e.g., free primary education, subsidized secondary education, and free health care for those who earn less than Z$150 (US$130) per month—more than 75 percent of the population.[27] A firm partnership unites Zimbabwe's avowedly revolutionary government with its capitalist elite, now valued by the government as an asset of incomparable worth for the pursuit of policies to cope with the exigent problems of poverty, unemployment, and exponential population growth—approximately 4 percent per year. (The estimated 1984 population is 8 million.) Long-term and stable partnerships between communist rulers and the capitalist elements of their countries are no longer exceptional. It only remains to be seen whether Zimbabwe will devise and perfect safeguards for the autonomy and genuine representation of small, as well as large farmers and businessmen. An even greater challenge to pluralists of Marxist-Leninist persuasion will be posed by the demand for trade union autonomy, a fugitive idea in the world of communist governments that could be rehabilitated by Zimbabwean communists.

The government of Zimbabwe has proclaimed its dedication to the goal of "a truly socialist, egalitarian, and democratic society in conditions of sustained growth and equity."[28] That aim implies a commitment to democratic pluralism; but, there are no examples of democratic pluralism in political systems constructed along Marxist-Leninist lines. At this stage, it would be premature to say that the die is cast for communism in Zimbabwe. Some, such as Lord Soames, the British governor during Zimbabwe's transition to independence (1979–1980), say that Mugabe's ideological "rhetoric" is only intended to placate impatient revolutionaries in his party.[29] However, that interpretation may underestimate the fervor of Mugabe's personal belief in Marxism-Leninism and the one-party state. Might it not be more realistic to ponder the possibility that his, and the party's, avowed political objectives will, in due course, be attained without expunging the idea of divided power from Zimbabwe's constitution and without detriment to the degree of economic and social pluralism that now obtains? Zimbabwe, then, would still be more liberal and pluralistic than either Tanzania or Zambia, both nondoctrinaire, one-party states of socialist orientation.[30] It would surely be more liberal and pluralistic than Malawi and no less so than Kenya, both one-party states of capitalist orientation. More than any other country in Africa, Zimbabwe would be a meeting ground for communist and liberal ideas in practice; its philosophy and form of government would institutionalize the debate between those rival ideologies and clarify, if not supercede, standard issues and arguments.

For some devout anticommunists, it is an article of faith that Marxism-Leninism cannot be reconciled with constitutionally limited government and individual liberty. At the opposite extreme, Marxism-Leninism is espoused by the faithful as an infallible guide to knowledge about the interests of working people. From that belief it is a small step to the conviction that governments controlled by Marxist-Leninists should be able to exercise power without let or hindrance by constitutional impediments. More pragmatic thinkers do not consign these matters to the realm of faith. Those who would rather learn from experience may now wonder: Will a Marxist-Leninist regime in Zimbabwe reaffirm the practice of judicial review, the independence of administrative tribunals, freedom of the press, the value of a pluralistic university with an open door to ideas, and freedom of action for the various interest groups that impart vitality to social and economic life? Experience may yet again confound the True Believers.

Notes

The author wishes to thank Leslie Rubin for his encouragement and critique.

1. A. James Gregor, *Italian Fascism and Developmental Dictatorship* (Princeton, N.J.: Princeton University Press, 1979).

2. Orville Schell, "A Reporter at Large: The Wind of Wanting to Go It Alone," *The New Yorker,* 23 January 1984, 43–85.

3. Justine De Lacy, "The Congo: Western Investors Now Welcome," *The Atlantic,* January 1984, 28.

4. *Report of the National Bipartisan Commission on Central America,* January 1984, 88.

5. Robert Mugabe, "The Construction of Scientific Socialism in Zimbabwe," *The Herald* (Harare), 10 July 1984.

6. I am indebted to Dr. John Hatchard of the University of Zimbabwe School of Law, who made copies of judgments involving constitutional rights and detentions under the Emergency Powers Act available to me together with his guidance. His professional study of those judgments, rendered by the Zimbabwe high and supreme courts, is in progress.

7. HC-H-313-83 (mimeographed).

8. 384 U.S. 436: 1966.

9. Constitution of Zimbabwe, Schedule 2, Section 2.

10. Bickle and Others v. Minister of Home Affairs, High Court of Zimbabwe, Bulawayo, 1983 (mimeographed); Minister of Home Affairs v. Bickle and Others, Zimbabwe Supreme Court 1984 (2) 439.

11. Author's notes on Bickle and Others v. Minister of Home Affairs, 18 (mimeographed).

12. ZSC 1984 (2): 450–51.

13. Granger v. the Minister of State, Judgment No. S.C. 83/84, Application No. 25/84 (mimeographed).

14. Constitution of Zimbabwe, Section 13 (5).

15. *Africa Confidential* 25 (8), 11 April 1984; *Manchester Guardian Weekly,* 20 May 1984, 8–9.

16. Colin Legum, "Southern Africa: The Road to and from Lancaster House," *Africa Contemporary Record* 12, 1979–80 (New York: Africana Publishing Company, 1981) A10–12.

17. Constitution of Zimbabwe, Section 84 (1).

18. *Africa Contemporary Record* 15, 1982–83, B898; Ronald Weitzer, "Continuities in the Politics of State Security in Zimbabwe," in Michael G. Schatzberg, ed., *The Political Economy of Zimbabwe* (New York: Praeger, 1984), 97–99.

19. Press Statement, Department of Information, 20 August 1984.

20. Schedule 2 (2).

21. *Africa Research Bulletin* (Political, Social and Cultural Series) 20 (11), 15 December 1983, 7055–56.

22. Carl J. Friedrich, *Limited Government: A Comparison* (Englewood Cliffs, N.J.: Prentice-Hall, 1974).

23. Jonathan Steele, "Atrocities in Zimbabwe: Sifting Fact from Rumour," *Manchester Guardian Weekly,* 20 May 1984, 8–9.

24. *The Catholic Commission for Justice and Peace in Zimbabwe,* no. 1, July 1983.

25. *The Sunday Mail* (Harare), 19 August 1984.

26. *The Herald* (Harare), 10 July 1984.

27. *The Economist* (London), 21 April 1984, 9.

28. Government of the Republic of Zimbabwe, *Growth with Equity: An Economic Policy Statement,* February 1981, 19.

29. *The Wall Street Journal,* 30 November 1984.

30. *See* Cranford Pratt, "Tanzania's Transition to Socialism: Reflections of a Democratic Socialist," in Bismarck U. Mwansasu and Cranford Pratt, eds., *Towards Socialism in Tanzania* (Toronto: University of Toronto Press, 1979), 193–236; and William Tordoff, ed., *Administration in Zambia* (Manchester: Manchester University Press, 1980).

W. A. E. Skurnik

16

Press Freedom in Africa: From Pessimism to Optimism

A government-controlled press is by its very nature a mouthpiece of those in power.

Hilary Ng'weno

The issues of freedom of expression and of press freedom have been part of a global debate for over a decade. They have been treated largely through the narrow lens of specific relations between national governments, on one hand, and news media, on the other. Many Third World governments, of which the single largest bloc is African, favor a new world order for information and communication; they have tried to use one international organization—the United Nations Educational, Scientific, and Cultural Organization (UNESCO)—to help legitimate control over news media by national governments, and thus to secure the imprimatur of the highly regarded United Nations system in the process.

This discussion uses a wider lens to raise some questions about past and present perspectives on press freedom. "Present Pessimism" reviews the findings of a number of well-known observers of the news media in sub-Saharan Africa, and two annual studies directing their attention to the larger topic of general freedom, but also paying some attention to freedom to the press. "Future Optimism" presents the views of an African historian, two novelists and one playwright as they raise questions pertinent to this inquiry. "The Credibility Gap" reviews a number of factors originating in African societies, which tend to produce serious, long range problems for governmental press control. Finally, the conclusion suggests that there are solid reasons to be optimistic about the future of press freedom in Africa. No doubt other perspectives—or academic disciplines—could yield fruitful and penetrating information in an overall effort to understand the role played by the news media in Africa. Research on the subject of press freedom in Africa, however, must be considered only in its "infancy," and the purpose of this effort is to make use of what is available in three areas—journalism, history, and literature. The emphasis here is on a comparison of what people say, what Africans complain about, and the credibility gap alienating people from government as a result of policies restricting press freedom.

The question of freedom of the press in Africa today appears in a state of suspended animation, as a result of the preferences and policies of incumbent political elites. Those who speak for governments on that issue are fond of deflecting criticism by invoking a barrel of intractable problems, and suggesting that the barrel would explode were the people whom they are presumed to serve to take such liberties as expressing their views or, even worse, the news media to find fault with government policy and disseminate blemishes to the people at large.

There is no question that African political leaders have to wrestle with myriad problems that frequently seem to be intractable. The governments' position against press freedom, however, is not nearly so convincing as their proponents would like. Their case rests largely on the belief that the new nations are as yet too fragile to withstand the presumed "assault" of news media—to the extent that media views differ from those of governments. The argument is curious. Freedom of speech, and press freedom (the latter a subset of the former) were justified during the colonial period on the grounds that they had to be used to further the legitimate goals of weakening and eventually overthrowing rule by aliens pursuing their own interests. Following political independence, it was assumed that incumbent governments, now no longer alien, would pursue the interests of Africa and of their national wards. Such an assumption would be valid only if there were only one universally recognized definition of the African national interests, and if the groups of political leaders who happened to control the levers of political power at any given time were the only national or subnational structure capable of identifying that interest. Empirical evidence suggests nothing of the kind. There is no necessary national agreement about what constitutes the national interest, and the pluralism that characterizes Africa is such that no single group can be regarded as having been blessed exclusively with the ability to identify it.

Most African governments fear the news media for essentially three reasons. First, the media might exacerbate existing sociopolitical tensions to the point where governments can no longer govern. The second reason is that the news media might reveal cases of malfeasance in office and thus lead to the removal of a leader or a government. The third is simply that they want to maintain themselves and their friends in power. None of these reasons is compelling as an argument against freedom of the press. Regarding the first, it would seem at first that withholding or disseminating news about existing tensions could place great stress on the "fragile" national political structures and their ability to extract help from and to remain on top of their nations. No doubt one could develop a flawless Cartesian construct to demonstrate the validity of that argument. Yet it remains too simplistic. It assumes that news media have the power to arouse national populations to overthrow governments; or that tensions are so strong, turbulent, and unpredictable that a newspaper article could, by itself, unwittingly or purposefully, cause the government to tumble. In reality, there is no solid evidence that newspapers alone have such power. The political tensions inhabiting Africa are not caused by newspapers, nor are they cured by them. Political dynamics in Africa respond to various forces, and these include the potent desire for more, not for less, freedom (twenty percent of the people of Guinea under former President Sékou Touré did not flee their country because it offered a climate of freedom).

The second reason for which incumbent elites fear the newspapers, *viz.,* that they reveal illegal or unethical conduct, should not really be dignified by taking it seriously as a legitimate justification for trampling freedom of the press underfoot. As for the third reason, it is not confined to Africa; it is a universal phenomenon characterizing elites in power, and should not stand as a reason for limiting the freedom of the people in whom ultimate sovereignty is believed to reside.

Present Pessimism

Media Observers

Western sources tend to convey pessimism concerning freedom of the press in Africa. One well known and astute observer of Africa, Colin Legum, stated simply and starkly that, in Africa, "the press is mostly an instrument of power, controlled and directed by the ruling groups." "Since independence," he added, "papers supporting the opposition . . . have been progressively taken over" by ruling governments. This does not augur well for press freedom, a concept which is "relevant only as an ideal" in the new Africa states.[1] One of the few American students of journalism with an interest in Africa, William A. Hachten, has made remarkably similar observations. He suggested that the control patterns established by African leaders after independence "will affect the African news media for many decades to come." One of the consequences is that there were, in 1970, "fewer independent or nongovernmental papers in Africa than at the time of independence." Another consequence is that postindependence newspapers "tell the government's story. . . . " A third consequence is that, unfortunately, ". . . each African government has become the gatekeeper and potential censor controlling the flow of news in and out of the territory."[2]

Finally, Hachten concluded that if press freedom is defined as "the right to fully report and criticize the conduct of government without fear of official recriminations, then there is precious little of that kind of freedom anywhere in Africa."[3] One might wonder if "that kind of freedom" is very much in evidence anywhere, and if the definition is not in fact a "straw man." More recently, Dennis Wilcox reviewed a variety of press controls in Africa and concluded that "it is doubtful that the present profile of press ownership and restraints in . . . Africa will change in the near future."[4]

Other Studies

To supplement the testimony of observers with many years of close experience, there are also efforts to present data in some systematic form. One widely available index of press freedom in Africa is contained in the annual report submitted by the Department of State to the U.S. Congress, entitled "Country Reports on Human Rights Practices." The latest available report was published in 1984 and covers activities in the preceding calendar year.[5] A reading of these reports shows a number of general indices about press freedom, which can be aggregated for a brief overview. Data can be extracted that fall into four categories, each bearing directly on the subject of press freedom. The first category concerns newspaper ownership and control. Among the states of independent black Africa (excluding South Africa and Namibia), there were thirty-eight instances where the government owned (or had a controlling interest in) print media, sixteen instances where there existed one or more privately owned newspaper, and six instances where a daily or weekly or biweekly newspaper was owned and operated by a Christian church organization. Moreover, in one instance the national political party owned a newspaper (the distinction between party and government ownership was not always addressed in the reports), and in another instance there was a clandestine newspaper operating sporadically.

A second category addressed the degree to which newspapers were allowed to criticize their governments. Two subcategories are used here to distinguish between (a) newspapers which were allowed to publish some criticism, mostly about the implementation of policy or about corruption at low- and middle-level government agencies, and (b) those which were not allowed to print any criticism of their government. The count by country included twenty-one instances where states allowed at least some criticism, and sixteen where criticism of the government was apparently not permitted.

A third question concerned the relative ease with which foreign print-news media were permitted to circulate within African states. The State Department report shows that foreign newspapers or news magazines were allowed to circulate freely in twenty-three countries, and were not normally permitted to circulate in five states (in two of these, only Marxist information was allowed).

Was there, finally, an apparent relationship between media ownership (governmental or private) and indices of press freedom? The data suggest a strong positive relationship in most cases. Privately owned papers were associated positively with thirteen cases when some criticism of government was usually allowed—in no case was criticism normally not allowed—and with fourteen cases where foreign news media circulated freely (in no case did such materials not circulate freely). Government-owned newspapers, however, displayed a pattern not nearly so bleak as might be expected. They were associated positively with twenty instances where criticism of the government was usually not permitted, but also with fourteen instances where such criticism was normally allowed. Moreover, government-owned papers were associated positively with nineteen instances where foreign news media circulated freely and only thirteen where this was not the case. It seems clear that these data underline the great diversity of the relative existence or absence of press freedom in sub-Saharan Africa.

It should be noted that these data must be used with some caution because of their lack of clarity and inconsistent use. The term "media" was frequently ill-defined, and many reports made no reference to ownership of print media. Some reports looked like careful studies, whereas others were superficial. Nonetheless, the countries reviewed included a number with considerable press freedom (e.g., Nigeria and Senegal) as well as some which allowed criticism under no circumstances. (In one case, the government prohibited private ownership of television receivers to prevent its citizens from watching news from a neighboring country.) One country was reported to have no national newspaper or newssheet.

Another source containing some information about freedom of the press in Africa is an annual volume, edited by Raymond Gastil, about global political and civil rights.[6] Extracting the states of independent sub-Saharan Africa from a table about "news media control" yields the following aggregate data. Of the forty-four states included, only three were classified as "generally free," twelve as "partly free," and twenty-nine as "generally not free." This review conveys a somewhat more somber impression than that of the State Department document. The Gastil book also enables us to make a quick general comparison between sub-Saharan independent Africa and the entire world. In this comparison, Africa looked much "less free". Its percentage of "generally free" states was 6.8 as opposed to 34 percent for the world; that for the "partly free" category was 27.3, compared with 25 percent for the world; and that for countries regarded as "generally not free" was 65.9 compared with 41 percent for the world.

Future Optimism

Reaching beyond the literature of journalism and political science clearly discloses that Africans have raised serious questions about freedom of expression, have articulated strong views about it, and echo comments made by working African journalists (as distinct from those who have elected to work directly for governments).

History

A glimpse of the work of an African historian and the feelings expressed by two novelists and one playwright conveys the flavor of their concerns. It is appropriate to remember in this context that the average African does have some notion of freedom, whether based on tradition, modern imports, or on a mixture of the two. Anyone having visited Guinea during President Sékou Touré's authoritarian regime can easily testify to the inexorable descent toward palpable and omnipresent fear, which scarred the country's postindependence period. It is perhaps fitting that a Guinean historian should speak out against tyranny and its consequences for peoples' freedom. Lansiné Kaba suggested that African governments need not discourage artistic creativity or individual freedom, and that such governments may subsidize freedoms without the hand of censorship.[7] Musicians and writers, he points out, at first thrived because of an "atmosphere of openness, trust, and dialog." Touré's regime was initially supported by such distinguished writers as Laye Camara and Fodéba Keita. But after about ten years, they and many others fell into official disfavor because "the Guinean regime turned into an autocratic system with a democratic facade, with Touré as the only spokesman." The country became "a one-man show, in which Touré served as the only director and actor, while others must dance, applaud, or sing for him, according to his whim." "The Guinean universe," Kaba added, "had become one in which freedom of expression and individuality had completely disappeared."[8] The significance of this finding is that freedom of expression was viewed not merely as desirable but also as antedating Sékou Touré.

Kaba went on to say that "rigid control over creativity" was undesirable, unnecessary, and opposed to the very notion of freedom in whose name the "revolution" had presumably been brought about; hence, he joins the theme stated by other Africans that leaders have betrayed the ideals which brought them to office, ideals which included freedom and expression and respect for the individual. "Guinea," he said, was a "classic example of what paranoia and autocracy can inflict upon a society and individual freedom." The effect of Touré's rule was, he added with some understatement,

> a deep sense of insecurity among those who are still living, and has taught them to be prudent. Instead of freedom of expression, in this context, one should rather speak of how to survive, and hence to conform to a dogmatic and coercive style.[9]

Literature

One of the clearest and most vivid African criticisms of African politicians after independence is Chinua Achebe's *A Man of the People: A Novel of Political Unrest in a New Nation*.[10] The novel stands out for a number of reasons. The least significant of these may well be that he anticipated a military takeover in his country, Nigeria, which took place during the month when the book was published. His political sensitivity was, to that extent, greater than that of the nation's government. The second reason for which it stands out is that it is addressed to an African, rather than an European, audience, i.e., the country's intellectuals, many of whom shared his views. The third is that it addresses directly not only some of the nature and dynamics of the political system, but also questions of freedom of expression and press freedom. Finally, as K. J. W. Post writes in his introduction, Achebe "remains supremely conscious of the fact that politics is about people."[11]

The political system is fairly representative of that of many African and Third World states. There is a strong undercurrent of frustration resulting from the disparity between preindependence promises and postindependence behavior of indigenous political leaders. These leaders are viewed with ambivalence. On one hand, they are tolerated to the degree that they redistribute material and moral rewards to their constituencies, through a system that Westerners would call corruption. On the other hand, the politicians are also "the villains of the piece" because they fill their bellies and bank accounts but, more important from the standpoint of the "system," they have betrayed the very ideals upon which they climbed to power, i.e., free and clean elections, respect for opponents, and peaceful change.[12] The scenario has been described in more formal terms by Aristide Zolberg.[13] Achebe tells that, for a variety of reasons, incumbent leaders are driven to hold on to their jobs almost at any cost; they begin with tampering with elections, preventing opponents from legally standing for office, and end up using government violence. "The thugs take control . . . as a kind of ever-present menace lurking just in the background."[14] Moreover, the thugs "get totally out of control and go on the rampage throughout the country," putting into practice against their mentors what they had been told to do to protect them.[15]

The notion of freedom and democracy that subsumes this novel may or may not be related to African precolonial traditions. But if we recognize that traditions do change and, more significantly, that modernization takes place and that this includes democratic values generally held to be universally desirable, then the Achebes are speaking for an important element of the people of the Third World. In the process, Achebe gives us one of the most searing and poignant indictments of the behavior of postindependence African rulers with regard to the notion of freedom of expression:

A handful—the smart and the lucky and hardly ever the best—had scrambled for the one shelter our former rulers left, and had taken it over and barricaded themselves in. And from within they sought to persuade the rest through numerous loudspeakers that independence required that all argument should cease and the whole people speak with one voice and that any more dissent and argument outside the door of the shelter would subvert and bring down the whole house.[16]

Critics may readily observe that flaws in this system must be placed at the door of the colonial power; the shelter is the constitution, the government, the political party, in other words, the new national political structure. Leaving aside the question of whether it should be automatically considered a "shelter," a prior question remains: Who forced African politicians to take and maintain these structures if they did not believe that they were appropriate? Regardless of the answer to this question, the fact remains that the people may have little choice but to continue to endure and to hope in the short run. As Achebe put it:

"Let them eat," was the people's opinion, "after all, when white men used to do all the eating did we commit suicide? Of course not. And where is the all-powerful white man today? He came, he ate, and he went. But we are still around." The important thing is to stay alive; if you do you will outlive your present annoyance.[17]

The verdict of African intellectuals about the old guard which led their country into independence and then stayed, holding on to power while bringing ruin to the new nation in the process, can also combine cynicism with a trace of pessimism, as in Armah.[18] Shortly before the overthrow of President Kwame Nkrumah, he portrayed Ghana as offering two choices: either join the corrupt government and benefit illegally and unethically from its largesse, or opt out and join the vast majority of the people who had been condemned to something less than somnambulism. As the hero of this novel put it, "All I remember clearly these days is that I have been walking along paths chosen for me before I had really decided, and it makes me feel the way I think impotent men feel."[19] The pathos of utter helplessness of independent Africa ruled by Africans is expressed also by another character, a teacher who is a friend of the hero:

I don't feel any hope in me any more. I can see things, but I don't feel much. When you can see the end of things even in their beginnings there is no more hope, unless you want to pretend or forget, or get drunk or something. No. I also am one of the dead people, the walking dead. A ghost. I died long ago. So long ago that not even the old libations of living blood will make me alive again.[20]

The betrayal of the people by their leaders is illustrated in a brief conversation between the hero and a party hack who had achieved high office. The functionary's wife leads into the subject as she says "it is this foolish socialism that will spoil everybody's peace." To which her husband replies that "It is a nuisance.... It is not possible here." "The old man himself [Nkrumah]," he adds, "does not believe in it."[21] Armah amplified the pervasiveness of this sort of betrayal by dismissing any hope that the military could bring about meaningful change. The brief conversation about military takeover in Ghana is worth remembering: "'So, you haven't heard.' 'On the morning shift we can't hear the news,' the man said. 'No 6 o'clock news this morning. Only some strange announcement by a man with a strange name.... They say they have seized power.' 'Who?' the man asked. 'Army and policemen.' 'Oh, I see. I thought they had always had power. Together with Nkrumah and his fat men.'"[22]

A third example of widespread dissatisfaction with African rulers who have betrayed their trust, suggesting an optimistic outcome, is a play by R. Philombe, *Africapolis*.[23] University students and their friends read it avidly in the late 1970s, and it was accordingly banned in several African states; the French government apparently cooperated with some of the African censors, and this made it all the more popular. The story is simple and direct: it pits a young, idealistic hero against an older, corrupt national king surrounded by syncophants. The usual arguments favoring a strong central government appear in the play, for the purpose of discrediting them. When the king learns of the formation of an opposition party based on strong popular support, he exclaims that "an opposition party in my kingdom . . . is inadmissible. To let it work freely is to sign my own suicide."[24] The author also suggests that postindependence African rulers have strayed from African tradition in their effort to sustain themselves in office and to deal with those who disagree with them. When the hero is brought to trial on false charges, because the king—quite rightly—sees him as a political danger, the attorney for the defense tells the court that the people, and not just the officers of the law, are involved in the process: "On the occasion of a palaver, the accused may address not only the judges, but also the public. The goal of this practice is to allow the people to bear witness, [the people] being the supreme judge of any human society. It is regrettable that our judicial system has not thought it necessary to adopt this valuable tradition."[25] When the hero of the play finally rises to defend himself, he articulates another strong indictment of postindependence African rulers:

> When the whites were in command in this country, all of us sighed: "Ah, if only we were independent." But we have been independent now for nearly nine years. And what do we see? We are looking at the macabre spectacle of a minority which is rich and armed to the teeth, which exercises

without pity its neocolonialist and even fascist dictatorship, over a majority without defense [and] which stinks of misery. . . . [26]

There is a final comment of special interest in the topic of foreign news coverage. "A foreign journalist was right," pleads the hero's defense attorney, "when he described as 'carnage' the series of legal executions which one witnesses in our country. . . ."[27]

The Credibility Gap

The public debates, associated with UNESCO, which have monopolized the world's attention since the early 1970s, have focused mostly on the consequences of government censorship of the news media. Relatively little has been said about the consequences to, or about the views and preferences of, the papers' audiences. Scratching beneath the thin layer of African politics shows that the behavior of African governments in looking over the shoulder of news media has created a very serious credibility gap. Let us recall the words of an African journalist, pronounced some ten years ago at a conference about press freedom in the world. Lateef Jakande of Nigeria said that, whereas "there are adequate guarantees of press freedoms in the constitutions of African countries [he probably meant most African countries]" attempts to control "or smother" journalists occur anyway; that "there is no press freedom" in one-party states such as Uganda; that the press "is allowed to nibble" at minor officials but "may not criticize the government or the president"; that in single-party states with private media ownership "there is a measure of press freedom but only up to a point"; and that even in multiparty countries where there is a "semblance of parliamentary democracy," press freedom only has "a chance—but this chance is under threat."[28]

One of the many puzzling questions about African newspapers is that they pay so much attention to foreign news. One obvious answer is that they want to get to know the rest of the world; yet they concentrate mostly on Africa and thus leave the remainder of the Third World in relative darkness.[29] It may be that foreign news coverage is also a function of socialization: it is covered because everyone is doing it. The U.S. print media, in a rare moment of reflection about the reasons for doing what they do, agreed that they should emphasize the context and explanation of meaning of events, rather than remain in the rut of printing spot news with splashy headlines, which most readers cannot integrate into a reasonably accurate cognitive structure. The American print media have made some—but only some—progress in that direction. Perhaps the Africans could give some serious thought to implementing routinely what others have agreed are more useful than the fruits of habit.

African incumbent elites cannot resist the temptations to inject "national interest" criteria into the selection of foreign news published in their national print media. Yet there can be little question that these news media suffer from a serious credibility gap in the eyes of journalists and audiences alike. This gap surfaces readily in informal conversations with readers, reporters, and government officials. Today it is fashionable to shift Africa's woes onto the shoulders of former colonial powers and their international surrogates (chiefly the United States). But something is clearly wrong at home, when average readers, as well as university students, would rather believe what they hear from Radio South Africa than from their national station.[30] In the context of holding extra-African forces and factors accountable for many of Africa's problems, it is of some import that this credibility gap must be ascribed to domestic, rather than foreign causes. These include: the existence of domestic communications channels antedating the introduction of print media; significant tensions between the professional objectives and values of journalists and government officials; the low social status given journalists by their governments; and the ready availability, in most African states, of foreign print matter and access to foreign radio stations.

Traditional Communications Channels

It is often overlooked that news about domestic and foreign events in Africa is disseminated through a variety of foreign as well as domestic traditional sources. If the president of a republic sends some of his children to school in the United States and spends some $2 million for one year's worth of education, or if there is a serious uprising several hundred miles away from the capital city, the ordinary African need not read his national newspaper or listen to his national radio station to learn about it. Chances are that the information is carried by shortwave stations and published in foreign newspapers or magazines entering the country. Also, this news is disseminated effectively and swiftly by a variety of traditional oral methods, including reports from travelers, traditional drums, or *radio trottoir* in urban centers. The average citizen in Africa is already well equipped to compare the content of foreign and domestic, traditional news sources with what government doles out or conveniently forgets to mention.

Tensions Between Journalists and Governments

There is a gap between expectations based on the governmental leaders' definition of what is important and what they allow newspapers to report. This is certainly evident in the coverage of foreign news. Official, stated priorities include a deep concern with what may be called "new issues" in international affairs: the North-South debate; decolonization; development; cultural; and economic relations, with an emphasis on trade over aid. One recent study compared the foreign news content of six African newspapers;

it found that national newspapers devoted only one-fourth of its coverage to such new issues, and that the remainder centered on more "traditional" issues of international relations (diplomacy, political/military conflict, foreign unrest and civil war, and the like.)[31] The same study also indicates that comparatively little attention was paid by these papers to economic relations with other countries, which made up only a small proportion of the total of foreign news printed. It may be difficult to quantify the importance of foreign economic relations as part of the national interest; but given the apparent widespread agreement of the importance of foreign trade, investment, and assistance, as well as of economic cooperation among African states, one might also reasonably expect that such topics be reported more fully.

The second factor contributing to the credibility gap, tensions between the values of professional journalists and those of government elites, can be illustrated also by the attitudes of African and French faculty and students at the Graduate International School of Journalism (ESIJY—Ecole supérieure internationale de journalisme) located in Yaoundé, capital of Cameroun. It was founded in 1972 as a regional organization and based on an international treaty between six states: Cameroun, the Central African Republic, Chad, the Congo [whose relationship is not clear], Gabon, and Rwanda. Both the treaty and the curriculum make ample room for emphasizing the connection between journalism and development.[32] The attitudes of faculty and students are a good indication of the degree to which they appear suspicious of their governments' pronouncements at international fora.

Personal interviews conducted in November 1979 show, for instance, that the school paid attention, in a descriptive mode, to the discussions about a new world information order. But that is, explained one African instructor, "something theoretical"; the faculty, including the school's executive director, suggested that talk about the new order is in reality "camouflage" for state control of the news. As professional journalists, they had serious reservations about such a prospect. Without sweeping under the rug the many shortcomings of Western news coverage, they believed also that not much can be gained by pretending that the West can, or should, be blamed for everything that is wrong with journalism in Africa. Both students and faculty were keenly aware of the credibility gap; faculty make special efforts to caution students about the differences between the professional criteria and objectives learned in school and the stark realities of working for an African government. They know from experience that the two are not always compatible, and that this creates occasional but significant problems in international cooperation. Thus, former Emperor Bokassa I withdrew his country's students, because he valued the inculcation of obedience to national government leaders more highly than the standards of a professional school.

Status

A third factor contributing to the credibility gap is the generally low status to which the journalistic profession is consigned. Reporters are poorly paid and held in low esteem by an officialdom who tend to regard them as mere hands whose fingers may—but whose brains should not—write the news. Some reporters complain that too many of their confreres are something less than a modern version of *griots*—less because a *griot* was able to influence his employer. In their view, this represents retrogression rather than progress. The consequences of this kind of credibility gap are serious enough to warrant attention: a combination of "internal emigration" and hope for the future. In the meantime, one also hears of a kind of "brain drain"; increasing numbers of journalists tend to gravitate toward direct government jobs. They can take "refuge" in a ministry of information, as press attachés, or in national news agencies where remuneration and status are more attractive than in the news media. One prominent Englishman generally critical of the West and sympathetic toward the Africans recognizes that "the sadness of the situation of the press . . . lies in the fact that journalists, unable to reach out for their potential, really lead wasted lives."[33]

It would not be far-fetched to suggest that a problem of lack of integration among various elites in Africa is being created today under our very eyes, although very few people are in the habit of articulating it or pointing it out as serious. To the extent that incumbent political leaders tend to view their own journalists as subordinates at best and craven at worst, they are sowing the seeds not merely for present and future discontent, but also for future action against them. Perhaps one simple way to express the problem is the time worn analogy of the genie being out of the bottle. Freedom of expression is, like the freedom to be nationally independent, one which cannot be returned to its former glass prison. I am reminded in this context of a conversation with a young African journalist, during which we explored the question of the state and future growth of press freedom in Africa. Near the end of our conversation, my interlocutor simply smiled and said, "the president of the republic is an old man. I am young, and Africa is very patient." It would be a mixture of folly and dysfunctional myopia for African political leaders, and their articulate but muzzled representatives at international conferences, to ignore the growing chasm between them and other elites on the issue of freedom of expression. Given the nature of journalism and its insistence on digging for the truth, as well as its intimate familiarity with events attributable to party and government elites, the malaise resulting from the climate of enforced silence is bound to grow, and politicians will be able to ignore it in the long run only at their own expense.

Comparing National and Foreign Sources

Another factor contributing to the credibility gap is the continuous comparison between foreign and national news media. What is frequently forgotten at international gatherings of media specialists, or blotted out from public lights, is the relatively free circulation, and hence presumably relative influence, of two kinds of foreign news media: (1) print media with a Third World perspective, and (2) radio broadcasts, which bring to their audiences much more international news than is found in national media. In the absence of studies attempting to discover the influence of such external sources on the credibility of Third World national news media, some empirical evidence nonetheless suggests the existence of a credibility gap for one segment of the national audience: students at institutions of higher learning. These are particularly important inasmuch as they are likely to serve as future government officials and intellectual leaders. This gap came to light during an anonymous survey conducted in the Ivory Coast.[34]

The survey included a section asking students at the University of Abidjan and the Ecole nationale d'administration to rank the reading or listening frequency, and the influence on their views about international affairs, of a number of reading materials: *Fraternité-Matin, Le Monde, Le Monde diplomatique,* and two African-oriented news magazines, *Jeune Afrique* and *Afrique-Asie,* as well as radio broadcasts (Radio-Télévision Ivoire, France-Inter, the BBC, and the VOA). Table 16.1 presents the aggregated rankings of high frequencies and high influence on their views.

The table demonstrates the existence of two rather striking gaps: one between the frequencies and the influence of the national media, and another between the national and foreign media. A large majority ranked reading frequency of the national newspaper and the listening frequency of the national radio station as very high (70.1 percent and 64.2 percent, respectively), but their estimate of the influence of these media on their views was a mere 14.9 percent for the paper and 28.0 percent for the radio station.

Yet another dimension of this gap emerges from a comparison of the relative importance attached by these students to the world's geographic regions with that appearing in *Fraternité-Matin.*

The difference between national and extranational media was equally striking. Whereas *Fraternité* was read with much greater frequency than was any other print medium, it was rated by far as the least influential among these sources. The pattern was similar for radio stations. A much larger proportion of students listened to Radio Ivoire than to any other source with a high degree of frequency, but ratings of influence placed Radio Ivoire last on the list, with about half the proportion of high influence attributed to the foreign stations. Reporting select news events is not, of course, necessarily identical with one's conception of the relative importance of regions. Still, a dramatic difference between students' views and what they see in their na-

TABLE 16.1   Ivoirien Student Evaluation of News Sources:
             Comparison of Reading and Broadcast Materials,
             High Rankings (in percentages)

	Frequency	Importance of Influence
Reading		
Fraternité-Matin	70.1	14.9
Le Monde	29.2	57.9
Le Monde Diplomatique	18.2	49.1
Jeune Afrique	59.2	47.8
Afrique-Asie	33.3	39.9
Listening		
Radio-Télévision Ivoire	64.2	28.0
France-Inter	47.6	56.5
BBC	30.4	54.3
VOA	42.6	54.7

Yet another dimension of this gap emerges from a comparison
of the relative importance attached by these students to the
world's geographic regions with that appearing in
Fraternité-Matin.

tional newspaper would suggest that the paper is out of tune with a significant element of its audience. In the study mentioned above, students were
asked to rank five geographic regions in order of "actual" and "desirable"
importance (Africa, the Americas, Asia, Europe, and the Middle East/North
Africa).[35] Table 16.2 recapitulates the "high" rankings given to the areas and
compares these with the distribution found in *Fraternité*.

Leaving aside the relatively small differences (except for Africa) between the "actual" and "desirable" ranking by the students, their perception
of the relative importance of geographic regions was much more evenly distributed than was the newspaper's coverage. Save for Europe and the Middle
East/North Africa, the difference between the students' estimate of the desirable importance of Africa (14.4 percent) and the importance attached to Africa by the newspaper (nearly 50.0 percent of all foreign news). The Ivoirien
government, through its national newspaper, does not seem to have made
much of an impression on these students. When this is seen in the context of
students—not exactly the role models for archconservatism—attributing
greater influence on their views to *Le Monde* than to the two Third World-
oriented news magazines, the suggestion seems inescapable that government-
controlled newspapers in Africa have cognitive maps of things international,

TABLE 16.2   High Importance of Geographic Regions:
             Actual and Desirable for Students, and
             Published News in Fraternité-Matin (in percentages)

Region	Students, Actual	Students, Desirable	Fraternité
Africa	9.2	14.4	49.1
Americas	27.0	26.2	5.2
Asia	19.2	20.8	1.7
Europe	24.0	19.3	14.5
Middle East/ North Africa	20.3	19.1	19.4

which barely resemble those of at least some important elements of their audience.

Concluding Thoughts

Ideally, many African governments prefer a world in which national sovereignty encompasses the news flow, about domestic as well as foreign events. Yet the doctrine of national sovereignty, like that of equality, is to some extent a polite fiction. The international news environment of most states does not conform to an image of impenetrable borders, not even for states like Guinea under Sékou Touré. News travels fast and relatively freely, particularly since the advent of the transistor, and tends to spread throughout a country even before its political leaders have a chance to react. Since many people, in addition to the official purveyors of news, have access to a flood of information from a variety of sources, they are in a position to compare the domestic with the foreign product. Not every thinking African is, or can be, indoctrinated by postindependence political elites. It is in this sense that total, national control over news lies outside the realm of possibility. Yet it is precisely the continued insistence on total control which, whatever the merits and the soundness of its justification, creates serious problems of disaffection and of credibility among journalists and others alike. As a journalist with long experience in Africa, and former spokesman for UNESCO, expressed it, "It is legitimate to ask if the loudly proclaimed will . . . to decolonize information is not that of controlling it better inside their own countries.[36]

For many journalists, this raises the fundamental issue of their professionalism, to the extent that it clashes with government control over news content. It is by now well known that African journalists are by no means in agreement with their government's thesis that they should be mere militants in the service of some vague national development priorities. Opposition is rooted not so much in a question of principle: they are likely to agree that they have an obligation to contribute to their country's development; let it not be forgotten that journalists, not governments, originated the very notion of development journalism. Their opposition is more practical and is rooted in the governments' takeover and monopoly of the idea of such service. Questions concern behavior if they are not convinced of the nobility or utility of the government's policy. The dilemma is real and painful. The views of journalists—not to mention opposition leaders—about problems of national development do not necessarily coincide with those of incumbent political elites. Should they then provide readers with alternative policy suggestions, or should they keep quiet and function as government mouthpieces? Is their obligation to the truth as they see it, or to the Truth as handed down by government bureaucrats? Let us listen to the distinguished African editor, Kenya's Hilary Ng'weno:

> In respect to the all-pervading power of the government, nothing has really changed from the bad old days of colonialism. Only the actors have changed; the play remains the same. Instead of a colonial governor you have a president or field marshal. . . . Newspapers were taken over and those which were totally opposed to being incorporated into the government propaganda machinery were closed down. . . . States tend to perceive the national interest as being merely another name for state interest. A journalist's perception of the national interest is by the very nature of his profession, unless he is a party hack or mere government functionary, broader. More important, it is tentative, undogmatic . . . and to that extent cannot be given meaningful expression within the confines of a state press.[37]

Mr. Ng'weno's arguments are difficult to dismiss. He suggests that Western bias is being replaced by "another, that of governmental or bureaucratic bias."[38] His is only one of many voices in Africa to claim freedom of expression and press freedom as a birthright. The African governments' preoccupations with news censorship should be seen also in a larger historical context. One observer has pointed out that "the itch to censor was government's first instinctive reaction to the threat it perceived from the printed word. Germany began censoring in 1529, and three decades later, the British limited printing to presses in London licensed by the Crown."[39] There is very little reason for Africa to repeat the mistakes that Europe made several centuries ago. And there is more than ample evidence that press freedom has African champions, who will eventually win against the small minds letting others guide the quills of censorship for them.

Some evidence shows that, whatever the legal basis of African governments' censorship authority, there is also pragmatic recognition that draconian measures against news media should not always be enforced. A few examples illustrate this point. In one country, the government *temporarily* prohibited the news media from mentioning France, because of a book published in Paris, which suggested that the African head of state was involved in a scandal about public funds. Another country adopted a law providing for death by a firing squad for such offenses as "influencing, opposing, castigating, or deriding" the government; individuals were tried on two occasions under this law, but their sentences were later set aside by the head of the government, following a verdict of guilty. The implementation of government censorship is also not without examples of humor. In yet another country, a reporter was charged with murder for writing a column suggesting that evidence of government corruption could go up in smoke; the following day, a fire at a government building cost three lives and may have consumed such evidence. The reporter was arrested, but subsequently cleared by a court of law. The prize for irony no doubt belongs to the country whose government prohibits criticism of its official ideology of "humanism."

We should not permit governments anywhere to forget that press freedom is a universal phenomenon which, like the desire for independence from oppressive masters, grows once let out of the bottle. Cross-cultural discussion among Third World elites can further this process. Correcting the imbalance of news within the Third World could easily produce another beacon of press freedom transcending the narrow horizons of too many political leaders. Ultimately, press freedom should not be bound by such notions as national news sovereignty, and there is good reason for believing that in the long run it will not.

The credibility gap, which atrophies the people's willingness to believe what their governments tell them, is a direct result of African government policies. Most of these governments use their news media destructively from the standpoint of national integration; they are also laying the groundwork for future opposition instead of national unity. Their policies toward news media are therefore dysfunctional. Western observers are frequently too critical or pessimistic, presumably because they fall into the trap of judging Africa on the basis of external criteria or insufficient knowledge of the social and cultural background. One effective way to help develop press freedom in Africa may be to demonstrate that existing government policies on that subject are dysfunctional. Another may be to suggest that incumbent political elites in Africa listen more attentively to their critics, particularly the "nonpolitical" elites, as they seek to understand what political elites are doing. A play or a novel may be worth a thousand government plans.

Notes

1. "The Mass Media—Institutions of the African Political System," in Olav Stokke, ed., *Reporting Africa in Africa and International Mass Media* (Uppsala: The

Scandinavian Institute of African Studies, 1971), 32.

2. *Muffled Drums: The News Media in Africa* (Ames: Iowa State University Press, 1971), 37, 39, 43.

3. Ibid., 47.

4. "Black African States," in Jane Leftwich Curry and Joan R. Dassin, eds., *Press Controls Around the World* (New York: Praeger, 1983), 209, 231.

5. U.S. Congress *Country Reports on Human Rights Practices for 1983* (Washington, D.C.: Committees on Foreign Affairs, House of Representatives, and on Foreign Relations, Senate, February 1984), 21–441.

6. Raymond D. Gastil, ed., *Freedom in the World: Political and Civil Liberties* (New York: Freedom House, 1984).

7. "The Cultural Revolution and Freedom of Expression in Guinea," *Journal of Modern African Studies,* 14:2 (June 1976).

8. Ibid., 208, 211, 212.

9. Ibid., 217–18.

10. (London: Heinemann, 1966).

11. Ibid., vii.

12. Ibid., viii.

13. *Creating Political Order: The Party-States of West Africa* (Chicago: Rand Mc-Nally, 1966).

14. Achebe, op. cit., xix.

15. Ibid., xii.

16. Ibid., 34.

17. Ibid., 136.

18. *The Beautiful Ones Are Not Yet Born* (London, New York: Collier, 1969).

19. Ibid., 59.

20. Ibid., 60.

21. Ibid., 134.

22. Ibid., 155.

23. (Yaoundé: Editions Semences africaines, 1978). Another play that touches on the issue of freedom and castigates some African leaders and their supporters is Wole Soyinka's *A Play of Giants.* It was reviewed on December 11, 1984 by Frank Rich in the *New York Times.* Mr. Rich writes that one of the four African leaders, representing Idi Amin, "and his cohorts may exploit the rhetoric of black liberation and antiimperialism to justify their mass murders and tortures, but there is no mistaking these leaders for anything other than deranged thugs." "The only character of integrity," adds Mr. Rich, is "the sculptor, who might well represent the playwright [Wole Soyinka]. . . . " Mr. Soyinka is clearly one of Africa's most outspoken and biting critics of African political elites, and he articulates a widespread desire for greater freedom by Africans.

24. Ibid., 33.

25. Ibid., 62.

26. Ibid., 78.

27. Ibid., 73.

28. Quoted in *World Press Freedom: A Wingspread Symposium* (Racine, Wisconsin: The International Press Institute; the American Society of Newspaper Editors; the Inter-American Press Association; and the Society of Professional Journalists, November 1974), 10.

29. Cf. W. A. E. Skurnik, "Foreign News Coverage in Six African Newspapers: The Potency of National Interests," *Gazette: International Journal for Mass Communications Studies* (Amsterdam, 1981) 28, 117–30; and "A New Look at Foreign News Coverage: External Dependence of National Interests?" *African Studies Review* 24:1 (March 1981), 99–112.

30. *See* W. A. E. Skurnik, "Ivoirien Student Perceptions of U.S. Africa Policy." *Journal of Modern African Studies* 17:3 (1979).

31. *See* Skurnik, "Some Observations About the African Press: National Interests and Credibility Gap," paper presented at the October 1980 annual convention of the African Studies Association, Philadelphia, Pennsylvania.

32. *Textes reglementaires.* Ecole supérieure internationale de journalisme de Yaoundé. Convention revisée instituant l'école supérieure internationale de journalisme de Yaoundé (no date, mimeographed).

33. Smith, Anthony, *The Geopolitics of Information: How Western Culture Dominates the World* (New York: Oxford University Press, 1980), 72.

34. *See* Skurnik, "Ivoirien Perceptions . . .," op. cit.

35. Ibid.

36. Bourges, Hervé. *Décoloniser l'information* (Paris: Editions Cana, 1978), 22.

37. Hilary Ng'weno. "The Third World Dilemma: Can a State Press be Free? *The Weekly Review* (Nairobi, 22 June 1979).

38. Quoted in Rosemary Righter, *Whose News? Politics, the Press and the Third World* (New York: Times Books, 1978), 196.

39. Leonard R. Sussman, "UNESCO: Getting Down to Cases," unpublished manuscript presented at an international conference in Talloires, France, 30 September 1983.

Davidson Nicol

17

African Pluralism and Democracy

The relationship between pluralism and democracy is of considerable importance to African development. Pluralism involves a wide range of categories—racial, ethnic, religious, class, and, within these, others such as kinship groups. One primary aim in Africa is to integrate all the disparate groups within a state system in a manner that will result in participatory democracy. According to much of the recent literature, the prospects for this are gloomy, and the achievements toward this have been meager; but, there remains room for optimism.

In African countries, where societal rewards are largely under the sole control of the government, a strong degree of rapprochement and peaceful government may be possible only under certain circumstances. These include a complete democracy with regular elections and changes of leadership when its citizens demand it; wise leaders of one-party states who hold opposing groups under enlightened control; a military or civilian leader of mixed ethnicity who cannot be claimed by any one group; a military or civilian leader from a minority group and who, therefore, may not be a threat to other ethnic groups; or, finally, a leader from a minority group that dominates the armed forces but who is wise enough to share the perquisites of office with the larger groups.

Although this analysis is concerned primarily with the African continent, it would be more balanced to consider it against an international background and thus within a more comparative framework. Parallel situations can then be detected in other parts of the world and the success of their attempts at solutions identified.

In Northern Ireland, a democratic solution is being sought in a pluralistic situation where sectarian and religious violence has already destroyed many lives. The conflict in Northern Ireland has historically been considered a sectarian and religious conflict between Catholics and Protestants. Might it not equally be an ethnic struggle between those of Celtic (Catholic) and Anglo-Saxon (Protestant) origins? Working towards a pluralistic democ-

racy in Northern Ireland, or in a united Ireland, has not so far been successful.

India, with outstanding attempts at a pluralistic democracy, is another
example. The senseless tragedy of the assassination of Prime Minister Indira
Gandhi resulted from the Sikhs' irredentist concept of an independent
Khalistan in a subcontinent where Pakistan and Bangladesh had previously
separated, raising thereby the hopes of other centrifugal groups. Just before
her death, Mrs. Gandhi stated that in a plural society, people must have a
single person, concept, or ideology to bind them together and act as a model
in the midst of their many differences.

Other non-African examples of these problems are in such places as
Canada, Switzerland, Belgium, Spain, Cyprus, and Yugoslavia. The devolu-
tion of the United Kingdom into England, Scotland, and Wales is relevant, as
are events in the gigantic socialist countries of China and the Soviet Union.

In the Western world, among the larger countries, the United States is
arguably the best example of a successful attempt at pluralism and democracy. Its central binding point is its Constitution; in an ethnically and racially
pluralistic society, the Constitution is generally accepted as the basis for defining law, government, social relations, and democratic process. As an
example, let me cite an analysis by the *Washington Times* of the 1984 presidential elections. It showed that a group of voters of northern European origins voted by 60 percent or more for the successful candidates. Those of
eastern European and Mediterranean origins gave a lower but still considerable percentage for those candidates; Hispanics were lower still in their support; but, lowest of all, were the 10 percent of Afro-Americans who voted for
the winning team. Despite their relative lack of support, it is extremely unlikely that the Hispanics and Afro-Americans would resort to armed violence
in protest against the new administration even though they compose
roughly 25 percent of the armed forces.

In Africa, the dissolution of colonialism introduced the nation-state system, with each state with boundaries inherited from the Congress of Berlin,
a century earlier. These states, now nearly all independent, contain plural,
national societies in which individual societies are sometimes contiguous
with and extend into neighboring countries, but remain divided by the arbitrary boundaries.[1]

A few independent African countries (Botswana, Lesotho, and Swaziland) are fortunate in being homogeneous and in having a common language and society within their borders. Others, in extreme contrast, have
had or continue to have violent irredentist episodes with their plural
societies. Nigeria has the former Biafra; Ethiopia has Eritrea; and the Sudan
its south. The rest contain plural societies in varying states of national integration.

The state system, inherited from colonial powers and sanctified by the
Organization of African Unity, has been largely accepted, although in the

western Sahara it has been challenged by allegations that this territory left by Spain was never a valid colonial possession and that it always legally belonged to Morocco. Along the northern borders of Chad, the Azou strip is contested by both Libya and Chad. These challenges are not based on the principle of self-determination of the inhabitants, but on legal references to treaties signed between European powers in the colonial era.

In the postwar period, the British, French, and Belgian governments, through the United Nations Trusteeship Council, granted independence to such trusteeship territories as Togo, Cameroon, Rwanda, and Burundi, sometimes by a process of self-determination. The British, earlier in the century, had insisted on the validity of the independent and homogeneous nations of Botswana, Lesotho, and Swaziland; after World War II, the British kept them as High Commission territories, and later granted them independence instead of handing them over to South Africa. Africans in Rhodesia (Zimbabwe), Namibia, and Zululand were not so fortunate; they were left under the control of white settler governments. They have either gained or are trying to gain their independence by armed struggle and negotiations.

Attempts by homogeneous societies to ignore frontiers and produce new, homogeneous nation-states have not been very successful. There had been a Bakongo kingdom, ruled by an emperor-king from Angola. This ancient kingdom was divided, during the nineteenth century, among the French (in Congo-Brazzaville), the Belgian (in Zaire), and the Portugese (in Angola). An attempt to revive it in immediate preindependence Zaire in the 1960s, through King Abako and President Kasavubu, was brief and unsuccessful. Somalia, as another example, maintains a five-pointed star on its flag to represent the goal of reuniting the people of Somali origin, who are now divided among five separate territories, including independent Somalia. This flag continues to produce tension, and in some cases, armed conflict in the region.

Although Crawford Young and others insist that the state system in Africa is permanent, voluntary economic and military alliances between states cannot be discounted.[2] For example, Senegal and Gambia may form a political confederation; Tanzania is a confederation of Tanganyika and Zanzibar. There were the brief Ghana-Mali-Guinea and Senegal-Mali unions, and recently there was an even briefer alliance of Chad (under Goukouni) and Libya. Future African Garibaldis and Bismarcks of the twenty-first century might attempt to bind small states into larger and more viable ones in the pattern of nineteenth-century Italy and Germany. This is one of the reasons why the UN and other international organizations are important. Their grant of membership gives visibility, validity, and a chance of survival to small states, which might otherwise risk being quietly absorbed by larger and more powerful neighbors.

Different ideologies have been professed within the African states. Britain and France tried to leave in Africa a system of liberal democracy, based on such thinkers as Burke, Rousseau, and Thomas Henry Green. The Portuguese and Spanish, occupied in freeing themselves from fascist authoritarian governments, had little time to build and leave a political system in their colonies. Portugal had to abandon the new governments of Angola and Mozambique to settling their own differences by force. However, they left a legacy of racial tolerance to those who had accepted the colonial-metropolitan idea, and an educated middle class of mixed Afro-Portugese origins, with a small group of blacks mostly trained by British and American religious groups.

Soon after decolonization, African states started to change their systems of government. They searched for systems based on African traditions, since the novel European parliamentary systems of government, with their opposition parties, had been in Africa, in most cases, for less than a decade and were considered alien. Regrettably, the new African systems of one-party rule and military government kept new leaders and their ethnic groups indefinitely in power and, in some cases, indefinitely enriched. Dissent or disapproval from other citizens of the state was equated with disloyalty and were dealt with by varying degrees of suppression—imprisonment, exile, or death. These one-party and military governments proliferated. (They could sometimes be useful if their leadership rotated among other individuals, especially those from other ethnic groups.) There were distinguished exceptions such as Senegal, Gambia, Cameroon, and, to a certain extent, Zimbabwe, which still maintains a democratic system.

What is democracy? Richard Sklar has outlined a spectrum of evolutionary democracy, which ranges from the developmental dictatorship derived from early 20th-century Italian revolutionary syndicalists and Marxists, to a liberal democracy that incorporates political liberty.[3] Guided democracy, for instance, is really a developmental dictatorship that takes into consideration leaders' accountability to citizens and, when the idea of social justice is introduced, produces social democracy. Participatory democracy is one form of government in which many would recognize the better traditional aspects of the societies and governments of precolonial Africa. Participatory democracy can then lead to consociational democracy.

Sklar's suggested developmental democracy, with its core values of social, participatory, and consociational democracies, and with an element of individual self-development, is preferable as a practical goal. Rightly or wrongly, his preceptorial democracy of leadership without political power and with a kind of refined and transformed guided democracy may be felt (perhaps pessimistically) to be too visionary and impracticable for pluralistic societies. These societies, within the definition of a state system, may call occasionally for a legitimate use of physical force by common consent of all pluralistic groups. Even Kenneth Kaunda of Zambia, with his philosophy of humanism, has been occasionally obliged to use force.

Unfortunately, modern Africa does not have many truly liberal democratic institutions. Crawford Young has summarized the existing systems loosely into three groups: the free market or capitalist (e.g., Zaire and Kenya); the populist-socialist (e.g., Tanzania); and the Afro-Marxist (e.g., Ethiopia and Benin).[4] All the fifteen states he discusses show dependency in their search for aid, foreign investment, and arms. He examines various indices of performance and the qualities required. It seems here that emphasis has to be laid on the quality of personal leadership and the competence of regimes.

In analyzing the search for national integration, Ali Mazrui has outlined factors in progressive order that may lead to success in pluralistic societies.[5] The initial step is toward coexistence with migrant traders and population movements, leading to closer contact; this, after cumulative experience of conflict resolution and discovery of areas of mutual compatibility, would lead to compromise. Eventually, there may be a merging of identities into a suprafactional community that would allow for centralization of social violence, when necessary, for that needed political unity; but, this has to be sanctioned by all groups.

Do African leaders and governments work towards these objectives of national integration within the political ideas discussed above?

Much depends on the personal qualities of leaders and their education. The lack of a formal education does not necessarily hamper a leader, but possession of one does enhance his leadership capabilities. Discrimination and the ability to choose wise advisers, and the periodic rotation of advisers, introduce ethnic and religious variety. (Rotation also minimizes the stealing of state funds and reduces bribery to a manageable and discreet level.) It is essential for the future to train the next generation of leaders in qualities of competence and integrity and to train them to moderate or sacrifice the emotional satisfactions and political claims of kinship, ethnicity, and religion for the larger and less immediately gratifying demands of a plural society seeking democracy.

This has happened already in Africa; it has been happening over the centuries. The colonial period was important in bringing Africa into the international industrialized era, but it is only a short epoch in African history. Long before the colonial era, Africans successfully worked towards harmony in a plural society. There were degrees of interethnic accommodation all over Africa: Arabs mixed with blacks to produce the Sudanese and other groups; the Hamitic people mixed with the local Bantu to produce the Buganda in Uganda; Fulanis of the jihad era mixed with Hausas to form the dominant caste in northern Nigeria; in Sierra Leone, a complex mixture of captive Yorubas, Ibos, Hausas, and Congolese mixed with the indigenous peoples, as well as immigrant black Americans and West Indians, among others, to produce the small group of Krios who supplied intellectual leadership in West Africa in the nineteenth and early twentieth centuries.

Even South Africa, in the last quarter of this century, has strived towards some form of pluralism in government under Vorster and Botha by instituting parliamentary bodies for colored (people of mixed racial origin) and Indians, in addition to the whites. Some illogicality lies in the political disregard of the urban black African, as well as in insisting on indefinite racial dominance by those of European descent. A more logical system of separate development in South Africa, instead of being organized by race, might be organized on a linguistic basis, separating English- and Afrikaans-speaking (including the relevant coloreds, Asians, and detribalized urban Africans), the Nguni group (which includes the Xhosa, Zulu, Swazi, and Ndebele) and the Sothos (the Tswana, the Pedi, and the northern and southern Sotho). This may be idealistic, but is more logical, if there is a continuing insistence that the groups must stay separate.

It is relevant that unions in South Africa have conducted successful strikes. It is important because these unions have transcended ethnicity by mobilizing groups, which were components of a plural society, into a unified negotiating entity.

South Africa is singled out here as an example because of its prominence in the media. However, in Africa, Nigeria appears to be the most advanced in working towards pluralism and democracy, even with periodic interventions by its military, which may indeed be part of the process. Its carefully worked-out constitution should be a model for states that seek democracy in pluralistic societies. It draws on the American model, and would appear also to have drawn on the Soviet model by having "consular" representation of its individual states at the center. However, it lacks the rotating, federal vice-presidency of individual states and the watchful representation by the center in state governments, which are present in the Soviet system. The insistence of the Nigerian constitution on a successful president securing a majority in at least two-thirds of the states helped to transcend fears of domination by any single ethnic group. The Nigerian constitution was not a failure; it was simply incomplete. It did not have sufficient control over financial expenditure or appointments to positions of power and control. It allowed manipulation of a president who might be too trusting and remote, and thus perhaps incorrectly described as "weak."

Larry Diamond has suggested a role for the military in a civilian government, which might avoid these defects, since the military would participate actively in elections and appointments and in judiciary and financial bodies.[6] The correct place for the military must be within a democratic government. There will be periods when civilian governments in a pluralistic society break down to a point where the introduction of a disciplined and corrective force is necessary; but, this interruption of the democratic process must be temporary and popular. Its period of office must be fixed at the outset, or else its anxiousness for perfection or an ideally (but impossibly) complete solution of national difficulties may lead it to prolong its stay beyond its period of necessity and popularity. It may also be encouraged to stay on by external major powers, which usually prefer stability, even if dictatorial, to a changing democracy. It can become, in effect, civilian government without checks, but which is backed by military force and soon becomes subject to Acton's precept of absolute power corrupting absolutely. It may leave no alternative for change but that of the same violent overthrow that brought it to power, thus beginning an indefinite cycle of violence and military regimes. Its original rectitude and discipline then changes into using its power to perpetuate the ethnic domination by its leader or its ruling officers of others by selective recruitment and promotion, or by removal or straightforward massacre of other ethnic elements in the army and their civilian counterparts.

In a pluralistic society, civilian corruption and disturbances can be halted by the military's intervention but cannot be indefinitely curbed or removed by it. The latter's role is most effective within the participatory democracy of a civilian regime.[7] But it can, as was the case of Kemal Ataturk in Turkey, provide a positive drive towards modernization.

Where a feeling of national unity is still in its preliminary stage, there is always a danger that, by their smallness of size, minorities in a plural society will suffer disadvantages. Where they differ markedly from the majority communities in race, religion, or in socioeconomic status, they may become victims of discrimination, prejudice, and sometimes oppression. Their position is even more serious when they are of the same race and color as the majority; their victimization may pass unnoticed, or, if noticed, may be shrugged off by local authorities and the outside world as being a regrettable consequence of history.

Under the pressure of rapid decolonization, the colonial authorities were faced with a dilemma about the treatment of minorities, and tended to adopt an attitude of sanguinary optimism that some postindependence accommodation would be reached. They enshrined in the independence documents articles regarding human rights, which were often later ignored. The result has been that, in the framework of national liberation, freedom, and democracy, some minority groups in pluralistic societies have been faced with autocracies and prejudices that did not exist during the colonial era, when all groups received equal treatment, whether good or bad. With independence, ancient enmities surfaced or perhaps deepened when the colonial authority had used the mechanism of control by divide and rule (a policy certainly not confined to white colonial governments).

For true democracy in a pluralistic society, minority groups must receive representation at the center regardless of their voting power, and should be given a measure of local autonomy at the periphery to retain their identity and alleviate any feelings of hopelessness and political suffocation.

Education, as an instrument in promoting democracy in a plural society, was initiated before independence by progressive colonial administrators. Such schools as the Lycée Ponty (Dakar), Katsina College (Nigeria), Achimota College (Ghana), Bo School (Sierra Leone), and King's School,

Budo (Uganda) brought together young people of diverse communities and religions. In doing so, they helped erase hostile and derogatory stereotypes, replacing them, through proximity, with friendship and sometimes admiration for the other groups, thus making possible identification with and loyalty to the nation-state, in addition to their communities. Government and church groups also instituted colleges which not only brought together different ethnic groups within a single territory, but also from other territories in the region.

Ironically, for national and regional unity, these mixed institutions may lose their distinctive characteristics with independence. Establishment of new, but more local and provincial, schools and universities is making the older schools more parochial and ethnic. They are being replaced as binding forces by federal schools, which insist on intakes from different parts of the nation, and by youth corps, where, after graduation, young people serve in parts of their nations other than their own provinces.

Facility in communication is important in a pluralistic democracy, and consideration should be given to the Scandinavian model of multilinguality, in which foreign languages are introduced early in school education. In Africa, this might entail beginning education in the child's vernacular, then introducing the territory's European preindependence language, and, later (or at the same time) introducing another national language other than the student's and, finally, adding another European language. A Temne from Port Loko in the former British territory of Sierra Leone would thus be equipped with the knowledge (and culture) of Temne, English, Mende (another Sierra Leone language), and French. A Bakongo student from Luanda would similarly by the age of eighteen be familiar with Bakongo, Portugese, Ovimbundu, and English. Forcefulness and determination on the part of political and educational leaders will be needed to overcome problems of parochialism, finance, and staffing. These changes will be building stones towards economic and political regionalism for future African leaders.

More immediately, adult education, literacy, and instruction in democratic procedures are urgently required in plural societies if democracy is to be achieved. The resolution, dignity, and patience of the average African, and the courage, intelligence, and integrity of African youth presages an optimistic future.

Democracy cannot survive the nation-states unless it is buttressed by a sound economy. Some African states are often not viable, and, in times of drought, famine, and economic recession, they frequently become client nations of northern industrial countries. The latter are becoming increasingly impatient with an African political rhetoric that continually harks back to the colonial past as a cause of the present state of economic disaster. Self-reliance and South-to-South cooperation, however, are honorable and dignified alternatives to the cycle of begging, borrowing, and indebtedness, and have been suggested by Samir Amin, the Egyptian economist.[8] By now, it is clear that a major shift of international trade and aid from the developed to the developing countries, as envisaged by Raoul Prebitsch, the Argentinian economist and first director of UNCTAD, will not be forthcoming. Neither will there be a marked stabilization and upward movement of commodity prices for the developing countries unless powerful cartels like OPEC can be formed.

There are alternatives: a free market economy that many Western countries favor, and which has had success in Nigeria, Kenya, Senegal, the Ivory Coast, and Morocco; or, a socialist economy, which has had success in Algeria and Libya, helped by their petroleum products. The variety of socialism in China, which accommodates some free enterprise, industrial zones, and a comprador class, may be the aim of Zimbabwe, where major agricultural successes have been achieved in maize harvests by both African peasants and white commercial farmers. Others have looked at the socialism of the Soviet Asian states, e.g., Uzbekistan, where feudalism has bypassed capitalism and gone straight to socialism.

The most pragmatic step at present appears to be internal accommodation and power-sharing within the African nation-state accompanied concomitantly by a drive towards multistate regionalism as an essential component of economic and political growth.[9] The colonial powers did attempt this, towards the close of their era, with bodies such as the East African Community; but, it seemed necessary for African countries to become independent first and then to attempt integration by their own act of will. The processes of dismantling and rebuilding these preindependence regional bodies were not always rational and delayed economic development. Within the framework of regionalism, national sovereignty with its powerful and vested interests can still be maintained whilst accompanied by the economic removal of the arbitrary borders of the Congress of Berlin.

Democracy has pluralistic elements even in a completely homogeneous society. In voting for elected representatives, an important right is being exercised by individuals who sacrifice their will to the common collective good of the immediate community and, beyond that, of the nation. Participating in democratic institutions is a fundamental human right and is the best goal in the predictable future for a satisfactory and lasting peace in Africa.

Notes

1. A. I. Asiwaju, ed., *Partitioned Africans: Ethnic Relations Across Africa's International Boundaries, 1884–1984* (London: C. Hurst & Co., and Lagos, Nigeria: University of Lagos Press, 1985).

2. Crawford Young, *Ideology and Development in Africa* (New Haven and London: Yale University Press, 1982).

3. Presidential Address, African Studies Association, U.S.A., 1981.

4. Ibid.

5. Leo Kuper and M. G. Smith, *Pluralism in Africa* (Berkeley and Los Angeles: University of California Press, 1971).

6. Larry Diamond, "Nigeria in Search of Democracy," *Foreign Affairs* (Spring 1984), 916–19.

7. There is extensive literature on military rule in Africa. *See* Samuel Decalo, *Coups and Army Rule in Africa: Studies in Military Style* (New Haven: Yale University Press, 1976); Victor Olorunsola, *Soldiers and Power* (Stanford, California: Hoover Institution Press, 1977); and Olatunde Odetola, *Military Regimes and Development* (London: Allen and Unwin, 1982).

8. Clive Archer, *International Organizations* (Boston and London: George Allen and Unwin, 1983).

9. D. Nicol, L. Echeverria and A. Peccei, eds., *Regionalism and the New International Economic Order* (New York: Pergamon Press, 1980).

18

Colin Legum

Democracy in Africa: Hope and Trends

Africa is very widely perceived in the Western democracies as a continent of virtually unrelieved tyranny, dictatorship, corruption, economic bankruptcy, administrative incompetence, and violence. Some of those more closely engaged in following African developments will usually qualify this stereotype of present-day Africa by citing exceptions to this overall gloomy assessment—such as Ivory Coast, Kenya, Morocco, Botswana, and Nigeria (except when it falls under military rule). If that is the image, what is the reality?

No meaningful discussion about the present-day condition of Africa or about the future prospects of democratic government is possible without reference to the major political and economic trends since the onset of independence less than a generation ago. These are summarized below.

• First is the widespread breakdown of the institutions inherited from colonial rule, and energetic experimentation with new political systems— mostly adaptive rather than innovative. Despite claims about instituting a peculiarly "African form of government," there have actually been very few attempts at creating unique political systems. On the whole, the response to institutional breakdown has been adaptation of the institutions that had failed, usually by an increase in the centralization of power, and often by increasing the coercive nature of this power.

• Constitutional adaptation and experimentation have been characterized by eclecticism, reflective of and inspired by all the known types of modern political systems: free enterprise capitalism (Ivory Coast, Kenya, Senegal, Gabon, Cameroon, Botswana, etc.); state capitalism masquerading as socialism (in the majority of African countries); evolutionary democratic socialism (Tanzania is the best, and perhaps only, model); Marxist-Leninist systems (Ethiopia, Angola, Mozambique); constitutional monarchy (Lesotho); Tudor or Hanoverian monarchy (Morocco and Swaziland).

• There has been a breakdown of law and order, widespread security problems and abuses of human rights in many of the new states. Mostly, these have been the direct result of (1) institutional breakdown; (2) the raw tensions produced by the process of merging clans, tribes, subnational and national communities into new nations within a modernizing development system; (3) power struggles among competing elites; (4) economic failure to meet the heightened expectancy aroused by the end of colonialism.

• Contrary to earlier predictions, there have been remarkably few major security problems over borders: a brief skirmish between Algeria and Morocco in 1963; a short conflict between Niger and Mali; quarrels of low military intensity between Nigeria and Cameroon and between Zaire and Zambia. The major border conflicts have been over Somali claims on Ethiopia and Kenya; over Morocco's stand on the western Sahara; and over the conflicts in southern Africa.

• Economic failure in most sub-Saharan countries is a phenomenon more remarkable because the first two decades after independence witnessed an average growth rate of 6 to 8 percent, declining after the mid-1970s to 2.3 percent, and then declining further to zero, or even to negative, growth rates in the early 1980s. The most alarming aspect of this economic failure has been the increasing failure of Africa to feed itself, with all that this means in terms of human misery, political disillusionment, and great burdens on foreign exchange reserves to pay for imported food. This failure is brilliantly described in the seminal OAU document embodied in the Lagos Economic Declaration.

• At the same time, population has continued to grow at an average of about 2.6 percent. In common with other Third World countries, most African countries have experienced a gargantuan urban population explosion. Both these developments make demands on limited resources that are impossible to fulfill, and so grow progressively more menacing year by year. (Population growth can be healthy in some African countries, provided only that their human and economic resources have been effectively mobilized.)

• A continuous but, as yet, elusive search for continental and regional security and economic answers is exemplified by the creation of the Organization of African Unity, the African Development Bank, the Economic Community of West African States, the Southern African Development Cooperation Conference, etc.

• Finally, and crucially, there have been the liberation struggles to complete the "unfinished African revolution," and the increasingly violent conflict situation in southern Africa.

The broad developments described above have had five major consequences: an unhealthy build-up of arms and armies, with expensive modern weapons of warfare; militarization of political systems; a huge refugee problem, with over 5 million seeking succor abroad, and millions more internally displaced; economic disruption and misdirection of resources; instability of governments and the perpetual threat of political and military coups.

Table 18.1 provides a useful way of looking at the process of breakdown and experimentation, of fission and fusion, as described above.

Some Myths About Democracy in Africa

Myth: Democracy Has Collapsed in Africa Since Independence.

No single African country was a democracy at its independence. While most had a semblance of democratic forms of government, all lacked the content, or even a skeletal framework of a true political democracy. The outward appearance of a democratic structure was simply alien flesh covering old bones; when the bones were rattled hard, the flesh proved to be only a flimsy covering lacking the muscle, fiber, and blood of a viable indigenous political system.

All the institutions of independence had been artificially created, and were not rooted in the indigenous society. Most were simply adaptations (or distortions) of metropolitan systems introduced to serve the needs and interests of colonial rule, which was itself heavily centralized. (Compare the role and power of the old colonial governor with that of his successor, the executive president.) What existed at independence, therefore, was a mixture of representative and authoritarian institutions. Local government was mostly nonexistent. There were seldom enough trained or experienced administrators and technicians to operate government institutions—other than the legal system. A new political class took over from the colonial ruler, with little or no experience of functioning alongside an independent civil service, which, in any event, was not itself independent under the colonial system; nor, on the whole, was the legal system. There were few internal checks and balances because the institutions were themselves in a state of imbalance. Some of the early postindependence consequences of this hybrid political system were: (1) institutional breakdown, e.g., removal of the chief justice in Ghana and, later, of other judges; but not yet a total breakdown of the judicial or legal system; the official requirement that civil servants should be loyal not to the government, but to the ruling party. In some cases, civil servants were required to become members of the ruling party; (2) increasing distortions within the institutions themselves while they remained outwardly democratic, in form, they were intrinsically undemocratic.

Myth: The Westminster or French Models of Parliamentary Democracy Were Imposed on the Colonial Peoples at Independence.

It is true that the colonial powers sought to bequeathe their own democratic values and systems (or version of it) to their former colonies; but, the almost

TABLE 18.1 Major Trends in the Political Process in Africa Since Independence

STAGE 1	A Multiparty Political System with Formal Trappings of Democratic Institutions[a]
	The movement that emerged strongest out of the anticolonial struggle is the new ruling party, confronted by one or more opposition parties. The army is still nonpolitical.
STAGE 2	The Ruling Party Splits[b]
	In the ensuing power struggle, opposition politics intensify and, on occsion, turn violent. Institutions become weaker, more distorted, and less efficient.
STAGE 3	Period of Growing Political Instability, Outbreaks of Violence (Often Tribal or Regional)
	Signs of weakening political authority; the ruling party loses its popular, mobilization role, and usually resorts to greater coercion.
STAGE 4	Three Different Trends
	a) emergence of single-party states; b) survival of some multiparty states;
	c) military regimes emerge
STAGE 5	A) Single-Party State Consolodates Its Power, or B) Military Regimes Take Over
	They adapt the old institutions and rule in partnership with civil service elites.
STAGE 6	A) Many ruling parties lose all claim to popular support and react in one of two ways:
	1. Some become more openly coercive or manipulative, relying increasingly on patronage and preventive detention;
	2. Others become more responsive and engage in liberalization of the political system and reform the ruling party.
	B) Some military regimes hand back power to civilians, but mostly only for brief periods. The army has become more politicized, and its role changes within the political society.
	C) The older established military regimes become incresingly dominated by a single charismatic army officer, or a small clique of officers; the government is increasingly civilianized, but the army remains the defender of the regime.

[a]In a few cases (Algeria, Egypt, Tanzania, and Mozambique), the ruling party had established its total domination by the time power had passed from the old system.

[b]There are a few exceptions, e.g., Botswana Democratic Party, Tanganyikan African National Union, Neo-Destour of Tunisia.

universal nationalist demand during their struggle for independence was for the transfer of Western institutions; they rejected any proposed changes or limitations as a sign of conferring something inferior on them: wigs and red gowns and high tables in universities were a feature of the practice of Nkrumah's Ghana and of the majority of sub-Saharan African states. Since the modernizing elite—the nationalists of independence—had as their first priority the establishment of modern institutions, they initially adopted the only ones they knew—Western models.

The reality is that none of the European systems of democracy had ever been developed under colonial rule, despite the claims made about their virtues. Nor were they introduced by the new political class (with a few isolated exceptions). However, some tried to incorporate aspects of European democratic institutions within fundamentally undemocratic political systems.

Myth: Traditional African Societies Were Democratic, Communalistic, and Operated on a Basis of Consensus: Hence the Justification for the Single-Party State.

This is a generalization; there are examples of both authoritarian and democratic systems in premodern times.

Moreover, systems appropriate to premodern and often shifting societies, comprising mostly small numbers of people, are wholly inappropriate to modern economic societies, especially since these new societies are heterogeneous and are only at an early stage of nation-formation.

Myth: Liberation from Colonial Rule Meant Democratic Freedom for the Former Colonial Subjects.

This view, propagated by the anti-colonial movement during the liberation struggle, confused two different aspects of liberty and freedom: freedom from *alien rule* (the raison d'être of the liberation struggle), and political freedom *after* independence. Because the nationalist leaders and their supporters in the West were waging their struggle against democratic nations, it was only natural that they should have based their case on achieving democratic rights for colonial subjects. In fact, though, the central argument in favor of ending colonialism was that, apart from the right of self-determination, the ending of alien rule was an essential prerequisite to the building of new democratic societies; but it was only the first step towards creating new democratic societies. Disappointment in the early failure to build and expand democratic states (as it is understood in Western societies) caused disillusionment both in the West and in Africa; but this disillusionment is due to a lack of historical understanding and perspective about the process of creating new nation-states.

What Went Wrong?

Virtually all the nationalist forces that emerged as the dominant political group at independence were coalitions of widely disparate ideological, economic, tribal, and regional interests. Almost without exception the ruling parties split soon after independence. Thus, central political power was threatened at a crucial, early stage. The breakup resulted in fierce internal power struggles, which frequently took as one of its forms tribal and/or regional rivalries. At times, it spilled over into violence and, if not to breakdown, then to a weakening of central political authority. A frequent response was to resort to coercive measures (arrests, preventive detention, and interference with the judicial process) in an attempt to restore political control and authority. Civil servants often took sides in these power struggles, resulting in their dismissal and, in other ways, weakening and demoralizing the public service.

This first postindependence political crisis, not infrequently, resulted in the outlawing of one or more opposition parties, and marked the start of the evolution of the single-party state.

In those situations where the dominant wing of the ruling party failed to rally effective support, or where its coercive measures produced violent political and/or tribal reactions, one outcome was army coups and military rule. This phenomenon usually occurred in situations of violence and institutional collapse and, especially, where economic hardship was an additional factor.

African Political Systems

The Single-Party State

Such states vary considerably in terms of their democratic content, aspirations, and the levels of coercion, tolerance, and respect for human rights within each of them. It is therefore important to distinguish between such states, and not to regard them all as fitting into a single political category. Examples:

More Democratic	Less Democratic	Authoritarian
Tanzania	Kenya	Zaire
Algeria	Ivory Coast	Gabon
	Cameroon	Guinea (under Sékou Touré)
	Somalia	Malawi

Hybrid Political Systems

In appearance these are pluralist systems but, in practice, they are single-party states. While they permit opposition political groups and political centers to exist in open opposition to the ruling party (and even to contest elections), these opposition groups are subject to differing degrees of constraints. It is therefore necessary to differentiate between: (a) Those that are engaged in experiments with *expanding* the right of parties to operate independently—e.g., Egypt and Morocco. (Senegal has gone farthest along this road of cautious experiment in legitimating a multiparty system.); (b) Those that are engaged in *contracting* the existing rights of opposition parties—e.g., Madagascar and probably also Zimbabwe.

Military Regimes

Africa's military regimes are usually a coalition between the army and civil servants, who have generally become alienated from the political class.

Unlike the earlier situation in many Latin American countries, there is no evidence yet of a tendency to develop a new military political class. The army is, in fact, closely allied to the supplanted political class (through familial relations), and these two classes mostly have similar interests and values. Only in a few exceptional cases (where the senior officer class has been replaced by junior officers or privates) have there been attempts by soldiers to make structural changes. When this has happened, it only began mostly with a commitment to improving the moral and disciplinary climate of the nation. (Ethiopia is currently an outstanding exception. Burkina Faso [Upper Volta] *may* be engaged in making radical changes. The efforts of Rawlings in Ghana have not, as yet, brought about any significant structural changes.)

The army rulers in Africa have, so far, seen their role as a transient one. Army rule has evolved in two directions: (a) after a period, the army itself suffers from internal divisions, corruption, popular discontent with its rule (reflecting the same kind of problems as those of the political parties they overthrew), and have voluntarily decided to withdraw to their barracks—usually returning at a later stage to restore discipline and order, once again. This has already happened three times in Nigeria and Ghana, twice in Benin (Dahomey), Sudan, and Upper Volta; (b) The army gradually loosens its hold on power, leaving a small military group (often in civvies) to control an increasingly civilianized government (e.g., Egypt under Nasser and Sadat, Sudan, Niger, Mali, Zaire, Algeria, Burundi, and Benin).

Some military regimes are decidedly less undemocratic than others; again, it is necessary to identify these differences in order to clarify the nature of military regimes and the possibilities of their acting as agents in a democratizing process.

Multiparty Parliamentary Democratic Systems

There are now a few *more* multiparty systems in Africa than five years ago. Even defenders and theorists of the single-party state are now more ready to adopt more flexible attitudes. A notable exception is Prime Minister Robert Mugabe of Zimbabwe, who appears to be determined to swim against this changing tide, while still accepting the democratic constraint of observing legal treaty obligations and the need for consensus. Other developments sympathetic to democratic ideas are the growing tendency to divide the role and responsibilities of the executive president and a prime minister; fewer restrictions are imposed on opposition parties in elections, and there is the offer of a more democratic choice of candidates. There is also a greater tendency to allow the growth of new political parties.

The following three categories of democratic parliamentary states observe the criteria of continuity and regularity of elections, a degree of freedom for opposition parties, and some fairness in the conduct of the elections themselves:

More Democratic	More or Less Democratic	Controlled Democracy
Botswana	Uganda	Egypt
Gambia	Tunisia	Morocco
Mauritius		
Zimbabwe (to date)		

Revolutionary Regimes

Despite all the political rhetoric, Africa has so far spawned only five revolutionary regimes, i.e., regimes that have violently destroyed the old political system and made some progress towards fundamentally restructuring social, economic, and political institutions and relations.

In Guinea, Sékou Touré used state terror to impose his own authoritarian rule, but failed in the end to create a durable, alternative society. After effectively destroying the economic, political, and social structures of the colonial regime, Angola and Mozambique are still at a relatively early stage of creating viable new institutions. Libya, under Qaddafi, has radically transformed the old monarchical system and transformed class relations, as well as establishing a new Islamic-culture value system in the country; but, how far this goes is still hard to say. Ethiopia is currently engaged in what might turn out to be the first fully structured Marxist-Leninist revolution on the continent. Swaziland is the single exception of an African country that has resorted to the monarchical institutions of premodern times.

Not all regimes that came to power by violence subsequently pursued their revolutionary methods or proclaimed objectives. For one reason or another (particular to each) the revolutionary momentum was arrested and diverted, e.g., Egypt under Nasser; Sudan before Nimeiry embarked on his new Islamicization program; Guinea-Bissau; Algeria, after the coup against Ben Bella.

Tyrannical Regimes

Strictly defined, there are no tyrannies left in Africa, since the overthrow of Amin in Uganda, Macías Nguema in Equatorial Guinea, and Bokassa in the Central African Republic. Except for Mobutu of Zaire and Nimeiry (until his overthrow) in Sudan, there have been no other leaders who can accurately be described as dictators.

Future of the Democratic Process in Africa

Africa's postindependence political institutions have been shaped largely by five major preoccupations of the postcolonial regimes: maintaining and consolidating the power of the ruling party; defending the unity of the nascent nation-state against fissiparous tribal and/or regional forces; safeguarding borders; promoting rapid economic and social development; lessening economic and political dependence on the former colonial powers.

These concerns still remain at the top of the agenda of most present-day African governments; but, there is now a much greater preoccupation with economic development, particularly in the rural sector. The political system throughout the continent is still characterized by fairly rapid changes in state institutions. Virtually none of the states has yet reached the stage where it is possible to define their political systems in terms of permanent state institutions. Experimentation in constitution-making remains the order of the day, reflecting the frequent failure of earlier institutional reforms to overcome the problems for which they were designed.

The political debate over appropriate structures to achieve stable government and economic growth remains a lively feature of most African societies. This debate revolves largely around three cardinal issues: the need to establish and defend basic freedoms and human rights; the nature of democracy in Africa; and how to achieve a better balance between the demands of an expanding modern economic sector and its modernizing elite and the demands of the peasant rural economy. There is a much greater readiness than in the past to question the central assumptions underlying the imperative need for, and the efficacy of, the single-party state.

The current African debate reflects fairly general agreement that, while Western institutions and forms of government are not relevant to the conditions of evolving nation-states, the principles and aspirations of democracy are universal and not peculiarly Western.

It is possible to extrapolate from contemporary African political statements a fairly general consensus about the requirements of a modern democratic society:

1. A form of representative government that allows for participation of all adult citizens.

2. A system of accountability by the elected representatives to the electorate; this requires regular elections, a method of nominating candidates for parliament through the popular choice of voters, full voting rights for all, and freedom to exercise the vote in secret.

3. Accountability by the elected government to the elected representatives through a parliamentary institution.

4. Accountability by the president and/or prime minister to a cabinet of ministers and to a parliament.

5. Accountability within political parties to their members.

6. Checks and balances between state institutions.

7. Separation of functions between the executive, the legislature, and the judiciary.

Although the major emphasis in the political debate is placed on the question of institutions, there is also a growing tendency to focus on the ideological aspects of democracy. Ideology is held to be especially important in nascent democratic political societies because of the importance of establishing aspirational goals for the evolving political culture, and of providing criteria by which to judge leaders—not just the politicians, but also others in responsible positions. Insistence on observing such criteria is held to be crucial to the promotion of democratic thought and practice. President Julius Nyerere has defined democracy as a "habit," which, like all habits, takes years to form. Thus, he argues, it is necessary to lay down rules of what is acceptable and what is reprehensible, which, in time, will produce an etiquette of democratic behavior, provided that the leadership itself sets a consistent example of such behavior. This concern over establishing rules of public behavior is reflected in the growing practice of drawing up codes of conduct. Even though these are not generally applied, at least they establish criteria which make it possible (and legitimate) to criticize the behavior of those in responsible positions.

The creation of single-party states in Africa is generally justified on three different grounds: that the multiparty system encourages tribal, sectional, or regional parties, which impede the process of national integration; that it is necessary for maintaining political stability, which is a prerequisite for sound economic development; and, that it reflects the traditional African pattern of decision-making by consensus. How valid are these three assumptions?

It is unarguably true that in multiparty states opposition political parties frequently resort to exploiting tribal or regional grievances to build up electoral support; but, it is also true that in single-party states the ruling party has used its power to promote the interests of particular tribes at the expense of others. Nor is there much evidence to support the claim that the single-party state has been more successful than multiparty states in promoting national unity. Nigeria is an outstanding example of a country where the process of national integration has made progress under a multiparty federal constitution, even though the party system has been disrupted for periods by military rule. Tanzania, on the other hand, is an example of a single-party state where tribal politics have played only a very minor role. But, then again, there is no evidence to show that, since becoming a single-party state, Kenya has made any more progress towards ending the alienation of the Luo—the second largest community in the country—than when it was still a multiparty state.

The second argument—that the single-party state helps to create political stability—is hard to sustain. One has only to look at the political instability in many of the single-party states to see that they are not more stable than the surviving multiparty states. Nor have the single-party states been significantly more successful than the multiparty states in promoting economic development. The case against those who seek to justify strong, even authoritarian, regimes in Africa as being necessary for political stability and economic development has been forcibly stated by Hilary Ng'weno, the editor in chief of the *Weekly Review* of Nairobi:

> This is no time for niceties of parliamentary democracy in Africa, we are told, and those who tell us so are not confined to leaders of repressive African regimes. We hear the same view from Western commentators and from international-aid donors whose emphasis is for the so-called 'basic needs' approach. Governments in Africa are judged these days not on the basis of the status of human rights and individual liberties that they accord their citizens, but on the economic well-being that they can assure their people.
>
> Just how far this criterion is removed from the question of democracy can be seen by the fact that it would place South Africa—with its abhorrent record of human rights—at the top of the scale of acceptability. Black African leaders as well as their sympathizers abroad often say that it really makes no difference what government is in power as long as the people benefit materially. From this kind of view it is only a short step to the dangerous prescription that what Africa needs is a system of benevolent dictators. These dictators, so the argument goes, should be free to order

affairs in their countries in such a way that material well-being can be secured. Then, and only then, should the people of Africa worry about such luxuries as human rights and individual liberties.

The trouble with such views, whether expressed by African leaders or by foreigners, is that they are blatantly paternalistic. Whereas the rest of mankind will not settle for less than economic well-being and individual liberty, the African people are expected to seek no more than material wealth. This, of course, is not the way the people of Africa—as opposed to their leaders—see things today. Time and again they have shown, in South Africa as well as in other areas of the continent—that their idea of democracy goes far beyond the desire to be materially well off.[1]

The third argument—that traditional African societies operated through a system of consensus—is a distorting generalization. An examination of historical evidence shows that premodern African societies were governed under a multiplicity of political systems, of which the practice of decision-making by consensus was only one type and, possibly, the least numerous. Besides, consensus was practiced mainly by small, homogeneous communities, and not by the larger heterogeneous societies. On the other hand, a country like Botswana—which is made up of a collection of small communities, who traditionally governed themselves through the *kgotla* system of consensus—has maintained a lively multiparty system since independence. There is the additional fact that, in olden times, an option was open to a minority group that refused to agree to a consensus view: they could express their opposition by moving away to new lands, where they were able to pursue their own ideas and way of life; in modern Africa this form of "voting by one's feet" is no longer practical.

Beyond all these arguments lies one inescapable reality: the existence of organized opposition political forces in every country in the continent. Despite every effort by the ruling parties of single-party states to eliminate them, opposition movements keep alive and some even manage to flourish.

One incontestable accomplishment of single-party states is that they spawn as much organized opposition as can be found in any of the multiparty states. The only difference is that in the latter they are, mostly, formally recognized whereas; in the former, they exist "informally"—either in exile or as clandestine movements.

At the first opportunity presenting itself, the sub rosa political parties sprout forth like flowers after rain in the Kalahari desert. When, after a decade of single-party rule in Senegal, President Diouf finally lifted the ban on all political parties (Senghor having only partially lifted the ban), no fewer than seventeen active parties appeared in the political arena, including seven different brands of Marxist parties. When the dictatorship of "Emperor" Bokassa was ended in 1979, nine political parties lined up to offer themselves for the new parliamentary elections. In Sudan, after the overthrow of General Nimeiry in early 1985, a dozen political parties stepped into the arena—most of them having maintained active organizations despite seventeen years of single-party and, latterly, dictatorial rule.

Needless to say, by no means all the opposition parties are themselves likely to behave more democratically than those they seek to supplant; but the experience of living under nondemocratic systems does appear to have strengthened the democratic spirit among many African political leaders, while, at all levels of African society, there is evidence of support for liberalizing the political system, and, above all, for greater protection of human rights.

The turbulence and diversity of political ideas and the numerous movements of dissent in the continent constitute possibly the most striking evidence that democracy in Africa (in the sense of multiparty systems) is potentially the wave of the future—in whatever form such systems finally take.

Note

1. *Newsweek,* Washington, D.C., 8 August 1984.

19

Dov Ronen

The State and Democracy in Africa

The prospects for the independence of African states was greeted with enthusiasm by African populations and with good wishes by almost everyone.[1] The attainment of independence brought pride, membership in the United Nations, and sovereign equality in the international system of states. Not accidentally, the ranks of Africanists swelled during the same period of the 1950s and 1960s, especially in the United States. Africanists set out to study and to analyze with new or renewed dedication the issues of democracy and economic development in Africa. Many among them, including this author, foresaw a road leading from African traditions to modernity—i.e., nation-building through a gradual process of integration, and the economic development of African states through foreign economic aid and assistance. Democracy and industrialization were seen by many to be just around the corner.[2]

The foreign policies of governments in industrialized countries seemed to reflect the attitude of Africanists and of other well-wishers. Bilateral and multilateral agreements for the support of development budgets and projects were signed with the governments of now-independent African states. Aid and assistance agencies were organized and private investment was encouraged.[3]

Although much positive has been accomplished in the more than two decades since the late 1950s, not all of the dreams for Africa have been fulfilled. First, the pan-African dream of an all-African unity, an idea that was born in the late nineteenth century and became a fledgling movement in the first half of the twentieth century, fell victim to nationalist state tendencies. Ghana's President Kwame Nkrumah's proposals for the political and economic unification of Africa (seconded by at least two African presidents, Sékou Touré of Guinea and Modibo Keita of Mali) were defeated by internal and external proponents of state sovereignty and interstate economic cooperation, rather than full integration, in the heat of the Cold War of the late 1950s and early 1960s. The founding of the Organization of African Unity

(OAU) in 1963 was no more than the creation of an edifice to the dream implied by name of the organization. In actuality, the OAU was a commitment to the existing African state system, since the inviolability of state borders was guaranteed in the organization's charter. Each independent African state remained separate and, at least on paper, politically and economically sovereign.

The coups d'etat in the early 1960s (the first occurring the same year the OAU was founded), followed by additional ones later in the same and subsequent decades, were probably the earliest explicit evidence that the projected state- and nation-building were troubled.[4] By the late 1960s, the planned economic takeoff had been aborted in many African states, and prospects for it in other states seemed more and more dim. It would be foolish to ignore that today many observers tend to view with equanimity the sudden takeover of a government by a handful of soldiers in one state, a fragile civilian regime maintained by repression in another, and the uncertainty of political continuity in most. "Political instability" and "economic poverty" in Africa confuse observers, frustrate foreign policy makers, disturb potential investors, keep away well-trained Africans, alienate segments of African populations, and confound scholars. Relative to the political situation in the industrialized countries, Africa is considered by many abroad to be unstable or potentially so. Whether "political instability" is or is not the most appropriate label to describe the actual *situation* in African states, this term and its connotations seem to reflect accurately the *views* of many outside observers. Their perception of Africa as politically "unstable" is, unfortunately, responsible for their apathy towards Africa.

Why have hopes and projections for economic development and democracy failed to the extent that they have? Why has the decade of hope of the late 1950s and early 1960s been followed, in the eyes of many observers (a view held, as well, by vast segments of African populations) by over a decade of frustration? If explanations are to be found, what can be done to reverse this trend?

In Search of Explanations

Assessments of the causes of the present political and economic failures in African states reflect a range of perspectives. One perspective views failures in both the political and the economic spheres as the deep and lasting effects of colonial rule, despite the arduous efforts by African leaders and populations to overcome this past.[5] Such an assessment can hardly be questioned, for the fact is that colonial powers did carve up Africa, did divide ethnic groups by artificial international boundaries, did favor one ethnic group over others, and did support one set of elites and not others. Further, they did channel local economies to meet the needs of European metropoles, and would not or could not work hard enough to bring about industrialization in their colonies. Although the record of one colonial power differs from another in the particulars, the many negative effects of colonial rule on political and economic development are present everywhere on the continent.

Possibly the most commonly shared Western public attitude toward the present situation in Africa is that "political instability" is an inconvenient, but perhaps inescapable side effect of the birth of all states, nations, and economies. The holders of this view maintain that, regardless of the detrimental colonial legacy in Africa, development and modernization cannot be achieved easily; the process, because of the tasks involved, is understandably lengthy. It has taken European and other industrialized countries hundreds of years to attain their present levels of political stability, of democracy, and of economic development. The same tasks in Africa may also take long years. Hence, according to the proponents of this view, the attainment of democracy and of economic development requires time and patience.[6]

The Marxist, pseudo-Marxist, and the so-called dependency-school perspectives argue that much of Africa's problems are due to the continent's being in the midst of a dialectic change of economic relations, as well as to imperialist manipulations of African elites, to the exploitation and expropriation of economic resources, and to the dependence of the economies of African states on the capitalist-controlled world market.[7] Here, too (for the proponents of these views at least), the facts speak for themselves. African economies are part of the international economic system, which is dominated by a world market based on the profit motive. The poor African states' economies are at a clear disadvantage, which has dire implications for both their political independence and economic development.

One may add many more assessments of modernization and development in Africa, especially if one allows for nuances among individual observers. The present difficulties may be rightly blamed on colonialism, as well as on wrong policies, weakness or absence of state institutions, on corruption of politicians, on insufficiency (or misallocation) of foreign aid and assistance, on too much (or too little) private enterprise, on (wrong) ideological commitments, and/or on a host of other factors. The validity of each of these arguments is amply demonstrated by their proponents.[8] The remedies proposed vary correspondingly: end the negative effects of colonial dependence by strengthening government institutions; end corruption; provide more and better administered foreign aid and assistance; increase (or reduce) private enterprise; change ideological commitments; pursue better economic policies; and so on. The recommendations of the World Bank on the one hand, as well as radical ideologies on the other, provide interesting evidence as to the variety of perspectives involved.[9]

In this chapter still another argument will be presented. First, I wish to preface it with a few remarks. The exclusive focus of this paper is democracy and the state. The crucial factor of economic development is unaddressed, not because economic development is unimportant, nor because it is irrelevant to democracy, but because democracy must be a goal in its own right. In my opinion, economic development cannot anywhere guarantee the implementation of democracy, and therefore both democracy and economic development must be concurrent goals. Furthermore, there will be no attempt here to offer comprehensive solutions; rather, I shall propose for discussion a rather unconventional argument for democracy. I shall try to demonstrate that what has failed or is failing in Africa, is not democracy, but rather many African *states*. The failure of the state has adversely affected democracy. I propose that the challenge today is not to fit democracy to African state, but to fit African state to democracy.

In order to accomplish this self-appointed task, I will have to deviate from what I think is a conventional approach to the subject. In any case, first democracy and then the state will be examined separately, and some tentative conclusions concerning Africa's future will be presented.

Democracy

Democracy is a Greek word which means "people's rule" or "rule by [the] people." The various scholarly definitions of the word have not been able to provide a better meaning. Accordingly, scholars have generally tried to explain or to define "democracy" by describing its *realization* or its *institutionalization*. Consequently, definitions have tended to emphasize representation and the process of choice and accountability, which include political parties, elections, public opinion, and so forth.[10]

If one returns to the *meaning* of democracy—"rule by [the] people"—two questions remain: what does "rule" mean, and who are "[the] people?" Definitions describing the *realization* of democracy have solved these issues by considering the *citizens* of a state to be "the people," and accountable elected representatives to constitute "rule." A more direct answer to the questions posed regarding "people" and "rule" was provided by Woodrow Wilson, the post-World War I champion of self-determination. For Wilson, the notion of self-determination (the very same notion that has survived to this day) was "entirely the corollary of democratic theory."[11] Wilson was a proponent of *democracy*, which he wished to offer and export to post-World War I Europe. For Wilson, democracy was self-determination. What Wilson apparently intended at the time was to rebuff and to counter Lenin's notion of self-determination, which had been propagated by Lenin both before and after the Bolshevik Revolution of 1917.

However, President Wilson never gave a comprehensive statement on self-determination either in his speeches or in his writings; he merely mentioned the term or alluded to it. In his "Message to Russia" of May 16, 1917, he wrote "We are fighting for the liberty, the self-government and the undictated development of all peoples. . . . [R]eadjustments after the war must follow a principle and the principle is plain. No people must be forced under sovereignty under which it does not wish to live."[12]

Article III of President Wilson's first draft of the Covenant of the League of Nations provides even greater insights into his intentions: "The Contracting Powers unite in guaranteeing . . . territorial readjustments . . . as may in the future become necessary by reason of changes in the present social conditions and aspirations or present social and political relationships, pursuant to the principle of self-determination."[13]

Wilson did not equate self-determination with sovereign statehood. Nor did the League of Nations equate the two; the Peace Conference, embracing the principle of Wilsonian self-determination that stemmed from the notion of democracy, offered protection to minorities, and advocated autonomy and self-rule for nationalities. This notion of self-determination aimed not only at ending Ottoman and Hapsburg colonization of peoples, but also aimed at the breaking up of these colonial entities. The mandate system introduced by the League was *not* intended to institutionalize territories whose boundaries had been formed by the occupying empires, but to prepare peoples for self-government. This Wilsonian notion, as adopted by the League, expressed the meaning and the essence of democracy. This referred to the liberation of peoples, not of territories; it reached out to the peoples over the heads of their governments; and, it championed human rights. Wilson and the League did not refer to parliamentary systems, elections, or multiparty systems in the context of self-determination; they referred to immediate or future liberation, freedom, and self-rule, which is self-determination (and, therefore, democracy). Although the League of Nations failed in translating this principle into action everywhere—especially in the case of Ethiopia—Wilsonian self-determination was not actually abandoned until the Second World War.

After the Second World War, a new approach was adopted; self-determination and democracy were separated. Self-determination has come to mean independent statehood; democracy has come to connote representative institutions, elected officials, political parties, and elections. The change was probably not accidental. Unlike after the First World War, self-determination also referred to Asians and Africans, not just to European peoples. Consequently, after World War II, the issue was *the belated recognition of the capacity, of the readiness of all peoples, including Asians and Africans, for self-rule.* Self-determination meant decolonization and the transfer of rule in Asia and in Africa to indigenous leaders, because African and Asian peoples were now deemed "ready." After World War I the "self" that was to determine itself was a nationality; after World War II the "self" was a decolonized territory that had been demarcated by colonial powers or, at best, was an amalgam of Africans and Asians *within* such boundaries. Self-determination implied sovereignty for the formerly colonized part of humanity; and, it came to mean not so much *self*-rule as rule *not by others*. It was thus, above all, separated and, in reality, virtually preempted from the democratic content that Wilson had attached to it—namely, territorial adjustments, protection of ethnic minorities, and, save in trust territories, referenda.

Democracy, separated from the idea of self-determination, after World War II, came to mean a method of rule, which was a clear alternative to Nazi, to fascist, and, later, to communist rule. Already in 1941, the Atlantic Charter referred to the rights of peoples to choose the form of government under which to live. Unlike Wilson, Roosevelt, and Churchill did not fight against Lenin's self-determination, but fought against Hitler's fascism. After World War II, and with the rise of the Cold War, democratic institutions and processes gained added importance vis-à-vis the Soviet system.

Although Africans fought for and eventually attained the right of self-determination, this did not lead to national self-determination. In Africa the right of nations to self-determination meant the right of a territorially-bounded plurality of peoples to it. After World War II, the demarcating lines on the map of Africa changed little; the only change was of title holders from Europeans to Africans. For the latter, however, the exercise of the right to self-determination did not break up socioculturally heterogeneous, or plural, entities.[14] African nationalists, turning their backs on pan-Africanism, contended over the inherited colonial boundaries. The civilian regimes that emerged after independence were faced with the challenge of ethnic or national heterogeneity. Ethnic conflicts were not postponed for long; they erupted in Nigeria, in the Congo, Dahomey (Benin), Cameroon, Sudan, Rwanda, Burundi, Uganda, and elsewhere as or under the guises of military coups, civil wars, "ethnic unrests," and actions that came close to genocide.[15]

The State

Unlike democracy, the word "state" cannot be translated to provide a meaning. At best, one might find the origin of the word "state" in the word "estate," which probably dates back to the image of a feudal holding. Since the meaning of the word itself is not clear, a plethora of definitions have been offered to explain what "state" means. In the absence of a consensus for a definition (or possibly, in spite of it), the word "state" both in speech and in writing is used interchangeably with "government" (and "administration" or "bureaucracy" in a wider sense), as well as interchangeably with "nation" and in reference to a territorial entity or a polity. Thus the state, as government, intervenes, collects taxes, is "on our back." The state, as a nation, is a member in the international community of states. As a territorial entity or as a polity, the state is a legal, sovereign entity. The state (the nation?) is said to go to war; but, the state (the government?) nationalizes banks and industries. Although African states are often said to be unstable, it is their governments that actually are.[16]

Another problem, mentioned above, is related to equating self-determination with sovereign statehood. If the exercising of self-determination in Africa means the sovereign existence of Nigeria, Ethiopia, Chad, or scores of other states *in their inherited boundaries,* then altering the boundaries of these entities, for whatever purpose, is to affect negatively the territorial integrity of these states—their sovereignty. Furthermore, if the boundaries of a state are not only defined by a nation but also define the nation, then national integration is not only useful for and instrumental to development, but it is also the imperative for sovereignty. If national integration is imperative, then the centralization of political power may be indispensable to its attainment.

I submit that self-determination as sovereign independence in Africa and elsewhere has not only *not meant* democracy, but that it has become the counterforce to democracy. This is because efforts to institutionalize democracy (i.e., political parties, elections, electoral competition for office, etc.) have awakened, strengthened, and even created ethnic or ethnonational identities, and thus have, in reality, countered the efforts of centralized power to integrate, unify, institutionalize, and define the nation. In this confrontation true "democracy" (civilian government "by the people") has been the loser in many cases.

Governments, whether elected or not, are neither nations, territories, nor states. Rather, a government is a group of people having the power, legitimate or not, to govern *within* the state, which in turn consists of both a demarcated territory and a population. The word "state" should not be used for both the governing and the governed. As illustrated below, it should be used *either* for the government or for the territory and population, or else the word "state" should not be used at all.

This illustration is not only applicable to Africa, but to any unitary (i.e., nonfederal, not confederal) entity anywhere. Furthermore, it should be applicable to any regime, system, or type of government. The illustration merely depicts any centralized political entity as an interactive relationship between two analytically, as well as practically, separable spheres. One may conceive of this interactive relationship as the challenge of one sphere ("the state") to which the other sphere ("regime") responds, thus initiating a dynamic interaction. It may be noted that this illustration implies that virtually any so-called "state activity," be it internal or external, political or economic, is a function of this interaction. For example, in reaction to the challenge of scarcity of resources, the government may introduce forced labor, or encourage technological innovations, or encourage foreign trade, etc. Similarly, in reaction to the challenge of plurality, the government might re-

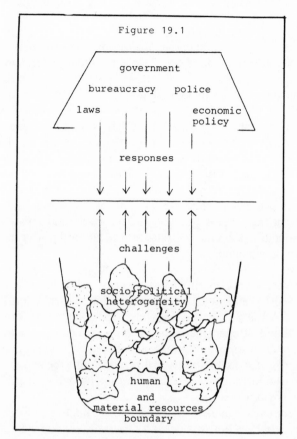

Figure 19.1

spond by exterminating part of the population, or by encouraging representation, or by expelling part of the population.

At independence, most colonial boundaries in Africa remained intact;
these boundaries enclosed a wide variety of ethnic groups, religions, and
political cultures, as well as limited human and material resources. The assumption that colonial rule eliminated ethnic diversity and indigenous cultures is largely a myth; although colonial rule repressed some ethnic groups,
it did promote others. It maintained a colonial government that used force,
intimidation, and cooptation of elites into the colonial culture. Colonial rule
later allowed the functioning of organizations and even of political parties
under tight control—elections of representatives under colonial rule produced political actors under the tight reign of colonial governors. Democratic institutions in Africa under colonial rule were a staged show; the actors
were picked from the community, the directors were European, and the
applauding audience was world public opinion. Police, as ushers at the
doors, were there to maintain order.

When the colonial rulers departed, the expectation of the onlooking
world was that the iron hand of the police would not be used again since the

government was no longer foreign. The expectation was that the theatrical democratic institutions would become real-life institutions, providing law and order themselves. There were also expectations that the ethnically and culturally heterogeneous population would gradually become a nation, and that all would participate in real-life democracy. The expectation was that democracy (as democratic government, representation, and party system) could be adapted to function in the sovereign state. This was not realized because the inherited frameworks of populations and of boundaries (or, in the customary vocabulary, the "state") were a dead end for democracy in Africa.

The State of Democracy in Africa

In Europe, the unleashed spirit of the right to self-determination had created (or "recreated") Hungarians, Serbs, Bulgarians, Germans, and many others. The very same spirit left the colonial, pre-World War II borders practically intact. The French Revolution had been followed by at least a partial *national* self-determination in Europe; World War II was followed by *state* self-determination in Africa.[17] In the eyes of educated Africans and non-Africans, nations were to be built from the remnants of "tribes," deemed to be leftovers of the antiquated past. Later on, even the word "tribe" was eliminated from the vocabulary because of its connotations of primitiveness and social retardation. In its stead the concept of "ethnic group" was introduced, not as a new term for nation or nationality, but as a new phrase meaning an amorphous cultural heritage.

The ethnic factor in African politics has often been dismissed, overlooked, or considered secondary by both African and non-African observers because the ethnic factor has been considered degrading.[18] Furthermore, in the context of the East-West confrontation, continuing schisms and conflicts have tended to be presented as ideological; one political force is seen (and thus presented) as pro-Western and the other as pro-communist.[19] Generally, the American, non-Marxist social scientist's perspective tends to see schisms and conflicts in terms of regional and sectional interests or as occurring between modernizing and traditional forces, while the "leftist" perspective tends to explain these in terms of class confrontation. Rarely is the ethnic factor totally dismissed, as it hardly can be, but it is usually presented as an undertone, an auxiliary element, or a side effect of conflicts. In light of the conventional image of the damage inflicted by colonial rule on African societies and of the conventional view of the impact of postindependence modernization on indigenous African systems, ethnicity is now conceived of as little more than just folklore and an exploitable tool in the hands of ambitious politicians, who promise its integration into a "national" body. Internal conflict in African states has been "modernized." It is presented as occurring between military men and civilians, among subregional interest groups, or, due to the present international atmosphere, as occurring between pro-Western and anti-Western, pro-communist elements.

The notion that ethnic groups in Africa and elsewhere are historical remnants is correct. However, the notion that they are no more than dispensable or malleable leftovers of primitiveness from a discardable past is a misconception. Every African and Africanist is keenly aware of the fact that many traditional customs, roles, and institutions still exist, and that many traditional, so-called "subsistence" economies (which include not only agricultural production, but also marketing and interregional trade) are still very much alive and provide livelihood for many. Furthermore, they know very well that ethnic groups in Africa are localized, and that each group lives (as did its ancestors, often for centuries) in a specific region of a now independent state—the same as nations or nationalities in Europe and in Asia. The overwhelming majority of African town dwellers *are* kinsmen and full-fledged members of various ethnic groups, with respective rights and obligations. Most conflicts in African states, whether political or armed ones, could not have reached their high intensity without the underlying ethnic factor. All these internal conflicts are basically ethnic conflicts; interests and ideologies are added factors and are often no more than a thin veneer.

In the eyes of contemporaries, African or not, the above statements are almost blasphemy when judged from the Western perspective, which considers the sovereign state to be the pinnacle, or at least a higher stage, of societal evolution. Even the Marxist conception of the state as an instrument of repression in the hands of a ruling class considers the changing African nation-state to be a higher stage of evolution than its primitive societal forms. In the Marxist view, the problems within the state can be solved only by the withering away of the state. Western social science maintains the exact opposite: problems within the state may only be solved by "democratizing" government-population relations. In the Western view there are two polarities, the stateless tribe and the nation-state. Once the nation-state emerges (as it did first in Europe, and then in Africa), the notion of the tribe disappears from the Western perspective and state-society relations replace tribal relations. The ethnic factor in modern times has been misunderstood or overlooked. One may note for example that secessionist movements and tendencies and ethnic movements in Europe in the 1960s and 1970s were looked at with genuine bewilderment. In the twentieth century, or at least since World War One, the existence of the nation-state was a "fact" taken for granted in Europe. It is evident, however, that the quest for personal freedom through *national* self-determination was merely dormant for some time in between the wars, and was dormant again, briefly, after the Second World War.

Ethnicity has continued to be a major factor also in African social and political life since independence. It is an ongoing manifestation of the human quest for self-determination and for democracy, and is a continuous counterforce to political centralization, which in many African states has led to arbitrary rule. Most African civilian leaders have little chance of attaining democracy because government-population relations in politically centralized entities can, only with great difficulty, handle ethnic diversity (heterogeneity) by democratic means. If Africans, and outside observers, keep regarding inherited boundaries as untouchable and national integration by centralized governments sancrosanct, or wait, as Marxists do, for the withering away of the state, political instability and economic poverty will likely continue to prevail in most parts of the African continent. Instead of bending human beings to fit the framework of the state, the frameworks of states in Africa ought to be fitted to human beings. The search for the key that could open the gates of democracy (and of economic development) should be concentrated on the unexplored area of *structural change* in and of states.

The Future of Democracy in Africa

All independent African states, at their outset, had civilian, secular, central governments. Their officials held a new type of authority and power that had no roots (and could not have roots) in the societal values and norms of all ethnic groups under their control. Central governments thus became entities in themselves, detached from the popular base with which they were supposed to interact. Since the state was ethnically heterogeneous, all ethnic groups not having a representative in the central government—especially a president—not only felt as though they were left without political leadership of their own. They also felt that they were ruled by the ethnic group that did have representatives (particularly a president) in the central government. Large groups of the population thus considered the central government to be equivalent to foreign rule. In a framework where the civilian central government is a small political island, any group of armed soldiers could easily eliminate the government, especially if they have the not so tacit good wishes of ethnic groups not represented in that government.

True, several "founding fathers" are still in power, and they do maintain a modicum of stability.[20] But it must be admitted that the peaceful transfer of power to their eventual successors is one of the major worries of both inside and outside observers. Early on, these founding fathers skillfully eliminated their political rivals, and have successfully kept others in check. Their respective populations thus tolerate and acquiesce in the rule of these presidents as long as he lives, especially since some benefits *do* trickle all the way down through the traditional channels of kinship ties, often through the use of "ethnic arithmetic." Some regimes, such as the one in Zaire, have lasted long without having had a founding father as president. This has been possible in Zaire because the regime, which started as a military one, has largely become an old European type of absolutist regime.[21] It is also true that, in some cases, political power has been peacefully transferred. The most notable examples are the governments of Kenya and, most recently, Tanzania and Senegal. However, these cases are notable exceptions, and their ultimate outcomes still remain to be seen.[22]

But the fact remains: Democracy has not failed in Africa. The making of democratic institutions and processes has failed in many of the forty-odd politically centralized, socioculturally heterogeneous, economically poor entities existing within inherited colonial boundaries. Democracy *as a specific political machinery of institutions, processes, and roles* has failed. In the ethnically heterogeneous African polities, all of which, save Nigeria, are unitary (i.e., politically centralized) the democratic process in the given frameworks has led to conflict and tensions, and often has resulted in military coups, single-party or no party systems, and in political repression. Democracy in the Wilsonian sense of self-rule and self-determination has yet to be tried in Africa. The implementation of Wilsonian democracy may require the decentralization of political power and the institutionalization of self-rule for nationalities that compose existing populations. It may thus require the transformation of unitary states into federal, confederal, or cantonal systems.

The Wilsonian principle truly expresses the meaning of democracy, for it is peoples' rule. People are members of ethnic, cultural, or linguistic groups. Human beings in these groups feel distinct from other groups because they sense they have in common *indigenously evolved* norms of conduct and of behavior, shared historical memories, rituals, language, and social customs. These legacies, more often than not, are much more than folkloric remnants, and such homogeneous communities, because of their internal cohesiveness, are capable of autonomous self-rule within a wider federated or confederated framework.

Anthropologists tell us that there are anywhere from a few dozen to hundreds of ethnic groups in most independent African states. Consequently, autonomy for each ethnic group would be impractical. True, but there are variations in the significance, size, and level of cultural distinction of each ethnic group, and many ethnic groups are so closely related through cultural and historical ties that their sociopolitical uniqueness has become minimal. However, there is no reason not to constitute several levels of flexible federal systems, where appropriate and desired by the prospective participants, so that any number of ethnic groups could have a degree of autonomy within another autonomous entity. The special arrangements may differ from case to case, as dictated by the principle of self-determination for all and as indicated by the will of the people. This should be the subject for systematic study, for no clear-cut evidence has been found to support the view that ethnic diversity is in itself the cause of political instability.

Ethnic diversity is not the cause of political instability in Africa or anywhere else. The utilization and manipulation of ethnic identities appears to be the single most important factor in political instability. This occurs when ethnic groups are mobilized by political leaders struggling to gain the *centralized* political power. If power were to be decentralized, the struggle for power would be bound to decline, and, with it, the intensity of political instability.

Towards Democracy in Africa

No regime morally acceptable to either the African people or the international community can for long maintain political unity, shared norms of conduct, or a national oneness if the government remains politically centralized. Regime or leadership changes, however ideologically suitable they may appear at the outset, will not suffice. It is time to recognize and accept the long-existing ethnic pressures for *structural changes* in and of states. Such structural changes are not sufficient in and of themselves in most cases, but these changes are necessary steps for attaining more democratic and humane polities.

The specific forms of such structural changes must vary from case to case. They may range from mere administrative decentralization to full internal federal arrangements—even secession in some rare cases. The specifics should be the subject of open-minded research, discussion, and examination of various existing theoretical and actual models. The widely held view, so emphatically propounded by political leaders in power, that the *idea* of secession (which is not advanced here) would open Pandora's box cannot be supported by historical evidence. Recent history has not shown that the idea of secession is contagious, only that the quest for self-determination and, hence, for democracy, is.

Since independence and before, African leaders by and large have been committed to democracy and economic development; African populations have always aspired to freedom and to economic well-being just like everyone else. African civilian and military leaders are unlikely to be more power-hungry or potentially more corruptible than other leaders elsewhere; the populations are unlikely to aspire less for freedom and for the amenities of life than do other human beings. Africans do not lend themselves more easily to mobilization against those who are perceived to be the sources of their discontentment than do other people. Although ethnicity is more often used in Africa than elsewhere, it is not because Africans are more "ethnic" than other human beings, but because ethnicity has played a more dominant part in the African colonial experience than in other places in the world.

Democracy is attainable in Africa, as it is everywhere, if it is accepted to mean, as it should, self-rule and self-determination.

Notes

1. The reference here and throughout is to sub-Saharan Africa, excluding South Africa.

2. This attitude is reflected in many of the studies published in the United States in the 1950s, and, to an extent, in the 1960s. *See* for example, David Apter, *The Gold Coast in Transition* (Princeton: Princeton University Press, 1955); Edward Shils, "Political Development in the New States," *Comparative Studies in Society and History* 2, no. 4 (June 1960); my own views were expressed in *Dahomey, Between Tradition and Modernity* (Ithaca: Cornell University Press, 1975).

3. For an assessment *see* Robert A. Packenham, *Liberal America and the Third World* (Princeton: Princeton University Press, 1973).

4. For an assessment of military coups see Samuel Decalo, *Coups and Army Rule in Africa; Studies in Military Style* (New Haven: Yale University Press, 1976).

5. The most explicit view is expressed in Walter Rodney, *How Europe Underdeveloped Africa?* (Washington D.C.: Howard University Press, 1972, 1981).

6. This public view may also be found at least as an underlining *leitmotif,* which in turn is probably anchored in the idea of progress. The idea of progress, whatever its origins may be, is an entirely Western (European) notion. For a modern-day interpretation of progress see Robert Nisbet, *History of the Idea of Progress* (Basic Books, 1980).

7. The arguments in the following books quite closely reflect this attitude: Claude Ake, *A Political Economy of Africa* (Longman, 1981); Samin Amin, *Unequal Development: An Essay on the Social Formations of Peripheral Capitalism* (New York, 1976); G. Arrighi and J. Saul, eds., *Essays in the Political Economy of Africa* (New York, 1973).

8. For a recent, perceptive assessment see Crawford Young, *Ideology and Development in Africa* (New Haven: Yale University Press, 1982).

9. World Bank, *Toward Sustained Development in Sub-Saharan Africa* (Washington D.C.: World Bank, 1984).

10. It does not mean, of course, that no other types of definitions of democracy exist. My argument is that there is an overwhelming tendency to use an *empirical* explanation rather than a theoretical one. For example, in a major textbook on American government, democracy is examined as a process and as institutions throughout the book, without providing a definition of the term. See Kenneth Prewitt and Sidney Verba, *An Introduction to American Government* (Harper and Row, 1974).

11. Alfred Cobban, *The Nation-state and National Self-determination* (New York: Thomas Crowell, 1945, 1969), 63.

12. Ray Stannard Baker and William E. Dodd, eds., *War and Peace: Presidential Messages, Addresses and Public Papers (1917–1924) of Woodrow Wilson* (New York: Harpers and Brothers, 1927), vol. 1, 50–51.

13. Rigo Sureda, *The Evolution of the Right to Self-determination: A Study of*

United Nations Practice (Leiden: A. W. Sijthoff, 1973), 28.

14. Plurality and heterogeneity are used here interchangeably. Both are taken to be the opposite of an indigenously evolved sociocultural homogeneity.

15. *See* Donald Rothchild and Victor Olorunsola, eds., *State Versus Ethnic Claims: African Policy Dilemmas* (Westview Press, 1983).

16. After several years of neglect, the term "state" is back into Africanist vocabulary and under their focus. Conferences are organized on the "state"; panels in conferences, articles and books are devoted to it. *See* for example, footnote fifteen; Thomas M. Callaghy, *The State-Society Struggle: Zaire in Comparative Perspective* (New York: Columbia University Press, 1984); John Lansdale, "States and Social Processes in Africa: A Historiographical Survey," *African Studies Review,* 24, 2/3 (1981); Larry Diamond, "Class, Ethnicity and the Democratic State: Nigeria 1950–1966," *Comparative Studies in Society and History,* 25, 3 (1983).

17. For an excellent analysis *see* Cobban, *Nation-state.*

18. *See* for example Rodney, *How Europe,* 227ff.

19. *viz.* recent (November 1985–February 1986) discussions in U.S. government circles concerning aid to UNITA in Angola. Most participants in the discussion have little or no knowledge of African realities, which in turn facilitates the casting of the issue exclusively into the ideological/strategic context; those knowledgeable about African realities and the history of the Angolan conflict tend to underemphasize the ethnic factor.

20. Kenneth Kaunda in Zambia, Félix Houphouet-Boigny in the Ivory Coast, and Hastings Banda in Malawi.

21. *See* Callaghy, *State-Society Struggle.*

22. It does *not* mean that these transfers will surely not succeed. It only means that it is too early to judge them as successes. In Senegal, Tanzania, and Sierra Leone, the former presidents are alive and at least socially active in the country, and, in the eyes of the respective citizenry, are part of the political scene. Only in Kenya is the former president no longer alive.

Contributors

Elliott Abrams

Mr. Abrams is the U.S. State Department's Assistant Secretary for Inter-American Affairs. He is also an attorney who has practiced in New York and Washington, D.C. In 1975, he worked for the U.S. Senate as assistant counsel to the U.S. Senate Permanent Committee on Investigations. He was special counsel to Senator Daniel P. Moynihan in 1977, and, from January 1978 until May 1979, served as Senator Moynihan's chief of staff. In January 1981, Mr. Abrams was named Assistant Secretary of State in the Bureau of International Organization Affairs. In December 1981, he was sworn in as Assistant Secretary of State for Human Rights and Humanitarian Affairs. Mr. Abrams is the author of numerous articles and appears frequently as a commentator on television news programs.

Austin Amissah

Presently a legal consultant with offices in Accra and in London, Mr. Amissah was Attorney General and Minister of Justice in Ghana from 1977 to 1979. He has at various times acted as Minister of Local Government, as legal advisor to The Economic Community of West African States (ECOWAS), and as a court of appeals judge. In 1973, Mr. Amissah was a fellow at the Woodrow Wilson International Center for Scholars in Washington, D.C. He is a member of various associations, including the British Institute of International and Comparative Law, and the United Nations Expert Group on Tax Treaties between Developed and Developing Countries. Mr. Amissah's most recent book is *The Contribution of the Courts to Government* (1981).

John A. A. Ayoade

Dr. Ayoade is currently a visiting professor in the Department of Political Science at the University of Pennsylvania, while on leave from his position as reader in Political Science at the University of Ibadan, Nigeria. In 1982 he served as Sub-Dean of the Faculty of Social Sciences at Ibadan, and was chairman of the Department of Political Science from 1982 to 84. He has published such works on Africa as: "The Administration of Development Plans in Africa," *Nigerian Journal of Economic and Social Studies* (1981); "Teaching African Politics," *Teaching Politics* (1980); and "Secession as a Redressive Mechanism in Nigerian Federalism," *Publius* (1973). In 1982, Dr. Ayoade was a Fulbright scholar at Boston University. Earlier, in 1972, he was a visiting lecturer at Williams College. He has also served as chairman of the Town Planning Authority in Oyo State, Nigeria.

Pauline H. Baker

Dr. Baker is currently a consultant with PHB Associates in Washington, D.C. She lectured in political science at the University of Lagos, Nigeria, and lived in Nigeria for eleven years. As a Rockefeller Foundation fellow she conducted research on the strategic situation in the southern Africa region, following the collapse of the Portuguese African empire. She subsequently became a staff member of the Foreign Relations Committee of the United States Senate, with specific responsibility as Staff Director of the African Affairs Subcommittee. She was a research scientist at the Battelle Memorial Institute. Dr. Baker is the author of *Urbanization and Political Change: The Politics of Lagos; Obstacles to Private Sector Activities in Africa;* and *The Economics of Nigerian Federalism.* She is coeditor of *African Armies: Force Modernization and Defense Policymaking in the Developing World* (with B. Arlinghaus, 1985).

Pathé Diagne

Dr. Diagne is Director of the Sankore Publishing House in Dakar. His fields of specialization include economics and linguistics. Dr. Diagne is currently a consultant for various international organizations, including UNIDO and UNESCO. Until 1972, he was professor of Linguistics at the University of Dakar. From 1972 to 1974, Dr. Diagne was a visiting professor at UCLA. He has published numerous works, including: *Le pouvoir politique traditionnel en Afrique occidentale* (1967); *Grammaire de Wolof moderne* (1970); *Pour l'unité ouest-africaine* (1972); *Introduction à la culture africaine*

(1978); *Europe philosophie* (1981); and *Histoire général de l'Afrique* (1981). He recently edited a volume entitled *Démocratie en Sénégal* (1983).

Ali Khalif Galaydh

Dr. Khalif Galaydh is presently a fellow at the Center for Middle Eastern Studies at Harvard University. He has held numerous ranking positions in Somalia, including Minister of Industry (1980–1982). From 1976 to 1981, he served as the Executive Chairman of the Juba Sugar Project, a $250 million development scheme, and was the General Manager of the Jowhar Sugar Enterprises from 1974 to 76. He earlier was Director General of the Somali Institute of Development Administration and Management (SIDAM). Dr. Khalif recently published "Instability in the Horn," *Harvard International Review* (1983). His research has focused on such topics as the public sector in Somalia, industrialization, and development administration.

John W. Harbeson

Dr. Harbeson is Professor of Political Science and Director of International Studies at the City College of New York. Previously, he held similar positions at the University of Wisconsin-Parkside, where he was concurrently on the faculty of the Land Tenure Center at the University of Wisconsin-Madison. Dr. Harbeson was a visiting professor at Addis Ababa University (1973–75) and at the University of Nairobi (1965–67). From 1979 to 1982, he worked for AID in the Office of Rural Development. Dr. Harbeson has published works on revolution in Ethiopia and on rural development in Africa, and is currently working on a monograph on development program management in AID. Dr. Harbeson's books include *Nation-building in Kenya: The Role of Land Reform* (1973) and *Military in African Politics* (editor, 1985).

Ilunga Kabongo

Dr. Ilunga is a Fulbright research scholar in residence at Howard University's African Studies and Research Program, and is jointly a lecturer at the School of Advanced International Studies, Johns Hopkins University. From 1974 to 1984 he was professor of Political Science and Director of the Interdisciplinary Research Center for Political Studies and Documentation at the University of Zaire, Kinshasa. Dr. Ilunga's publications include: *Crise politique: Concept et application à l'Afrique* (1965) and *Pluralisme et integration: Reflections sur la dynamique politique en Afrique noire post-coloniale* (1967).

Lansiné Kaba

Formerly professor of History and chairman of the Department of Afro-American and African Studies at the University of Minnesota, Dr. Kaba is now professor of History and director of Black Studies at the University of Illinois at Chicago. From 1981 to 1982 he was a senior Fulbright research professor at the University of Dakar. He has written extensively on African history, and, in 1975, received the Melville Herskovits Award for his book *The Wahhabiyya: Islamic Reform and Politics in French West Africa, 1945–1960* (1974). Other publications include: *Sonni Ali, empereur du Songhay, 1464–1492* (1978); *The Rise and Fall of an African State in the XVIth Century: Songhay and Its Civilization* (1984); and *L'Etat, la société et l'humanisme du Songhay* (forthcoming).

Colin Legum

Mr. Legum is editor of the *Africa Contemporary Record* and of the *Third World Report*. He is the former editor and Commonwealth correspondent of the London *Observer*. Among Mr. Legum's special interests are the Third World, particularly African independence movements. Mr. Legum is the author of numerous books including: *Pan-Africanism; After Angola: The War over Southern Africa; Vorster's Gamble in Africa;* and *Still Only the Whirlwind*. More recent works have included *The West's Crisis in Southern Africa; Africa; Reshaping the Horn* (with William Lee); and *Africa in the 1980s: A Continent in Crisis* (with Zartman, Langdon, and Mytelka). Mr. Legum is currently completing a book titled *Apartheid on the Rocks*.

David N. Magang

Mr. Magang is a member of the Parliament of Botswana where he serves on the Standing Committee on Law Reform, on the Committee on Privileges, and on the Committee on Public Accounts. A practicing attorney, he is a member of the Central Committee of the Botswana Democratic Party, and is chairman of Premet Building Botswana, Ltd. Prior to his election to Parliament, Mr. Magang served as a member of the President's Economic Opportunity Commission (1981–1982). He was also a member of the Senior State Counsel as the Register of Companies (1971–1972) and as State Counsel (1969–1971). He has recently published *A Look at Botswana's Future Economic Prospects* (1981).

Bona Malwal

Mr. Malwal is currently a senior research fellow at Columbia University's School of International Affairs. In 1976 he was elected to the Politburo of the Sudan Socialist Union, a position he held until 1982. He served as Political Supervisor of the Administration of Bahr Al Ghazal Province (1976–1978), Minister of Culture and Information (1976–78), Minister of Industry and Mining (1980), and Minister of Finance and Economic Planning, the Government of Southern Sudan (1980–1981). Following dissolution of the Government of the South in 1982, Mr. Malwal was dismissed from the Politburo, his passport was withdrawn, and he was banned from leaving the country from July 1982 to June 1984. He was arrested and held without charge or trial for eight months between May 1983 and January 1984. Mr. Malwal was editor of the *Sudan Daily,* and from 1965 to 1969, was founder and editor of the *Vigilant Newspaper.* During this time he was arrested and prosecuted. Mr. Malwal is holder of the Sudan's Order of the Nile, First Class. He is author of *People and Power in the Sudan: The Struggle for National Stability* (1981).

Davidson Nicol

Dr. Nicol is Honorary Fellow at Christ's College, Cambridge and lecturer at the Graduate School in International Relations. He is also a guest scholar at the Hoover Institute at Stanford University. From 1950 to 1968 he taught in Sierra Leone, Nigeria, Ghana, Canada, and in the United States. From 1966 to 1968, Dr. Nicol served as Vice-Chancellor of the University of Sierra Leone. In 1968 he was appointed Sierra Leone's permanent representative to the United Nations. He became his country's High Commissioner to the United Kingdom in 1971. In 1973 Dr. Nicol was appointed director of the United Nations Institute of Training and Research (UNITAR). He has also held positions as chairman of the West African Council for Medical Research and as chairman of the Sierra Leone Public Service Commission. Dr. Nicol has received many honorary degrees and awards, including his nation's Independence Medal. His most recent publications include: *Paths to Peace: The UN Security Council and Its Presidency* (editor, 1981); *Regionalism and the New International Economic Order: Studies Presented to the UNITAR-CEESTEM Club of Rome Conference at the United Nations* (with Echeverria, editors); *The UN Security Council: Towards Greater Effectiveness* (et al., 1982); and "U.S. Foreign Policy in Southern Africa: Third World Perspectives," *Journal of Modern African Studies* (December 1983).

Victor A. Olorunsola

Professor Olorunsola is chairman of the Department of Political Science at Iowa University, a position he has held since 1977. Among his recent publications have been: *State Versus Ethnic Claims: An African Policy Dilemma* (1983); *Soldiers and Power* (1977); and *Societal Reconstruction in Two African States* (1977).

Dov Ronen

Dr. Ronen is the Director of the Center for International Affairs' Africa Research Program, Harvard University. He is presently chairman of the "Ethnicity and Politics" research committee of the International Political Science Association. His publications include: *Dahomey: Between Tradition and Modernity* (1975); *The Quest for Self-determination* (1979); and *Ethnicity, Politics, and Development* (coeditor with Dennis Thompson, 1986).

Richard L. Sklar

Dr. Sklar is a professor of political science at the University of California at Los Angeles and is former president of the African Studies Association. He was a visiting Fulbright professor at the University of Zimbabwe during the summer of 1984. He has also taught at Makerere University College, Uganda (1967), the University of Zambia (1966–68), and the University of Ibadan (1963–65). Dr. Sklar was Simon Visiting Professor at the University of Manchester (1975), and a fellow at the Harry S. Truman Research Institute, Hebrew University, Jerusalem (1979). He has published numerous works on African politics, including *Nigerian Political Parties: Power in an Emergent African Nation* (1963) and *Corporate Power in an African State* (1975). He recently published "Democracy in Africa" in the *African Studies Review* (1984).

W. A. E. Skurnik

Dr. Skurnik is a professor of political science at the University of Colorado. In 1976 he was a Fulbright professor of International Relations at the University of Abidjan. Dr. Skurnik has lectured at the Universities of Niger, Sierra Leone, Guinea-Bissau, Senegal, Togo, Gabon, Congo, and Cameroon. Dr. Skurnik's most recent books are: *International Relations: Sub-Saharan Africa* (1977); *The Foreign Policy of Senegal* (1972); *Soldier and State in Africa* (with Claude E. Welch, 1972); and *African Political Thought: Lumumba, Nkrumah, and Touré* (editor, 1968).

Winston B. Tubman

Mr. Tubman is an attorney for the Tubman Law Firm in Monrovia. He served as legal advisor to the Ministry of Planning and Economic Affairs from 1966 to 71, and as legal counselor to the Ministry of Foreign Affairs from 1971 to 73. From 1975 to 76, he was legal advisor to the United Nations Environment Program, and from 1979 to 81 was appointed permanent representative to the UN. He was the Liberian Minister for Justice from 1982 to 83, when he returned to private legal practice.

Index

DATE DUE

MAR 2 7 1991			
FEB 1 7 1998			
MAY 2 1 1998			